The Making of
an Army Psychologist

The Making of an Army Psychologist

From Fighting in Vietnam to Treating Fellow Veterans

BOB WORTHINGTON

McFarland & Company, Inc., Publishers
Jefferson, North Carolina

ISBN (print) 978-1-4766-8753-7
ISBN (ebook) 978-1-4766-4802-6

Library of Congress and British Library
Cataloguing data are available

Library of Congress Control Number 2022059906

Lieutenant Colonel Bob Worthington, Army psychologist
(US Army photo); background illustration of soldiers in combat
(Shutterstock/Zhelunovych)

Printed in the United States of America

McFarland & Company, Inc., Publishers
Box 611, Jefferson, North Carolina 28640
www.mcfarlandpub.com

Anita Elliott Worthington
1938–2021

Loving companion and best friend for 64 years

Halfway through writing this book, my wife Anita died.
Then three guardian angels took over.
Our three daughters, Susan, Julie, and Karen,
made sure I was not alone.
They tackled chapters I had difficulty with,
offering suggestions and edited versions.
They helped select the photos in this book,
and hid short notes in my sock drawer,
taped to salsa jars in the cupboard,
or slipped between the pages of books I was to read.
All exhorted me to exercise more, eat healthier,
and remember that I am not alone.

Acknowledgments

As a writer I depend on several others to help me make my books as interesting as possible. To this end I ask friends of mine, experts in many different ways, to read my manuscript and point out errors, let me know when my prose becomes boring, or suggest ways to improve my writing.

Greg Laskow, a retired Army psychologist, noted where my descriptions of Army psychology were either wrong or didn't make sense. His comments forced me to rethink what I was trying to say and review what I had written. His observations and remarks were greatly appreciated, compelling me to instill more clarity into my writing.

Award-winning author Ted Spitzmiller combed through every word and every chapter, suggesting better ways to say something, and identifying English mistakes I seemed to repeat often. His ability to rightfully question what I said required me to consider what I was trying to say and revise a better way to get my point across.

Some parts of this book simply did not work. What I wrote did not read well. Daughter Karen Worthington, a professional writer, spent considerable time going over my poor prose, offering suggestions which eliminated my problems. One chapter in particular proved difficult, yet her comments allowed me to make it readable.

So, thanks to these readers who contributed so much to help me tell the story of how I became an Army psychologist.

Preparing the final manuscript in the correct format, type size and font challenges my meager computer skills, so I rely on Margie Graham to do this. This is the third book we have worked on. Thanks.

As a writer I want to spend my time writing. Producing a book, though, requires more than an author with a manuscript. The staff at McFarland has done an excellent job turning my texts into marketable books, several times. I appreciate all your efforts on my behalf.

Table of Contents

Part IV—Return to Practicing Psychology: July 1976 to September 1981

Part V—Doing What I Love Most: Community Psychology: July 1978 to September 1981

Preface

The Army in the early 1970s was undergoing challenging times. America's involvement in the Vietnam War terminated in early 1973. At that time the draft ended, and the Army became an all-volunteer military force. Now the Army had to attract and retain qualified men and women. Additionally, the size of the Army to support fighting in Vietnam was far larger than necessary for peace-time missions.

Added to these arduous tasks was the homecoming of several hundred U.S. military men, incarcerated for years as prisoners of war by the North Vietnamese and their communist allies. Their evaluations and safe return to their lives after captivity were supported by Congress as another responsibility of the military.

Clearly the Army faced demanding undertakings ahead, often requiring the knowledge and assistance of behavioral scientists to smooth the transition from a bloated conscript organization into a leaner fighting force comprised entirely of members serving because they wanted to. Assisting the adjustment of the repatriated POWs from prisons to freedom would also fall to military psychologists, psychiatrists, social workers, and other mental health professionals.

In the 1960s and 1970s, the field of psychology underwent vast changes. Over this time psychologists were moving out of the typical medical practice of seeing patients in their offices, instead utilizing their skills of understanding how humans behave in different situations in a variety of non-clinical areas. Psychologists found that their theoretical expertise became particularly useful in a variety of endeavors such as sports, industry, management, aviation, law enforcement, organizations, and leadership. This movement in civilian psychology was mirrored in the military.

During these times, clinical psychology education was also undergoing considerable transformation. Until the late 1960s, PhD programs in psychology focused on research, rather than clinical skills. During the 1970s, practical experiences (like attorneys, dentists, and physicians received) were demanded, so clinical training was added to the research education. In fact, some schools created a new degree, emphasizing practical studies, called the Doctor of Psychology degree. The American Psychological Association required students seeking an APA-approved PhD degree to serve a one-year practical internship in a clinic or hospital.

Throughout this book, reference is made to both clinical and counseling psychologists. From a practical point of view, they are similar, and their job functions are identical. From an academic stance the clinical education stresses theoretical orientation, while counseling emphasizes humanistic approaches. Typically, clinical psychology is taught by psychology departments, while counseling psych is taught by schools of education. My PhD was in counseling psychology, with a minor in clinical psychology.

Additionally, the practice of clinical and counseling psychology was moving into new territories, using behavioral science education and skills to work with professionals in areas of athletics, aviation, forensics, management, and gerontology, just to mention a few. Clinical psychologists also desired more freedom to practice independently, not always under the supervision of a psychiatrist (who is a physician). Focus was directed on having clinicians certified and licensed to practice their profession, independently, without supervision of a physician. Requirements were strengthened to regulate the profession in the same way as physicians, lawyers, and dentists.

Military psychology in the 1970s was both similar to yet distinct from clinical practice in the civilian world. Military clinicians provided the same services as did their non-military counterparts. Educational backgrounds were similar. Practicums and internships were in both civilian and military facilities. Military and civilian clinical psychologists followed the same practice approaches.

So what was the difference between civilian and military practitioners? What set the military psychologist apart from his/her civilian counterpart? The distinct differences were the populations served and the environments each practiced in. Civilian clinical psychologists worked in a variety of organizations, from private practices to medical facilities to state and non-military federal organizations. Military psychologists worked within the structured armed forces framework. Most were stationed at military medical facilities. Some served as members of various military units, such as Army combat divisions or Air Force and Navy major commands.

Military rules and regulations required these psychologists to be part of the military themselves. This meant wearing uniforms and training to be an officer. It also required them to understand and expect other assigned duties as a part of the military unit they belonged to. A benefit to a military patient or client is that they would be able to receive whatever help was necessary and available, regardless of cost. Most often, civilian psychology practices were controlled by either insurance or budget limitations regarding what services could be provided.

Another challenge both military and civilian behavioral scientists addressed was post-traumatic stress disorder (PTSD), a mental condition caused by experiencing or seeing a traumatic event such as war and combat. The media (and anti-war professionals) predicted that most Vietnam veterans would suffer some degree of post-service adjustment problems. This myth was debunked by repatriated American military POWs and a major, Congressionally-mandated psychological study of veterans in the 1980s.

A non-draftee Army meant a different Army. The end of a war and a reduced need for men and officers would lead to the downsizing of the force and leadership challenges. The return of the repatriated POWs required long term physical and psychological evaluations, rehabilitation, and probable changes in training for combat.

Behavioral scientists were embracing a concept known as Organizational Development (OD). In the Army this was called Organizational Effectiveness. This science-based effort was designed to evaluate the effectiveness of an organization, and then create programs to enhance strong areas and improve weak areas through the usage of behavioral science and human interactive techniques, from the bottom up. The Army had OE enthusiasts such as General Bernard Rogers and other flag officers. It also had its detractors: old-line senior officers and NCOs who believed that command is only a one-way street, from the top on down. Army OE staff members were assigned to Army posts and combat divisions to help commanders more effectively deal with command and organizational issues.

These ordeals for all branches of the post-war military would require the services of more people trained in behavioral sciences such as psychology and social work. To accommodate this need, the Army created a program to procure these people.

The Army sought out former combat officers who were entering doctoral programs in the behavioral sciences. The program brought them back on active duty, and allowed them to complete their doctoral education as officers in the Army, receiving full pay and benefits. For psychologists, this typically involved three years of education and practicums followed by a year's internship at an Army medical center, culminating in a PhD and assignment as a clinical psychologist in the Army.

This program proved successful, with several graduates remaining in the Army until retiring. One officer in this program was Howard Prince, a 1962 graduate of the U.S. Military Academy (West Point). As an infantry commander in Vietnam, he was wounded twice and highly decorated for valor. His injuries prevented him from returning to the infantry, so he entered the psychology graduate program. His first assignment, as a major, was to West Point as a counselor. In 1978 he was selected to serve as the head of the newly-created Department of Behavioral Sciences and Leadership, becoming the Army's youngest full colonel. He retired from that position as a brigadier general.

As a disgruntled Army infantry major, and a veteran of two combat tours in Vietnam, I left the Army and earned a master's degree in psychology. After working for a year as a psychologist, I was admitted into the Counseling Psychology doctoral program at the University of Utah. I applied for and was accepted into the Army psychology graduate program, so I returned to active duty as a major.

I left the Army in 1969 because of what I perceived as poor senior leadership. I realized that with the ending of the Vietnam War and the draft, the Army would have to change. Returning to the Army as a psychologist would offer me the opportunity to work within the system to institute change and restore the leadership to what it should have been. During my decade as an Army psychologist, I advanced from being a student, to a clinician, to quickly becoming a very senior psychologist, involved in a variety of military evaluation programs.

This is my story of what I did and how I did it.

PART I

Graduate School
August 1969 to August 1973

1

Graduate School

I tossed another letter in my desk drawer, where it landed on top of a pile of several others. Dejected, I eyed the growing stack of correspondence, all saying the same thing. Each one detailed why I was not seen as a worthwhile candidate for entering a PhD program in psychology.

In August 1969, I left the Army as an infantry major, upon completion of my second tour as a combat advisor in Vietnam.[1] I immediately began a master's degree program in Guidance and Counseling at Northern Arizona University in Flagstaff.

By the spring of 1970, I was almost finished with my second semester in graduate school. Recently I had applied to psychology PhD programs at several schools across the Southwest.

Every doctoral psychology program had turned me down.

One school said that, because I had spent twelve years in the military, I was no longer capable of thinking. A second pointed out that my undergraduate C grades at Dartmouth College were not sufficient for me to successfully compete at the doctoral level (even though I had graduated more than nine years previously). A third was amazed that I would even consider entering a PhD program in psychology when I had no degrees in psychology, nor had published any professional papers on the subject. Another informed me that I had no experience in practicing psychology nor any certification in the field.

Every letter denied my application to their doctoral program in psychology.

My Dartmouth major was art (I had worked as a commercial artist while in college). College was not of interest to me, so at the end of the first semester of my sophomore year, I dropped out to enlist in the U.S. Marine Corps in February 1957.

During my two-year tour I experienced combat during Operation Bluebat, when the Marines landed in Beirut, Lebanon in July 1958. Upon completion of my adventures in the Marines I returned to Dartmouth and joined the Army ROTC program.

While in the Marines, I dated Anita Elliott, a native of Washington, D.C. That led to our getting engaged, and we married just before I began my junior year. Shortly after graduating in June 1961, I was commissioned a second lieutenant in the Army and went on active duty. While a clerical error initially replaced my Infantry commission with one in the Chemical Corps, that was soon corrected, and I moved into the Infantry.

During the next eight years I was trained in counterinsurgency and counter-guerrilla warfare, becoming an expert in unconventional warfare (today called special operations). Sent to language school at the Defense Language Institute in California for Vietnamese, I served two separate years in the Vietnam War as a combat advisor.

Because of my disillusionment with the upper leadership in the Army and the Army's refusal to send me to graduate school, I elected to leave active duty and attend graduate school on my own.

During my first semester I learned that if I ever wanted to be my own boss as a psychologist, I had to obtain the doctoral degree. A master-level psychologist always works for a psychologist with a doctoral degree.

So, upon completing my first semester of my master's degree program, I applied to several schools offering doctoral degrees in psychology, only to be told "no" by every single program.

These rejections created doubts about my ability to succeed as a graduate student. But one day, almost a year later, fate decided to befriend me.

2

Northern Arizona University

From Combat to Classes

In August 1969, upon returning stateside from my second tour in Vietnam as a combat advisor, I left the Army. My plan was to attend graduate school, get credentialed as a school guidance counselor and become active in the Army Reserves. I was released from active duty at Fort Benning, Georgia, where my family remained while I was in Vietnam. We left Benning with two vehicles, a small travel trailer, three daughters, and a cat, looking forward to the future. Destination: Flagstaff, Arizona, home of Northern Arizona University, where I would begin my master's degree program in Guidance and Counseling. Upon arrival we needed to find a home, enroll two daughters in school, register me at NAU, and find me a job.

All was accomplished quickly. We bought a ranch style house, right across the street from the girls' school. I was lucky to get hired as the office manager for an electrical contractor, Howard P. Foley, out of Phoenix. The firm was in Flagstaff to install all the electrical wiring for a new particle board plant being constructed as an addition to a local sawmill. The job was expected to last about 12 months. I was not needed full-time, so was able to set up my work schedule around my classes. It was a perfect arrangement for both the company and me.

My swift transition from combat soldier to graduate student was abrupt and, in many ways, unbelievable. Most of my fellow students were single, in their mid–20s and came directly from undergraduate school. All possessed either degrees in psychology or minors in that field. My undergrad degree was in art. Most had never held a full-time job, having been students throughout their lives. Only nine hours of graduate courses composed a full course load, and that is all most of my colleagues took. As I was coming from a dangerous 24/7 work background in Vietnam, grad school was a piece of cake, so I took a minimum of 18 hours each semester.

Without an academic background in psychology, I was at a serious

Bob holding Karen, with Anita, Julie, and Suzi in front of home in Flagstaff, 1970.

disadvantage. Most of my professors had served during World War II or Korea and had an affinity for a combat veteran. Some of them suggested I sit in on some of their undergraduate psych classes. I also found I could get up to speed by getting several books from the library on a single, specific topic and reading all the books to help me understand what I was learning. Both the classes and the books helped considerably, keeping my student head above water.

One class I audited was an advanced psychology course taught by my advisor. One section covered coercive persuasion, also known as brainwashing. Knowing my background, the professor inquired about my experience in brainwashing. I explained that I had gone through several Army E & E programs (Escape and Evasion techniques) and additionally taught evasion courses and how to perform if captured. Similarly, I served as a guard or officer in enemy prisons we had set up for soldiers captured during the 12- to 24-hour practical part of E & E training, where soldiers must successfully transit (on foot) several miles of wild terrain while avoiding capture by enemy (aggressor) troops. Additionally, I was a graduate of a classified military program for officers assigned to combat positions which could lead to being captured during a war. The professor asked if I would teach the two-week section on brainwashing. I said yes, and I did. The students were thrilled to have part of their course taught by an outside "expert."

During my first semester I took a course on the principles of guidance counseling. Our term project was to create a guidance counseling program for a school (grade school, junior high, or high school). We were to write our plan and turn it in. Most students wrote 10 to 12 pages. My paper was 80 pages (yes, overkill, but I wanted to learn as much as possible about the actual role of a guidance counselor).

My proposed guidance program was for a private prep school, where the students live on campus while being educated for colleges (and in New England, where I grew up, the intended colleges were predominately Ivy League). The course covered what guidance counselors really did. Much of our class time was spent visiting various local schools and seeing the programs in action. At other times, various school counselors would come to class and discuss the functions of their job.

Much of my time in the military was devoted to counseling and mentoring enlisted men or junior officers. I enjoyed this kind of interaction and found satisfaction in helping others achieve what they were capable of. Therefore, I wanted to learn how to be a school counselor, to help students.

This course was the most important one of my graduate education. It showed me why I did not want to become a high school guidance counselor. As I mentioned, interacting with others as a mentor was enjoyable. Guidance counselors, however, did little of this. Much of their time was spent proctoring national tests and explaining the results to students' parents. Considerable time was consumed performing administrative duties. Not much time was devoted to one-on-one interaction or mentoring. This was not the career I envisioned.

My professors understood my plight and were able to rearrange my program to focus more on counseling psychology than guidance counseling. My curriculum changed from education to psychology. I took several classes in various psychological testing methods and various practicums in testing, vocational counseling, and individual counseling.

It also became apparent that to head a clinic or counseling

program, a psychologist must possess a doctoral degree, like a Doctor of Education (EdD) or a Doctor of Philosophy (PhD). Thus, even before the first semester ended, I began to examine various doctoral psychology programs in the Southwest. Frantically, I began researching universities and programs. I completed and mailed applications to about 10 universities in the Southwest. Applying to graduate schools for a master's degree was rather simple, and being accepted was no problem. Thus, I thought that it would be the same for a doctoral program. Boy, was I wrong!

Every school I applied to turned me down, essentially saying I was not a viable candidate for a doctoral degree.

Media Assertions and Vietnam Vets

As a Vietnam veteran, I could not help but be aware of the media hype presenting the myth that anyone who served in Vietnam arrived home psychologically broken. Normal readjustment back into the civilian world was being described as virtually impossible for those who served in Vietnam. Magazine articles, newspaper stories and several books cited case after case where service in Vietnam rendered veterans depressed, lonely, and unable to successfully return to their former lives.

Newspapers printed stories about soldiers returning stateside in uniform and being spit on, booed, and jeered for being part of the war in Vietnam. My problem was I never saw this. I was never treated like this upon my return, nor were any of my friends.

The media described veterans fearing loud noises, facing sleepless nights, being unable to interact with others, and resorting to drugs or alcohol to escape their demons and depression. The media portrayed any vet who experienced combat as being the worst off. The conclusion was that the more combat one encountered, the greater the difficulty adjusting upon return home.

This bothered me. I endured two years of extensive combat in Vietnam; was wounded and injured more than once; and was decorated several times for my actions in battle, yet never experienced any adjustment problems. Loud noises did not bother me; I slept fine. I was not depressed. I did not encounter difficulty interacting with others, nor did any of my close fellow officers.

I questioned the validity of these media assumptions. I began to cut out newspaper and magazine articles on the subject, and bought books decrying the same topic. As a student, I did not have time to explore this in more depth, but my interest in the truth led me to start a collection on this media saga. I considered this a subject to delve into, sometime in the future.

Active Reserve Duty

With 10 years of active duty and three years in reserve, I did not want to just throw away 13 years of military service. I wanted to join an active reserve unit to remain a part of the Army.

Upon arriving in Flagstaff, I found an Army Reserve unit: a military police company, commanded by an MP captain. But the captain did not want a combat infantry major attached to his company, so I had to look elsewhere. I discovered a Navy Reserve Surface Unit on the NAU campus. It was commanded by Lieutenant Commander (same as a major) F.R. Kuchem, who was delighted to have me join his unit. Because of my time aboard a Navy ship when I was in the Marines, I was familiar with Navy customs. In March 1970 I was brought on board to run their weapons qualification courses, provide instruction in the Code of Conduct, deliver seminars on counter-insurgency warfare, and teach military leadership classes. My time with the unit was fascinating, but short. In September I left to join a Navy reserve school as a student.

While we only met one weekend each month, my duties required much more time preparing for what I did. When I completed my degree requirements (in August 1970) and took a full-time job, I sought a less time-consuming way to receive reserve credit.

The Navy had a reserve school in Phoenix. Once a month, on a weekend, officers from the school would travel to Flagstaff to teach a portion of the Naval War College, a course in national and international security. The one-year course began in September and finished in June 1971. While the Navy unit and school enabled me to acquire reserve credit, I also wanted active duty in the summer as a reservist.

I discovered an Army Reserve unit, the 75th MAC (Maneuver Area Command), headquartered in Houston, Texas, which specialized in annual evaluations of Army Reserve and National Guard units. In July 1970 I went on two weeks of active reserve duty as an evaluator at Fort Chafee, Arkansas, where a brigade of the 36th Infantry Division of the Texas National Guard underwent their annual training tests.

The Army Command and General Staff College at Fort Leavenworth, Kansas, is recognized as almost a prerequisite for promotion to lieutenant colonel for combat arms officers. There are three ways to take this course. Active-duty officers must be selected to attend this course. It prepares mid-level field grade officers for higher staff and command assignments at the battalion, brigade, and division levels. A second option is to take the courses by attending classes taught by an Army Reserve school. Finally, the C & GS College is also available by correspondence to all officers. In the fall of 1970 (in addition to the Naval War College classes) I enrolled in the C & GS correspondence program.

A requirement for correspondence and reserve school C & GS students is to attend a two-week active-duty school run by the Army Reserve. My two weeks in July 1971 were spent on the Reno campus of the University of Nevada. Few of the reserve students had as much experience as a company commander or battalion staff officer as I did. Much of what we were being taught presumed a thorough background in both command and staff time as a captain and major, which I had. Many of our classes were difficult for the reserve officers, so extra study time was arranged in the evenings and over the weekends. I did not need the extra study time. My family accompanied me to Reno, and we had ample time for sightseeing. In the evenings, Anita and I spent time in the casinos. For many, this two-week school was not easy, requiring considerable hours doing homework outside of class. I found the classes effortless, so the reserve school at Reno was just like a paid vacation.

Additionally, I spent two weeks at Fort Sheridan, Illinois, with the 75th MAC evaluating the 12th Special Forces Reserve. My two weeks of active duty would earn me more money than I would make in a month at my regular job.

On 10 March 1970 (during my second semester at NAU) I was requested to attend a ceremony at the nearby Army post, the Navajo Army Depot, a repository for munitions used in the Vietnam War. I was asked to wear my uniform, as I would be decorated. My wife and oldest daughter attended with me. I was awarded the U.S. Navy Bronze Star with the combat "V" (for valor) and the U.S. Navy Achievement Medal, also with the combat "V." Each was awarded for separate combat operations where I was assigned to a Navy advisor unit, advising a Vietnamese commando company almost a year prior. The Navy could not decorate me after the action because I was Army. The award went up the channels to the Secretary of the Navy, who offered it to the Secretary of the Army, and eventually worked its way down the commands to finally reach me.

The local paper thought this was a newsworthy event, so they prepared signs with "GO NAVY," which they asked my wife and me to hold for photographs.

A few months later I was again requested to attend a ceremony in uniform, where I received the Army Commendation Medal. I had requested the medal instead of a third Bronze Star because I wanted quantity (more decorations as I did not have an ACM) instead of quality (another Bronze Star).

Anita (holding "Go Navy" sign) as Bob is decorated for valor by U.S. Navy, 1970.

Bob looks at Suzi as he is decorated for his service on his second tour in Vietnam (U.S. Army photo, 1970).

My time in the reserve components while at NAU proved varied, interesting, and very worthwhile. I found several different means of achieving credit from the reserve besides being attached to a local Army Reserve unit.

Rejection Is Not Fun

As mentioned, I had applied to several doctoral programs. All said no for a variety of reasons. Bear in mind that in 1970–1971, the U.S. was no longer tolerant of the war in Vietnam or the military. This was especially true in academia.

By late spring of 1970, during my second semester, rejections began arriving. Some made sense while others were just mean. One school rejected me because "You have spent so much time in the military that you can no longer think"; others reflected on my military background, believing that it rendered me not a suitable candidate for graduate work at the doctoral level. One pointed out (correctly) that I had no education in psychology, and no degrees in the field. Another noted that I had no psychology experience; I had published no papers in psychology; and I simply had no background in that vocation. One school said that my C+ grade average at Dartmouth clearly showed I would not be able to successfully compete at the doctoral level.

Every school rejected me. What is interesting is that every school presented a different reason for denying me entrance into its program. Overall, the rejections did have two similarities as to why I could not succeed at the doctoral level: one was the fact that I had spent several years in the military, and the other emphasized my lack of education or experience in psychology. I seriously began to question my decision to leave the Army for graduate school. Doubts about my ability to succeed in graduate school arose with every rejection letter.

Despite no one wanting me, I soldiered on with my studies. I did have one great advantage over the other grad students. Most had entered grad school straight from being an undergraduate. They were well versed in psychological theories, human behavior courses, and principles of counseling. Yet most lacked any practical experience dealing with people. On the other hand, I had been managing people and overseeing all aspects of behavior for over a decade. It was not difficult to learn theories or principles and relate them to my experiences with people.

Part of my program required different practicums where I would do a short internship, working at some local agency. One practicum was with the Flagstaff office of the Arizona Department of Vocational

Rehabilitation. I would assist in evaluating clients for vocational aptitude and abilities. We would counsel clients and develop training or educational programs to meet their vocational needs.

Another agency I worked at was a counseling/job placement clinic for the local American Indian tribes. I was assigned a client, a young (18-year-old) female who had no vocational skills (or interest in working). I tried placing her in various entry-level jobs at volunteer agencies as a paid worker. She was provided a hotel room to live in, but had problems getting to work on time, or had difficulties being supervised. She was lazy and didn't like work. The goal of the agency was to help her to be self-sufficient and earn a living. Every attempt I made to assist her in achieving this goal was met with failure. My class requirement was to write a paper describing my experience as a counselor.

When she didn't work (and did not get paid), we noticed that she did have money. We learned that she became a freelance prostitute where she lived, working nights, so she could sleep during the days. She was making enough money to support herself, so the agency deemed her employed and terminated her as a client. And my paper, describing my failures with her, received an A.

The second semester terminated, and I entered summer school. On 22 August 1970 I completed all studies to receive my Master of Education degree, majoring in Guidance and Counseling. Because I took so many hours each semester, I completed all degree requirements quickly. My grade point average was 3.924 (out of 4.0), so I graduated with honors and was inducted in Phi Kappa Phi honor society in November 1970.

While I did not have the graduation ceremony until the following May, I did have the degree, so now what? During the last summer session, I began to look for work. Two positions became available, both for master-level counselors. One was at a local mental health clinic and the other was at the Institute for Human Development at NAU. There were two of us graduating in August, seeking a local job. Me, a 33-year-old married male, and a vivacious classmate: a mid-twenties, single, red-headed female with the actual name of Flame Valentine. She drove a bright red VW Bug. Each of us applied to both positions. The heads of each organization met and decided who would accept whom. Flame went to the clinic and I joined IHD.

Fun Time in Northern Arizona

Our two years in Flagstaff were not only school and work. With a four-wheel drive Jeep and a small camping trailer, we still found time for plenty of fun. Northern Arizona is an outdoors paradise. The surrounding area was dry, but covered with pine forests. South of Flagstaff were several mid-sized lakes stocked with pike and trout. Ancient Indian ruins were scattered around, all within a half day or so drive. Abutting the northern edge of Flag was the 12,633-foot San Francisco mountain, a winter wonderland with excellent skiing.

Because Flagstaff in the winter is snowy, with days of sub-freezing temperatures, we would hitch the trailer to the Jeep and head south to Sedona. This small town was home to 2700 people with a rich heritage of art and culture, and plenty of rugged Jeep trails. Through the area ran Oak Creek, a cold, clear creek, tumbling out of the higher elevations north and west of Sedona, and filled with rainbow trout. Sedona, almost 2000 feet lower than Flagstaff, is reached via a 27-mile canyon road. When Flagstaff experienced three feet of snow and backyard temperatures of 10 to 15 degrees, we would descend to temperatures in the 50s to 60s, enjoying camping, fishing, and four-wheeling in the unpopulated outdoors.

As a family we explored all of the northern half of Arizona. From the Indian tribal homes to abandoned gold and silver mines and old western ghost towns, there was never an end to the exciting weekend trips we would enjoy throughout our stay in Flagstaff.

My First Job as a Psychologist

The Institute for Human Development was located within the College of Education. It provided a variety of counseling, educational, and psychological services for northern Arizona. It did psychological and educational testing for several American Indian schools across northern Arizona. It did vocational testing for various state agencies, and it ran a special educational program. IHD had counselors who could also do psychological testing, high school level teachers and vocational evaluators.

It had a partnership with Flagstaff High School. Certain high school dropouts could qualify for a special educational program at IHD. Students completing the program could receive a diploma from Flag High. IHD teachers would teach the dropouts. The program was devised to meet the needs of each student. Counseling was part of their requirements. This was an innovative way to rescue dropouts and get them through high school. All of the dropouts had psychological issues; thus, the required counseling.

I continued taking additional graduate courses, obtaining my Arizona certification as an Assistant School Psychologist and a School Psychometrist. IHD was awarded a contract to establish a Veterans

Administration Counseling Office for Northern Arizona, and I was selected to head it. This was a part-time endeavor, so I still had my regular duties as a counselor.

My work consisted of conducting intake interviews for new clients; doing psychological, vocational, educational, and personality testing; traveling to various American Indian schools (mostly Navajo) to test children; and providing the VA counseling and evaluations. It was the kind of work I enjoyed. Our boss, Bill Amberg, a former Navy officer and diver, had his EdD and ran IHD. We worked with a variety of mental health clinics around town, and every boss had a doctoral degree. I still wanted a doctoral degree, so in the late fall of 1970, began to apply once again for doctoral programs

This Time Around Everyone Likes Me

My approach this time was quite different. I had graduated with honors, I was certified, and I was employed as a psychologist. This time I avoided applying only to the most prestigious programs. My first application, in the fall of 1970, went to the EdD program in Counseling Psychology at the University of Northern Colorado, historically a teacher education school. I received an early acceptance into its doctoral program. Now, no matter what, I was in a doctoral program.

I then applied to several more schools, including schools which had rejected me a year prior. All American Psychological Association-approved PhD programs I applied to required me to take the Miller Analogy Test (MAT). This is a standardized test of logical and analytical reasoning used for admission into graduate school.

Not being familiar with the exam, I bought a guidebook for the test. It consisted of explaining how the test worked and provided several sample tests. The test questions would go something like this: apples are to oranges as beets are to _____. This would be followed by four possible answers, and the test taker would have to select the best response. In this case one answer was carrot, which was correct. Apples and oranges are fruits, and beets and carrots are vegetables.

For over a month I read the guidebook several times and took the sample tests. Each test seemed to have a singular focus, such as English or history or math. Despite my reading and test taking, my scores were always low, around the 60th to 70th percentile, suggesting that 30 to 40 percent of the test takers scored above me. These scores would never get me into a doctoral program, and most schools required this test. Again, doubts about my wanting graduate school yet not getting MAT scores high enough festered. But stubborn me, I refused to quit or give up.

On the day I was to take the MAT at the NAU counseling center, I took the last test in my book during my lunch hour. This test was different. It was a general topics test. I did very well, achieving the 90th percentile. Feeling good, I went to take the real test. I was flabbergasted. The "real" test I took was a replica of the test I just completed during lunch. My final score was at the 95th percentile, meaning I did better than 95 percent of the test takers. On this day, fate was certainly on my side. My doubts about being qualified for the PhD began to dissolve.

I was accepted at every school I applied to. Most appealing to me was the American Psychological Association-approved PhD program in Counseling Psychology in the College of Education at the University of Utah. I visited the school, met my proposed advisor, and accepted their offer. I enjoyed sending a perverse reply to those schools that initially rejected me. I said that their program was not good enough for me and would not attend.

Anita holding Karen in front of the Worthington home in Flagstaff, 1969.

The summer of 1971 was a remarkably busy time for the Worthingtons. Once I accepted Utah's offer to enter their PhD program in Counseling Psychology, several things had to be accomplished. I still had the G.I. Bill for schooling, which provided funds for school and family. Because I would enter the doctoral program with an A average from my master's program, Utah would provide me with a full academic scholarship covering all university costs. If I maintained an A average at Utah, I would retain the scholarship (which I did). We had to sell a house, travel to Salt Lake City, find a place to live, enroll the girls in school, and investigate a part-time job.

In August 1971 the family and I packed the trailer (this time a 31-footer I purchased and rebuilt), the two vehicles, three daughters and now, two cats, leaving Flagstaff for Salt Lake City. We had purchased our house in September 1969 for $23,000 and sold it (within days) for $27,500.

3

The University of Utah

Moving to Salt Lake City

In early 1971, when I received acceptance into the doctoral program at the University of Northern Colorado, I began to consider returning to active duty as a clinical psychologist. Over time I contacted the Navy and the Air Force, inquiring into what it would take to join their branch as a psychologist. The Air Force responded by stating that when I received my PhD, it could initiate a branch transfer and commission me as a lieutenant. Going backwards, rank wise, was not acceptable to me. The Navy offered, upon graduation, a branch transfer with the rank of lieutenant senior grade (the same as an Army captain). Again, not acceptable.

The Army, though, had a totally different option. In 1971, the U.S. involvement in the Vietnam War was winding down. The Army was planning to convert to an all-volunteer force, with the draft disappearing. The Army realized that once it eliminated conscripted recruits, the service would have to render volunteering attractive, which may become a challenge to senior officers and senior NCOs. One way to enable a smooth transition would be to recruit combat-experienced officers to receive advanced degrees in the behavioral sciences. Army Psychology already had a program in place.

As an Army infantry major, I became so disenchanted with the senior leadership that I left active duty. I was a small fish in a very big pond. Essentially, my ability to enact change was very minuscule. But as an Army psychologist (now Doctor Worthington), I believed that I would be in a position to assist in the transformation I felt the Army needed. I believed, as a behavioral scientist, I could effect change.

Like many medical specialties, the Army would encourage qualified students to apply for final graduate or medical schooling as an active-duty officer drawing full pay and allowances. The payback was to serve in their specialty for a few years. Psychology students accepted into an APA (American Psychological Association) approved doctoral program could apply for commission as an officer to complete their education. Typically, the student would complete the academic portion of the schooling (while some would also have completed their dissertation), and as a requirement of the APA-approved degree program undergo a one-year internship at a designated Army Medical Center.

The students accepted into this program came from civilians, active-duty and reserve officers, and former officers. Those who were already commissioned would enter active duty at their current rank. I applied to this program.

In late August I received notification that I was accepted into this program. On September 16, 1971 I returned to active duty as a Medical Service Corps major, assigned to the Sixth Army headquarters (in San Francisco) with duty at the University of Utah for a maximum of three years.

Now I no longer needed to seek work. I had the G.I. Bill, a full academic scholarship and the pay and allowances of a major. All of this added up. I was making more than most of my professors.

We thought selling our home in Flagstaff could be a problem. A local real estate agent made an offer we could not refuse, agreeing to sell

Home in Salt Lake City, 1971.

the home; if it did not sell within 30 days, the agent would buy it at an agreed-upon price. Within a couple of days, it was sold.

In late August we moved to Salt Lake City and by early September we had a contract on a house, near the university. The two oldest girls enrolled in local schools. The youngest, at three and a half, entered a nearby Montessori school. When we married, Anita had an AA degree, so she decided to continue her education and get her bachelor's degree in Fashion Merchandising at the U of U. By the end of September, all five of us were students somewhere.

Grad School at the Doctoral Level ... Getting Started

Prior to starting school, several things had to be accomplished. The graduate school had to determine what courses in my master's program would be acceptable for the PhD. Then I had to connect with my advisor. Lastly, a degree program had to be defined. All my master's courses were acceptable, which meant all my courses at Utah would be at the doctoral level. My advisor and I established a schedule for all the classes I needed, practicums, and an internship. I decided to take an overload of courses (15 to 21 hours each quarter) to complete the degree as quickly as possible. We developed a two-year viable plan, which included the dissertation and the required one-year APA internship.

PhD programs require their students to have a doctoral committee to guide the student through the requirements for obtaining the degree. This committee oversees the student's progress and keeps the student on track. Additionally, the steps required to move forward are established and evaluated by the committee, as well as the dissertation. At the beginning the student is assigned an advisor. As time passes, the student must ask other faculty members if they would serve on the student's committee.

At Utah, the committee consisted of five faculty members. When I had to select professors to serve on my committee, the school had so many doctoral candidates that there were not enough faculty to go around, so the required number of committee members was dropped to three faculty. This became great for me.

In addition to the academic classes, the student must pass a comprehensive exam on their specialty (psychology) which is devised by the committee. Additionally, this committee oversees the PhD dissertation.

I am a practical man by nature. I wanted the PhD to practice psychology, not to be a teacher or researcher. The typical tenured university professor is very academic and research oriented (and not very well grounded in the practical aspects of his or her field). I needed faculty members on my committee who actually practiced psychology. And now I only needed three.

My advisor was a psychology professor who was now assigned as the Dean of Freshmen (a practicing psychologist). The Chief of the Psychology Service at the local Veterans Administration Hospital was a practicing psychologist and an adjunct professor of psychology. The man who evaluated and supervised my practicum at the local mental health clinic was the Assistant Director of the University Student Counseling Center, a psychology professor, and a practicing psychologist. I asked all three to form my committee, and all agreed.

The PhD program in psychology, as approved by the American Psychological Association, consists of four separate components. First is the academic part: classes covering all aspects of psychology as a behavioral science. Second is the comprehensive exam: a verbal and written evaluation of what has been learned thus far. Typically, in the College of Education Psych program in Utah, the candidate is given 40 or so books to virtually memorize and then regurgitate their contents. My committee and I did not see this as a worthwhile exercise, so my comprehensive exam focused on my practical experience, detailing what I had learned, not a rote memorization of textbook facts. Third is the dissertation: a written document that describes a major research project completed and conclusions arrived at. The final component is a one-year internship in an APA-approved institution or clinic where psychology is practiced.

Even though the Army would provide the internship, I decided to incorporate it into my studies. Since Salt Lake City had a local VA hospital with a large psychology service, I met with the chief of the service and explained what I wanted. The VA offered paid internships on a competitive basis, so the chief already had an ongoing internship program. Since I was not competing for a paid scholarship, I would enroll as a VA hospital volunteer, assigned to the psychology service. Using my PhD course plan, we developed a strategy where I would do my internship at the VA hospital in a function most closely aligned with my classes. For example, when I was taking most of my psychological testing classes, I would be assigned to the hospital psychological testing unit. The internship program for me consisted of part-time work such that in two years I would have officially completed a one-year internship and all requirements for my APA PhD.

The classes were interesting and readily handled. Math and statistics were not my strong suit. I was not alone, and our statistics prof realized this. All stat students were divided into two groups. One for those students like me, mathematically challenged; and the other for those who craved numbers and equations. Those students became heavily immersed in computing statistics, while folks like me focused on understanding the importance of statistics and what they meant. Throughout my PhD program I received three Bs. Two came in statistics, and one in a personality theory course. The professor in the personality course had a pronounced dislike for a particular personality theory. The class required a lengthy paper on the proposal and defense of a personality theory. I selected the theory he hated and got a B in his class.

Along with the academic classes I was assigned as a counseling psychologist (I was licensed as an Assistant School Psychologist in Utah) to the Granite Community Mental Health Center, in its Adult Day Care Unit, where I saw patients. So, I attended classes, served an internship, and worked as a counselor at a local clinic. My plate was full, but it all merged smoothly. While my testing classmates were scrambling for subjects to test, I had all I needed at the VA testing unit. Throughout my stay at Utah, my internship duties melded beautifully with the classes I was taking. Essentially, my internship also became my homework.

Other Classes Taken

For fun and exercise, I also enrolled in both judo and karate classes, each taught by competition-winning instructors. After a year in these classes, I was eligible to compete on some weekends. Twice I was injured in these matches. In a karate competition, I made a kick at my opponent, who quickly raised his leg to block the kick. My toes hit his shin, breaking a couple of them. In a judo match, my opponent tried to throw me over his shoulder but instead dropped me, and fractured my clavicle. In karate, I had achieved my green belt and was up for my brown belt but, finished with my academic classes and drafting my dissertation, I had to terminate my sports classes.

Enjoying Utah

As in Arizona, our family spent considerable time wandering around the Wasatch Mountains, just east of the city. We now had two four-wheel drive vehicles: a six-cylinder red Jeep CJ-5 and a larger red International Harvester Scout (with extra-long range gas tanks for extended family trips). The mountain stream fishing was excellent, and on day trips our family would enter the mountains on 4WD trails for a "Swiss picnic" with fresh baked bread, some cheese, and a thermos filled with hot chocolate.

One trip will never be forgotten. Our oldest daughter, Suzi, was going to do a school paper on the 1860 Pony Express Trail which traversed Utah. Entering the state northeast of our city, it crossed through the city, turned southwest below the Great Salt Lake (where Interstate 80 is), continued further southwest and then turned west across the desert. During a spring break, we decided the family would follow the old trail for Suzi's paper. Loading the back of the Scout with tents, sleeping bags, cooking equipment, water, and food, we began our trek. Suzi had marked our route on a map. We would go all the way to the Nevada border. At one overnight stop, we arrived in the afternoon at an unimproved campsite. As Anita and I were setting up camp, the three girls were wandering around, exploring.

A young man working nearby suddenly dropped his rake; jumped over a small fence; rushed to Karen, our four-year-old daughter; swooped her up; and jumped away. Not understanding what was happening, Anita and I started to run to him until he shouted, "Rattlesnake." He noticed a snake slithering toward Karen and ran to grab her away from the rattlesnake. We thanked him profusely, and kept the girls close to us until we left early the next morning. Suzi wrote her report, citing her first-hand knowledge of the 110-year-old Trail. She received an A.

The Comprehensive Exam

Most of my academic classes were completed by the end of 1972. For my comprehensive exam I prepared several examples of my academic, clinical, and research accomplishments. For the clinical component, I had clips of audio counseling of a married couple undergoing marital difficulties. Accompanying the audio were summaries of the counseling sessions. For the academic section, I created a one-semester graduate course in community psychology, covering every aspect of the class. The research part was remarkably interesting, and very atypical.

The VA Hospital in Salt Lake had two monozygotic (identical) twins hospitalized with the diagnosis of schizophrenia. Both had some college and dropped out, enlisting in the U.S. Air Force at the same time. A year or so into their tour, each experienced a psychotic break, within hours of each other. What was interesting is that one twin was stationed in the U.S. and the other in Japan. Being medically discharged from the Air Force, they became patients at the Salt Lake City VA Hospital.

Monozygotic twins appear in three or four out of 1,000 births. Initially they have similar DNA, but over time, as they grow in different environments, their characteristics can change. While I did not know this at the time of my research, monozygotic twins do not share the same risk factor for disease.

Schizophrenia is a mental disease affecting how a person feels, behaves, and thinks. It is characterized by disorganized expressions and thoughts that are out of touch with reality. While the explicit causes of schizophrenia are not known, it is thought that genetics, brain structure/chemistry, and the environment play a role in the disease. What is unusual with my twins is that, while their breaks occurred almost simultaneously, they were in two distinctly different environments (albeit both were in the same Air Force).

I conducted an intense series of many psychological tests and inventories. The results: both had similar findings, almost like two test batteries given to the same person.

Upon compiling my comprehensive exam materials into a single document, each committee member received a copy. Individual meetings with each one elicited questions for me to respond to during the exam. On a Monday I was told the exam would be on Friday morning. At the same time, I was told that Friday evening there would be a celebration for passing my oral and written comprehensive exam, and I would then officially be a candidate for the PhD. I asked if it wasn't premature to plan a party when I had not even taken the exam. The response was, if the committee thought I would not pass the exam, I would not take it. Now that is the kind of committee every doctoral candidate should have. Obviously, I passed.

My last class was individual child evaluations. This was a seminar lecture course that included practical experiences. Up to this point in time, all my clinical work at Utah had been with adults. This intensive course was taught at the University Child Treatment facility. While I had plenty of experience evaluating children working in Arizona, this class expanded my knowledge and capability for working with special needs kids.

Now I could begin my dissertation.

4

Dissertation

The Demise of the Army

While I was in graduate school, the U.S. Army was rapidly falling apart. I left the Army in 1969 because of my perception that the senior leadership was failing, being more interested in themselves than their men. Their self-serving behaviors, therefore, were contradictory to the people and organizations they were to manage. This perception, by the early 1970s, became front page reality, time and time again.

From 17 November 1970 to 29 March 1971, the U.S. Army endured the longest court-martial in its history. The defendant was First Lieutenant William Calley, a former platoon leader in combat in Vietnam. His platoon was on a search and destroy mission in the spring of 1968 in the hamlet of My Lai 4, as part of a battalion-size task force. The mission ended with numerous unarmed civilians (some as young as 12 years old) being massacred. Calley was found guilty of murdering 22 Vietnamese, yet some counts of the dead were as high as 504 killed. Calley was described as a marginal student prior to the Army and had difficulty completing Officers Candidate School. His defense was that he was just following orders. During his trial I was in graduate school at NAU and followed the trial closely. I knew two of the officers on his jury (one, Major Charles McIntosh, I served with; he was a captain, and I was a lieutenant). I knew that Calley's defense (that he was only doing what he was told) would never be accepted by the two jury members I knew. His behavior was not what the Army was teaching its young leaders.

Several members of his company, including the commanding officer, were also charged in the massacre, but only Calley was found guilty. Yet the trend of poor leadership did not end with Calley. The brigade commander, Colonel Oran Henderson; one assistant division commander, Brigadier General George Young, Jr.; and the division commander, Major General Samuel Koster, were all charged with covering up the mass murders at My Lai. Henderson was acquitted, Young was censured and Koster was demoted. The task force commander, Lieutenant Colonel Frank Barker, died in a helicopter crash three months after My Lai, before the investigation began.

While the entire My Lai massacre was a huge blot on the action of Army leadership, more was to follow. In 1971, Daniel Ellsberg released to the public a history of the U.S. involvement in the Vietnam War. Covering some 47 volumes from World War II to 1968, the 2.5-million-word document, called the *Pentagon Papers*, clearly showed that what was being done to expand the war was being withheld from its citizens.

More scandals became public, all testifying to the hidden trend of the Army's top brass participating in illegal deals to feather their own nests. Between 1965 and 1969, several top non-commissioned officers were committing fraud in their management of NCO clubs in Vietnam. Eight NCOs were charged with fraud and bribery, one being the senior NCO of the Army, Sergeant Major William Wooldridge (the first Sergeant Major of the Army).

The retired Provost Marshall of the Army (1964 to 1968), Major General Carl Turner, was found guilty of soliciting firearms from the Chicago Police Department and trading or selling some for his personal gain. He was also charged with tax evasion (1965 to 1968). He spent a year in prison. He was additionally involved in hindering the investigation into the Vietnam NCO clubs scandal.

In April 1970, U.S. and Vietnamese combat units moved into Cambodia, around the Angel's Wing (where I was wounded) and the Parrot's Beak. The mission was to locate and destroy all North Vietnamese units lying in safety between raids into South Vietnam. For those of us who fought on this border, it was a mission long overdue. For too many Americans, this was just another step in expanding the war by invading Cambodia.

The Army in Vietnam was suffering tragedies never experienced. The hippie peace symbol was appearing on helmets and web gear everywhere. Some U.S. combat units refused to fight upon learning they were in line to return stateside. Another phenomenon appeared called "fragging." This involved fragmentation hand grenades being used to injure and kill officers.

In 1971, the *Washington Post* published a series of investigative articles by Haynes Johnson and George Wilson describing the crisis in the military. They wrote: "Today's American Army is fighting its most threatening battle, a struggle for survival as an institution." Award-winning author of *The Ugly American* (co-authored with Eugene Burdick, 1958), retired Navy Captain William Lederer, foresaw exactly what I experienced regarding the poor leadership in the Army. In his 1968 book, *Our Own*

Worst Enemy, he relates: "There is a conviction held by many Americans that our leaders will do almost anything to salve their pride and protect their careers." Military researcher and writer Shelby Stanton, in his 1985 book, *The Rise and Fall of an American Army*, referring to the end of the war in 1973, explained: "the United States military had to build a new volunteer army from the smallest shreds of its tattered remnants." Clearly the demise of the Army was not seen by me alone.

On 27 January 1973, the U.S. signed the Paris Peace Accords, terminating America's combat in the Vietnam War. Essentially, U.S. ground troops would leave Vietnam, and North Vietnam would return all American prisoners of war. The Viet Cong and North Vietnamese did not win the war. But they did not lose the war. They just refused to quit, outstaying the Americans, who did quit.

This was the Army I re-entered in the fall of 1971. I left the Army because as an infantry officer, I had little chance of making this institution better. But as a senior psychology officer, I believed I might be able to improve the Army. And as I was to learn, I could.

The Media Myth of the Vietnam Veteran

In the late 1960s and early 1970s, in addition to the failing of the Army, the mass media was continuously presenting the theory that military service in Vietnam would prevent soldiers from successfully returning to civilian life. Their war experiences caused such a trauma that normalcy was a state few achieved. Magazines, newspapers, and books touted the concept that being in Vietnam, in the military, rendered vets unable to return home without facing severe adjustment difficulties.

Initially I sensed that the media portrayed the Vietnam vet as unlike any other vet. *Army Times* describes the vet returning home: "to find jobs scarce, GI Bill mortgage money hard to find, and many of their civilian friends hostile to the military and the Vietnam War" (*Army Times*, 7 October 1970). Ernestine Forrest wrote in the *Los Angeles Times* (16 November 1970): "While veterans of previous wars had a united country's appreciation to help them obtain employment, Vietnam-era veterans are finding job hunting difficult."

Numerous other experts, articles and books constantly flaunted the belief that the Vietnam War and its veterans are unlike wars and their veterans of any other period in America's history. Next came articles and books indicating that most who served in Vietnam would suffer difficulty rejoining civilian society. These books became best sellers, most likely based on the credentials of their authors. Most of the writers based their pronouncements on their interaction with a very few vets or conversations with other mental health professionals. None were the result of a scientifically controlled study of a large group of Vietnam vets.

College teacher Murray Polner wrote *No Victory Parades* (1971), a book addressing the difficulties of nine Vietnam vets whom he met in 1967 while teaching at a community college outside New York City. He stated: "All nine were somewhat ashamed of the war.… Most of them have retained forms of guilt." Prominent Yale psychiatrist Robert Jay Lifton admits in his 1972 book, *Home from the War*, that he did not conduct a study from a representative group of veterans but explored "feelings and images brought back from the Vietnam War." In testimony before the Senate Subcommittee on Veterans' Affairs (27 January 1970) he told the members: "I think we will see patterns of depression and paranoia, and I think we will see disturbed relationships with other people."

While these are just a few examples of what professionals were saying about the problems Vietnam vets were experiencing upon returning home, the media grabbed them as evidence that most Vietnam vets would not be able to successfully re-enter society without dire consequences. And all of this bothered me.

I am a Vietnam vet. I endured two intense combat tours in Vietnam, yet I did not see myself as having psychological problems. Loud noises did not bother me. I did not have nightmares; slept soundly. I was not feeling guilty, and was proud of my service in Vietnam. I was also a successful graduate student. And my friends who experienced similar tours in Vietnam also reported no difficulties upon returning stateside. So what was the truth? Who was right? Were Vietnam vets finding it difficult to return to civilian life? If so, how pervasive was this issue? Apparently, this was a question which was not addressed by a scientific inquiry.

This question became the perfect enigma for my PhD dissertation.

The Dissertation … the Research

By most accounts, the doctoral dissertation is the greatest hurdle to getting the PhD. Many students simply quit, as the work required is not seen as worth the effort. Some never finish, as they cannot seem to ever collect enough data. Some create a project which is too complex to ever complete.

A key to successful completion of the dissertation is the student's doctoral committee. This group can hinder or assist the candidate in the quest to conclude the research project. In my case, my committee served more as consultants than evaluators. They went over every step of my project, and as each chapter was completed, provided me with needed corrections and then approved it as done. Many committees had their student complete the entire dissertation, and then tore it apart, requiring more work by the student. This approach also had a demoralizing effect on the candidate, where some would just abandon their desire to get their PhD. My committee was vastly different; they were there for me, all the way. My dissertation was completed from the initial design to the printed copies in six months. And the completed research resulted in two professional journal articles[1] and a chapter in a clinical book[2] which is still used as a reference source well into the 21st century.

During the entire time I worked on my dissertation, I met with my committee every Friday afternoon. If I had problems, the committee members resolved them. If I had questions, they answered them. They were with me the entire way, and the total process of doing the dissertation was a pleasurable learning process, unlike the drudgery many of my classmates recounted. Our meeting place was quite unique.

On the east side of the university sat Fort Douglas, an Army Post slowly being decommissioned. It was home of the 96th Army Reserve Command and the U.S. Army Deseret Test Command (a unit that managed testing of biological and chemical weapons, but not at Douglas). It was also home to many support facilities found on any military post, such as a gas station, small post exchange, and an officers' club. Every Friday my committee joined me at this officers' club.

The main portion of my dissertation (*The Vietnam Era Veteran, Adjustment, and Anomie*[3]) consisted of five sections (Introduction, Review of Literature, Method, Results and Discussion, and Summary). The process of the dissertation was to create a scientific inquiry to either answer a question or solve a problem. In my case I wanted to know if most Vietnam vets suffered difficulty upon their return to civilian society.

The first step for my dissertation was to submit a proposal to the committee for its approval. The next step was to develop a research protocol in which the question is proposed and the methodology to find an answer is defined. Then I would review all the research conducted prior to my project and explore any data published which would have a bearing on my study. This would be followed by doing the heart of the research: collecting and analyzing this information, and finally, summarizing the results.

The readjustment process of the recently-returned Vietnam-era veteran appears to be a phenomenon of which little is systematically known. Although an abundance of anecdotal and descriptive information has been compiled to describe the veteran and his adjustment problems, scientific understanding is limited.

Another issue I questioned was the assumption that the Vietnam vet was totally different from veterans of other wars. The popular media portrayed the Vietnam vet as unique, with experiences unlike any veterans of other conflicts. Army physician Major Ronald Glasser, in his 1971 book *365 Days*, describes his one-year tour in Japan, during which he observed the arrival of medevaced soldiers from Vietnam. He noted that these veterans had no clubs, no unit reunions, and no one cared about where they had been or what they did, like it had never happened. Only the 18- to 20-year-olds have to worry, and since no one listens to them, it doesn't matter.

My research compared the 1945 "coming home" experiences of World War II vets to those of the 1970s Vietnam vets.

Several studies and popular books (such as Washington Irving's tale, *Rip Van Winkle,* or even Homer's *Odyssey*) recount how people returning home after extended or traumatic experiences return to a changed society, one now foreign to the homecoming vet. Pulitzer-Prize combat illustrator and author Bill Mauldin, in his 1947 book *Back Home,* describes how the World War II vet was perceived by the society he returned to, and how the vet was negatively portrayed by the media. "But the sad fact was that such headlines gave added impetus to the rumor that always appears in every country after a war-that the returning soldiers are trained in killing and assault and are potential menaces to society" (page 55). He continues by recounting what the World War II veterans face: housing problems, employment problems, training-camp romances and marriages, and the realization that for many, the ex-GI was an object of resentment by civilians. From my point of view, the homecoming experiences of the Vietnam vet were no different from those of the Second World War (or other wars).

The Dissertation Research Design

The purpose of my study was to investigate the reported feelings of Army veterans after release from active military duty. The nature and extent to which Army veterans may have experienced certain effects of anomie were studied. The concept of *anomie* was selected for two reasons. *Anomie* refers to an individual's psychological state of feeling meaningless, a lack of purpose, a sense of despair, a personal breakdown of moral values, a rejection of the normal social bonds. These conditions mirror the media theory of what was happening to Vietnam vets. Second, the feelings of anomie could be measured with specific paper and pencil psychological instruments (tests).

Basically, my study attempted to determine the degree of anomie present in Vietnam-era veterans, and if these feelings were related to service in Vietnam. I selected those psychological tests best suited to measure anomie. Then I developed a method to evaluate and determine what feelings related to service in Vietnam. To do this, though, I had to locate and evaluate a sample of Army personnel recently released from active duty. Creating a sizable sample of specific individuals could be a challenging task. Once located, evaluating them would be a very labor-intensive endeavor.

The testing instruments selected to evaluate the reported feelings of the veterans were parts of the Elmore Scale of Anomie, parts of the Tennessee Self Concept Scale, and the Socialization Scale of the California Psychological Inventory.

Two design factors were selected. One was the veteran's assessment of his military tour (like or dislike). The second factor was where the veteran served: Vietnam or not in Vietnam. The reported feelings of anomie (by the psychological tests) were then related to the two factors. Essentially, I was dividing the veterans into different groups: those who liked or disliked their service time, and those who did or did not serve in Vietnam. Then I would evaluate their feelings of anomie relative to these two factors. Analyses of these variables were processed by a Univac 1108 computer at the University of Utah Computer Center and performed by a computerized multi-variate analysis of variance (MANOVA).

The former Army members tested were located using a computerized personnel roster of soldiers who had been released from active duty between April 1972 and March 1973. Since gender was not noted on the rosters, I had no idea how many veterans were women, but none on the list I obtained were female. The list of soldiers was obtained from a local Army Reserve headquarters. The original inventory contained the names and addresses of 227 Salt Lake County Army veterans. Two rosters existed, one for enlisted and the other for officers.

Telephone numbers were obtained for most veterans who were contacted by phone. During these calls, I explained the study and clarified the time required to take the tests (30 minutes). Requesting their help, I said I would come to them with the test and wait as it was completed. Those vets with no known phone numbers were visited and then asked for their help.

With the 227 names, 32 were found to have moved out of the county. Of the 195 soldiers remaining, nine refused to participate, six were unable to complete the study (mostly due to limited reading abilities), and 33 were never located. Therefore, this group consisted of 147 male veterans (75 percent of the eligible veterans).

After appointments were arranged for my visits, I spent most days (and many evenings) for several weeks driving over 500 miles each week, gathering my data.

The veterans who completed the tests ranged in age from 19 through 29. They were well educated: only 5 percent had not completed high school, 42 percent had some college, and 18 percent were college graduates. The majority were drafted (54 percent), and 18 percent were officers. Fifty-nine percent served between one and two years, while the active time ranged from under six months to three years. This final sample represented 91 percent of the 147 veterans contacted.

I am not a computer expert in any fashion. The analytical process of MANOVA is still pretty much Greek to me. I had a general understanding of what the statistical analysis was, but the process between collecting the data and the results from the computer punch cards totally eluded me. One of my committee members was a MANOVA expert (and he convinced me to use it); he had a friend who knew how to use the process. A statistician and computer expert at the Salt Lake City school district was paid by me to take my data, transfer the information to punch cards, crunch the data on the Univac, tabulate the results, and then teach me enough to understand what I needed to be able to make it part of my dissertation (and to verbally defend my results).

The results were not surprising to me.

The Research Results

The working hypotheses predicting differences between those veterans who had served in Vietnam and those who had never served in Vietnam was not supported by the data collected. It needs to be mentioned that the conclusions do have their limitations, and it is prudent for me as a scientific investigator to point these out.

The sample served in Vietnam in the early 1970s, at the end of the war, a time when combat operations were becoming fewer and less costly in human injury or death. The size of the sample and its geographic location also limits a broader understanding of the results. Additionally, the sample came from a Mormon population, one where military service was viewed as a traditional and honorable accomplishment.

Twenty-six percent of my sample had served in Vietnam, with almost two thirds of them having experienced combat. Of the sample who served in Vietnam, 34 percent received combat awards for valor, from the Distinguished Service Cross down, with eight percent being wounded.

Numerous mental health professionals had portrayed the Vietnam veteran as unable to adjust upon his return home. Their beliefs were not supported by any scientific studies, and no carefully calculated statistics have been employed to add credibility to their statements.

Within the limitations defined, the following conclusions may be drawn from my research:

1. There is no evidence to support the theory that Army service in Vietnam is strongly related to feelings of anomie.

2. Army veterans who reported liking their service time differed from those who disliked their tour, with the former receiving lower anomie scores on their tests.

Overall, this study also concluded that these Salt Lake County veterans are not viewed as having any serious readjustment problems after military service.

This study collected much demographic data that was not processed as part of my dissertation. A second statistical computer analysis was designed to determine if any of 26 demographic factors collected were related to post-service adjustment.

News article citing Bob's research on the adjustment of Vietnam-era veterans, 18 October 1981.

A Second Research Project on Veteran Adjustment

A year after my dissertation, I was in a post-doctoral fellowship program at William Beaumont Army Medical Center located at Fort Bliss, in El Paso, Texas. While there I was also completing my last year of Command and General Staff College at an Army Reserve school in nearby Las Cruces, New Mexico. The head of the program was Reserve Lieutenant Colonel Robert Baird, a civilian director of the computer center at the Army White Sands Missile Range, outside of Las Cruces.

WSMR began on 9 July 1945 as White Sands Proving Ground, one week before the first atomic bomb was exploded in the area known as

Trinity Site. After World War II, the base became the national test range for military and other government rockets and missiles. It is the largest military installation (by size, not people) in the U.S.

One evening, between a class break, I was discussing my research project using MANOVA and explained I had quite a bit more data that I wanted to analyze using a computer program. Becoming very animated, Colonel Baird questioned what I intended to do. I said I was going to obtain a specific behavioral science analysis of variance program to examine my data regarding the post-service adjustment of Vietnam vets. As we talked, Baird said his computer experts could do that for me. When I asked where he could get the behavioral ANOVA program, he said he would not. ANOVA (analysis of variance) is a computer program designed to determine if differences between groups of data are statistically significant. His computer scientists spent all their time using computer programs calculating ballistic data, so they would really enjoy designing their own ANOVA program as a pleasant break from their work.

I gave him my data and described what needed to be accomplished. His experts designed their own program and processed my information, again utilizing a Univac 1108 computer. This time the research was to determine if any significant differences existed between the veteran's responses on the three psychological tests (measuring degrees of adjustment) in the original study, and any of 26 selected demographic items (not yet evaluated). The ANOVA detected that eleven demographic areas were significantly related to post-service adjustment. The criteria used to identify differences were high scores (on the tests), meaning favorable adjustment, with low scores indicating adjustment difficulty.

The eleven items were:

1. Married veterans received the highest scores, while those divorced or separated received the lowest scores.

2. Veterans with no religious affiliation received the lowest adjustment scores.

3. High school dropouts received the lowest scores.

4. The vets in post-service professional occupations received the highest scores, while those being unemployed received the lowest scores.

5. Enlisted vets received the lowest scores, while officers had the highest (most officers served for six months or less).

6. The vets released at the lower enlisted grades (E-1 to E-3, i.e., private, or private first class) received the lowest scores (most soldiers leaving after two years would exit as E-4s).

7. The vets who reported disciplinary action while serving received the lowest scores.

8. The vets who were in college or a trade school prior to service received the highest scores, and those waiting for the draft scored lowest.

9. Vets 21 or older upon entering service received the highest adjustment scores.

10. Veterans reporting no authority problems prior to service received the highest scores.

11. Those who served a church mission (members of the Church of Jesus Christ of Latter-Day Saints) prior to the military scored highest.

Service in Vietnam Did Not Cause Post-Service Adjustment Difficulties

My first research project suggested that post-military adjustment was not related to serving in Vietnam. This second set of analyses of the demographic data and the scores on the various adjustment (anomie) tests suggested that post-service adjustment difficulty could be attributed to social, educational, or vocational problems not connected to military service. It also suggested that those veterans experiencing post-service adjustment problems also experienced adjustment difficulty during their tour of duty and prior to military service.

Both studies tended to refute the commonly accepted notion that serving in Vietnam was responsible for the inability to successfully return to a normal life after the military. They also suggested that prior-service behaviors might be more of a cause for post-service adjustment problems than the military.

These findings whetted my appetite to continue my research into post-service adjustment problems and prior-service behaviors.

Leaving Utah

My wife, Anita, spent the summer of 1963 typing my 128-page dissertation, as she had completed all classes for her degree. Despite spilling a cup of coffee on several finished pages, she did complete the manuscript with zero typo errors. The document was then approved by the committee members, the chair of my major department, and the dean of the graduate school. I received my PhD in August 1973, while my wife received her undergraduate degree with honors.

The Army psychology PhD program provided the one-year APA-required internship at some Army medical centers around the U.S., as an integral part of preparing doctoral students to enter the field of clinical psychology in the Army. One day, in early summer, I received a call from the Army Psychology Consultant on the Surgeon General's staff. He explained that I would be assigned to William Beaumont Army Medical Center to complete my internship prior to receiving my PhD. I countered, saying that I had already completed my internship, and would receive my PhD in August. Clearly, another internship was not required. The colonel said he would get back to me.

A few days later he called again. He said I was to report to William Beaumont on 25 August 1973, but not as an intern. Upon graduation from Utah, I would receive the MOS (military occupational specialty) of 3620, Psychologist. In the mid–1970s, the MOS of commissioned Army officers changed from four numbers to two numbers and a letter, so Army Clinical Psychologists would become 68S. I would be assigned to Beaumont for a one-year post-doctoral fellowship in community psychology. Having no clue what a post-doc fellowship is, I asked my committee members what it was. After all, I was now an Army psychologist and I wanted to start practicing as one.

All members said a post-doc is a much sought-after extension of one's PhD educational training. It was the icing on the cake. They explained that most post-docs allowed the student to create a specific program to further develop and hone one's clinical and research skills. They convinced me that this was an exceptional opportunity, not to be taken lightly.

Our daughters were sent to their grandparents on the East Coast. We sold our home to one of Anita's classmates in June (her husband was a local attorney) for $33,000. We'd purchased it for $28,500 in September 1971. Ironically, the value of the home in 2022 was one million dollars. The summer was spent completing the dissertation and preparing for the move to El Paso, Texas. We drove the Jeep and our camping trailer (packed with various household items), and parked it at Fort Bliss. Flying back to Salt Lake a week later, we returned in the Scout to our next Army assignment.

Four swift years ago I was in Vietnam, fighting the Viet Cong. One constant, since then, as a civilian, was the ongoing bombardment of the mass media (newspapers, TV, radio, books, and magazines) telling me that my service in Vietnam would most likely render me incapable of returning to a normal life. Yet, in those 48 months, I was an honor grad student, a successful working psychologist, a researcher who earned his PhD, and now invited to take up a post-doc fellowship. What is wrong with this picture? The media is telling me and other Vietnam vets that life after Vietnam will be encapsulated in psychological trauma, rendering us unable to adjust to post-service life.

This was not me. This was not my combat-experienced friends. Most important, though, was my research, which showed that most Vietnam vets did not experience difficulty returning home. My appetite was whetted; I wanted more evidence to disprove the media and the behavioral scientists who postulated those same beliefs. I wanted to continue my research into the adjustment of Vietnam veterans. I wanted more evidence that my normal life after two Vietnam combat tours was common, not an exception.

PART II

Post-Graduate Fellowship
August 1973 to August 1974

5

Post-Doc Fellowship

31 August 1973 to 31 August 1974

During our first trip to Fort Bliss, in early August, Anita and I met with a real estate broker (a retired Army major who understood exactly what we needed) and began seeking a house to buy. On arriving the second time we located (and bought) a single-story, four-bedroom house in a nice, new neighborhood (the area was growing so fast that we were almost next to the desert, and when we left a year later, the new houses stretched several more blocks toward the desert). In East El Paso, it was a 20-minute drive to Beaumont Medical Center, the longest commute ever for me.

Commuting was an issue. My father lived in southwestern Connecticut but worked in New York City (as did many other professional neighbors). He drove 30 minutes to the train station, then took a two-hour commuter-train ride to Grand Central Station and a subway ride to Wall Street, where he managed a bank. I knew I could never spend five hours a day just commuting back and forth to work. He justified this by saying he loved living in rural Connecticut and thoroughly enjoyed his job in the city.

With a home in El Paso, our three daughters returned, and we set up house again. They were enrolled in local schools; Anita began her volunteer involvement with the local Girl Scout chapter. On 31 August 1973, I reported to the Psychology Service at William Beaumont, to begin my one-year post-doc fellowship.

What Are Army Psychologists?

The Army Medical Department recognizes three types of psychologists: clinical psychologists, research psychologists, and behavioral science associates (people who have completed all doctoral degree work except for the dissertation).

Clinical psychologists (who can also be counseling psychologists) primarily work in Army hospitals or medical centers, or hold a post at Community Mental Health Services or the medical battalions of combat divisions. There are also limited individual positions, such as psychology consultants to various major Army commands or teaching in various Army schools.

Research psychologists serve in a variety of positions in the Army's research and development community solving challenging Army problems. These areas include medical research, human factors, environmental issues, social psychology, aviation psychology, and pharmacology. The Army in the 1970s had seven medical-related research institutes and three other Army research institutes where medical research psychologists may serve.

The behavioral science associate typically is in a holding position until completing the PhD, so serves mostly as a master's degree clinician. Usually, this person is assigned to a hospital setting, working for other psychologists who have their doctoral degree.

The Army psychologist, after completing graduate school, begins as a captain, and most clinicians leave as a captain as soon as their commitment ends. In the field of Army clinical psychology in the mid–1970s, there were few field grade officers. The senior psychologist was a colonel and served as the Psychology Consultant to the Army Surgeon General in the Pentagon. Dick Hartzell, the Chief of the Psychology Service at William Beaumont Army Medical Center, was the only lieutenant colonel clinical psychologist. I was the senior clinical psychologist major. In the next couple of years, though, there would be several Army clinical psychologists serving as majors and lieutenant colonels. Most, like me, were already majors when brought back on active duty as doctoral students. While most clinical psychologists only served about five years, the research psychologists often remained until retiring.

William Beaumont Army Medical Center

As in all Army Medical Centers, the psychology service is part of the hospital's Department of Psychiatry. William Beaumont was a new, 460-bed, 12-story modern building just completed in 1972. It is on a high slope on the eastern side of the 7192-foot Franklin Mountain (which splits El Paso in two). Beaumont is on the high west side of Fort Bliss, with the stark north-south ridge of the Franklin Mountains on its west side and the mostly unused World War II yellow wood buildings of the old William Beaumont General Hospital stretching down toward the Fort Bliss main post. While the old and new hospital are both part of Fort Bliss, they are geographically separated by a major highway.

While the Department of Psychiatry is located high up in the new building, the psychology service is set up in one of the old World War II hospital buildings. Also a part of the Psychiatry Department is the Fort Bliss Community Mental Health Service, located on the main post, with the chief being a psychiatrist.

On our first day, the interns and I met. One intern I quickly became good friends with was Jerry Nowak, being 10 years younger than me and brand new to the Army. Average in height, lean with thick dark tousled hair and an engaging, outgoing personality, he appeared eager to learn and to assimilate into the military culture. His wife, Linda, a smart blonde, was very agreeable to be with. As a couple they were enjoyable to interact with, and Anita and I would spend a lot of time together with them. Both were from the East Coast, but he was to receive his PhD in Counseling Psychology from a university in Texas (his school was one that initially denied my acceptance). We remain friends today.

Roger Schroeder and his wife Kathy had children and didn't interact with us as much as Jerry and Linda. Rog was close to my age, a former enlisted Army EOD (explosive ordnance disposal) specialist, very tall, gangling, and bald, who went to Arizona State (another school that rejected me, but I did not reapply). He was truly knowledgeable, wise, and probably the most serious of us. Ironically, though, he did not appear to have the demeanor to warmly interact with patients.

Last was Sam Getz, an Arkansas boy, appearing very rural in mannerism, sort of camouflaging his character and intelligence. Sam was married, with his family also at Bliss. He was an Army reserve officer, on active duty to complete his year at Beaumont. Wry, funny, and always finding amusement in everything he did, he was average in size, bespectacled, and had light-colored, sandy hair.

This was our group of four. I was the oldest, with the most military background, and the only one with the PhD. The other three would receive their doctoral degrees upon completion of their internship. For the next 12 months we would work together, study together, play together, and take short TDY (temporary duty) learning trips together. We all were amazingly comfortable with each other and got along extremely well during our year together.

The Psychology Service Chief, Dick Hartzell, was also the Director of Internship Training. A unique individual, Dick was until recently an assistant tennis coach and instructor at the U.S. Naval Academy as a Navy lieutenant senior grade (an Army captain). He is built like a Division III football linebacker: of average height, but muscular and burly, with

Psychology staff and interns at William Beaumont Army Medical Center. Lt. Col. Hartzell, chief of psychology service, is on the far right, and Bob is to his immediate right (U.S. Army photo, 1974).

short-cropped blond hair and glasses. Physically fit, he thoroughly enjoyed most sports.

While at the Academy, he received his PhD in psychology from American University in 1968. He arranged a branch transfer into the Army as a major, and was assigned to Walter Reed Army Medical Center for his clinical internship. Upon completing his internship, he was promoted to lieutenant colonel and assigned to Beaumont as the Psychology Service Chief.

I found Dick outgoing, friendly, athletic, fun, always in motion, and quite easy to work for. Throughout my year at Beaumont, he genuinely cared for me and for my introduction to practicing psychology in the Army. He encouraged every portion of my post-doc and was invaluable throughout the year. I admired what he had accomplished and who he was: a mentor, a colleague, and a friend.

Duties of a Post-Doctoral Fellow

The typical Army clinical psychology internship consists of four core skill areas: clinical, consulting, teaching, and program evaluation/ research. Within this framework are opportunities to receive specialty training and experience in child and adolescent psychology, biofeedback, hypnosis, marriage and sexual counseling, and behavioral treatment modalities. The internship emphasizes an individualized approach to training with frequent supervisory opportunities.

As a post-doc fellow, though, I had already completed the internship, so my year would be spent expanding my knowledge and practice of psychology. Because my fellowship was being conducted within the internship framework, I could still partake of the training and seminars presented by outside consultants.

With Dick Hartzell, a one-year agenda was developed. I explained what I wanted to learn, and Dick described what facilities and resources were available. We created a program that involved four major areas: clinical, consulting, research, and special training.

Clinical Experiences

The clinical experience had me placed in two settings. I was to join the El Paso Child Treatment Center as a part-time staff psychologist. The Center was a day facility which provided a variety of assessments and evaluations for children with special needs or psychological problems, and then offered treatment. My specific duties involved evaluating children, developing treatment programs for them, and then supervising the programs. The Center was also a location for the University of Texas at El Paso (UTEP) nursing students to do a rotation as part of their pediatrics training. I was to supervise their training at the Center. My supervisor was a PhD psychologist, the director of the Center.

A second part-time clinical assignment was as the staff psychologist at the William Beaumont Trauma Unit. The Beaumont Trauma Unit was located near the hospital emergency room, but a complete unit by itself. It had its own ER and intensive care unit situated such that it had no windows; thus, the staff had no way of monitoring the outside weather, giving the area sort of a gloomy atmosphere. The Trauma Unit was the only unit in El Paso, so it received a variety of patients.

A trauma unit is an emergency room which is specifically designed for patients with multiple injuries from automobile accidents, gunshot wounds, knife injuries, falling, or other incidents causing severe damage to the body. For example, a car accident victim may have broken legs or arms requiring an orthopedic surgeon, a skull fracture needing a neurosurgeon, and damage to the internal organs necessitating an internist. Therefore, the patient requires the skills of multiple surgeons, simultaneously.

One aspect of the trauma patients is they tend to be young adults and have multiple injuries, such that many may never fully recover from the bodily damage. Often this becomes a psychological problem for the patient and their spouse or parents. Additionally, working in the windowless trauma environment, among a daily diet of death and human destruction, also gets to the staff. My job was to provide psychological support when and where needed.

Command Consultation

My focus on consulting was to the community of the 3rd Armor Cavalry Regiment, recently assigned to Fort Bliss (a year previous) from Fort Lewis, Washington. An armored cav regiment is a self-supporting unit consisting of seven squadrons (each the equivalent of an infantry battalion) of which four are combat units and three support teams. Its mission is to provide reconnaissance, surveillance, and security for other Army combat units or within a geographical area. My job was to provide command consultation to various squadron or troop commanders regarding behavioral problems the commanders might encounter. With my infantry command and combat background, I would understand the problems of command.

Research

My interest in research was a continuation of studying the behavior and adjustment of soldiers, focusing on Vietnam veterans. My previous research suggested that problem soldiers entered the service with a difficult behavioral background. I wanted to continue to explore this thesis. Additionally, I wanted more tools to evaluate military units and render assistance intervening to effect change. To do this I partnered with two organizations.

One was a local Army behavioral science research organization, assigned to Bliss. A second was the Army Forces Command Organizational Effectiveness headquarters at Fort Ord, California. The Army OE program is what civilian psychologists call Organizational Development. Essentially, in the Army, it is a chain of command effort to assess, strengthen, and improve how an organization accomplishes its mission. I wanted to become a part of this program.

To better understand theories of how groups function, I took a graduate course at the University of Texas at El Paso, Organizational Behavior, to study how an organization functions and how to intervene to alter its behavior. The professor was a new acquaintance who shared my interest in organizational research, so he assisted in my research efforts with OE.

In addition to conducting research, I began authoring papers on completed research for publication or presentation. I did have two articles accepted for publication in a noted professional journal and two papers accepted for presentation at conferences in 1975 and 1976.

Specialty Training

Lastly, I wanted to become skilled in different clinical methods dealing with undesirable human behavior. One skill I wanted to achieve was clinical hypnosis, a successful form of clinical therapy. Another area in which I sought additional schooling was couples' marital sexual dysfunction. In both my master's and doctoral practicums in marriage counseling, I realized this was a clinical area I needed to learn more about. Therefore, training in areas of sexual dysfunction counseling, using the Masters and Johnson techniques, was requested, and provided.

This was my planned fellowship for the next year.

6

My One-Year Fellowship

Two things became very apparent during my year at Beaumont. First, since I did not have one job and a single work location, I spent a lot of time driving around both Bliss and El Paso. Second, I worked for a lot of different bosses. I had, of course, Dick Hartzell (who wrote my Officer's Efficiency Report); the head of each clinical site where I practiced psychology also was my boss. Then came the squadron commanders in the 3rd Cav, to whom I also reported.

Time management was a necessary tool which somehow, I was able to successfully control. The variety of places I worked were both challenging and stimulating. The experience of this post-doc served me well throughout my career as a clinician, and much of what I learned continued to aid me even when I changed careers. This was an extremely valuable year at the beginning of my time as an Army psychologist.

Clinical Work

Working in the Trauma Unit was fascinating. Much of my time was spent counseling young patients and their families attempting to deal with the acute, sudden loss of so many physical attributes. Often, I would use my people skills assisting parents to recognize and accept the fact that their offspring may never regain the natural abilities once common to the patient. One patient in particular will never be forgotten.

Some 120 miles northeast of Beaumont lies the Mescalero Apache Indian Reservation. One night, a horrible auto accident brought a young Apache male to the Trauma Unit. His body was torn asunder, brain damaged, and barely held on to life. I was present when his parents were brought in from the reservation by a relative.

Comprehending truly little of modern medicine, the parents relied on the tribal medicine man for health and physical issues. He was accepted in the Apache culture as the leader in spiritual healing. In this individual the parents placed their faith. They knew their son was dying, and their beliefs required the blessing of their medicine man to provide a proper passage from life to death for the young Apache.

The relative explained the parents' desire to have their medicine man conduct a final ceremony in the presence of their offspring. I explained this request to the physician in charge of the Trauma Unit, who described the dangerous introduction of germs into his sterile environment. I discussed this with the relative and inquired if we could dress the medicine man in hospital attire and have him wear a surgical mask. The parents began a serious discussion; the relative turned to me and said yes, most probably the medicine man would agree to do this to accommodate the patient and his parents.

I returned to the physician, explaining what the parents wanted, actually needed. To them the Trauma Unit was totally foreign, way beyond their experience. Their culture required the blessing of their medicine man for their son. My job as the staff psychologist was to provide the unit with my expertise in dealing with human grief, and these parents sought the only help they understood: their medicine man. I continued telling the physician we could dress the medicine man in hospital scrubs, mask, and hair cover, and we could move the patient's bed into another room for the ceremony. Finally, he gave in and agreed.

As I told the relative that we could have the ceremony, I could see a cloud of despair slightly rise from the parents. Arrangements were made to hold the ceremony the next day. The patient, his bed, and all attached medical equipment were moved into a vacant room. We kitted the medicine man in clean hospital clothes and ushered him into the young man's room. Curiosity got the best of the unit staff, so watching through a window were a nurse, the doctor and myself. In the room were the dying patient, his parents, the relative and the medicine man. The ceremony began with the medicine man slowly moving around the bed, chanting in a foreign tongue, waving around sticks with feathers attached in each hand. The ceremony did not last very long.

Everyone in the ceremony left, feeling much better regarding the patient's future. The patient in his bed, with his hospital apparatus, was returned to the unit ICU. While I was ignorant about the Apache culture and the power of the medicine man, the bedside ritual calmed the parents. It must have worked, as the patient did recover, and after a few weeks, went home.

My work at the Child Treatment Center consisted of evaluating children by using psychological tests, observations, and interviews; explaining the results to the parents; and discussing my evaluations with the staff, so that together we could create a treatment plan. But the most enjoyment

I received was mentoring the UTEP nursing students. Being tutored by the staff on each child's psychological or special needs issues, I would explain that conditions exhibited by the child suggested what tests needed to be used to confirm and detail each child's condition. I would then detail how the treatment plan is put together, using physical and psychological data to define what help the kid needs. Because the nursing students had almost no instruction on the use of psychological instruments to quantify a person's behavior, they were amazed at what we could learn. As one of their teachers, I was pleased with their attitude and motivation to learn. My time at the Child Treatment Center significantly increased my sphere of knowledge in children, their behaviors, and possible therapy options. It was a learning experience that became most beneficial while at my next duty station.

Command Consultation

No doubt, command consultation with combat troops and their officers was clearly at the top of my list of professional practices. As a former company commander and battalion staff officer, I had trod in their shoes and was fully aware of what pressures motivated their behaviors. I left the Army four years before and now was able to help instill changes to make the Army a better place to function.

The purpose of command consultation is to provide commanders with the expertise of a behavioral scientist to evaluate a unit and suggest changes to improve the efficiency of the organization. Sometimes an Army unit has problems, while at other times a commander just wants to become more effective. In either case the performance of an organization is directly related to the behavior of its members. This is where I can help.

I was a student of the employment of organizational development (OD) as a means of working with a military unit. Essentially a behavioral scientist discusses with a unit commander the problems within his unit. The OD process involves the assessment of the unit to uncover real or perceived problems. Then the OD practitioner and the commander create a program to change the behavior to reduce or eliminate the problems. This change procedure concentrates on the interpersonal interaction between the members of the unit. Changed individual behavior patterns can restructure the behavior of an organization. The Army calls this intervention Organizational Effectiveness (OE). This is what I can do.

A major project[1] I initiated in two troops of the 3rd Armored Cavalry Regiment was to design and conduct a nine-month OE project to assess the effectiveness and/or the efficiency of the human interaction within the units. Then with the unit commanders, I would develop a program to improve the human interaction skills of the organization's members. This project would be completed in four phases: assessment, planning, implementation, and evaluation.

In the assessment stage, the members completed a questionnaire regarding their feelings about their relationships to their unit as well as personal demographic information. Additionally, a small sample (10 percent) of the unit participated in individual interviews, and their responses were recorded on a form. It must be emphasized that the OE process begins at the bottom of an organization to understand how the workers perceive their organization and how they function within it. The data was analyzed via computer and the results broken down into horizontal layers (i.e., officers, senior NCOs, junior NCOs, and enlisted). The results were divided into both weak and strong areas within the units. We wanted to emphasize the strong areas and strengthen the weak areas.

Noted were indications of areas that needed changing, both within the total unit and broken down by rank. Understanding what changes were preferred, the unit commander and I created a plan to intervene with the implementation of different human interaction skills. For example, if a major area of dissatisfaction by the enlisted members related to their NCOs requiring too much skilled work from too little training, a solution would involve improved and expanded training. This is phase two: planning.

Phase three, implementation, begins with a briefing to the organization explaining the evaluation results and the plans for change. Strengths and weaknesses are explained and the goals for change presented. Then the interventions begin. Often this process involves improved communication between all the members of an organization, and convincing those at the bottom of the importance of their contributions, leading to the overall success of the unit. These training exercises are called team building.

For the evaluation stage, the same tools used in the original assessment are used again. The data is analyzed by computer and the results statistically compared with the initial testing to see if any significant differences occurred. In this study, statistically there were no changes but ... both commanders said that the projects did make major improvements in the unit's performance and human interaction.

One commander cited that after initiating the intervention techniques, his troop won "The Best Unit" award, three months in a row. The other commander believed that change did occur, in that the interaction between the officers and NCOs, in his opinion, did improve considerably.

My ability to create these two projects was achieved through schooling and training, in several separate ways. The UTEP graduate class in Organizational Behavior solidified my theoretical understanding of how organizations act and what it takes to change the way they behave. But most of my education was obtained from the seminars and publications of University Associates.

In the late 1960s, two men at the University of Iowa founded University Associates. John Jones (PhD professor in Counselor Education) and John William (Bill) Pfeiffer (instructor and PhD candidate) became leading experts in the field of organization development (the study and practice of evaluating organizations, utilizing survey and feedback tools, implementing change via team building and problem solving). University Associates initially started as a publishing house for sharing various OD training and intervention methods. As their fame increased, they moved into consulting and seminars. In 1973 they moved to La Jolla, California (just north of San Diego), where University Associates became their full-time job.

I was a regular subscriber to many of their publications and a couple of times attended their OD seminars in La Jolla. Once Jerry Nowak, Dick Hartzell, and I (and our wives) attended a five-day seminar as part of our education at Beaumont. The seminar was excellent and added extensively to my tool kit of OD abilities. More memorable, though, was a moonlight yacht cruise in San Diego Bay. John had somehow arranged to take the seminar attendees and spouses on a borrowed yacht for an evening tour of the bay. Unfortunately, the guy selected to pilot our boat was not a perfect yachtsman, and while attempting to exit the marina, crashed several times into the dock and several other expensive yachts. Damage was slight, so Jones decided to continue, and make amends later. The night was a romantic trip watching the moon rise and the lights come alive in San Diego.

The training I received in OD later became a mainstay of a management consulting business Anita and I founded in the late 1970s.

Jerry Nowak took to the military like a duck to water. With my military background, I was sort of seen as a military mentor. Fellow intern Sam had his reserve background, and Rog his enlisted time, but I had over 16 years in the Marines and Army (and three combat tours). Jerry enjoyed accompanying me on my command consultation visits. Upon our return to Beaumont after our first visit to a 3rd Cav unit, he commented that when I was talking to a unit commander, to Jerry we were speaking in a foreign language. He was referring to our usage of common military acronyms and abbreviations.

Discussing our tours in Vietnam, in our conversations we would use words like eye-corps (I Corps) or Kilo Alpha India (KIA) or el-zee (landing zone) or see-eye-bee (combat infantryman badge) or dee rose (date expected return from overseas) or are-com (Army Commendation medal) or are-vin (ARVN), all foreign to Jerry. But Jerry did recognize that being part of the "real" Army did earn respect from those men and officers in the combat arms. My military background made entrance and acceptance as a psychology consultant comfortable, and established instant camaraderie with the soldiers with whom we consulted.

This awareness must have made an impression on Jerry, because after his first assignment as a psychologist he requested assignment to a combat division (in the Medical Battalion as the division psychologist). After graduating from Parachute School, he joined the division, where he earned his Expert Field Medical Badge (one of the hardest Army qualification badges to earn, with a pass rate of less than 20 percent). These honors are achieved by few Medical Service Corps officers, and most likely never by an Army psychologist. He remained on active duty to retire as a colonel, quite a military accomplishment.

Research

Probably the most important single thing I learned this year was the ins and outs of medical research. I discovered that medical facilities have money to finance appropriate medical research, and the funds to cover all travel costs to a conference to present research findings. This meant that the more research one conducts which is accepted for presentation, the nicer places one can visit on the Army's dime. During this year I traveled to several conferences, research forums, and training seminars, all over the country, paid for by the Army.

I worked with the Fort Bliss branch of Army Human Research Unit # 5, an organization of mostly civilian (with some military) psychologists, statisticians, research associates, and administrators assigned to conduct psychological research in support of the Army Air Defense Artillery (ADA) School and Center. Their office was located on the main post, in an old World War II wood building. The major portion of their research involved examining the ADA education and training programs and their interaction with humans. As such they had a decided interest in the Army's new Organizational Effectiveness programs.

Organizational Effectiveness is the Army's concept of organizational development. During the summer of 1947, in Maine, a three-week training seminar was held (partially funded by the U.S. Navy) providing information on the use of behavioral science in organizations. This seminar later became the National Training Laboratory. Until the 1960s, the use of behavioral science to effect change in organizations was a little-known procedure. By the late 1960s and early 1970s, OD became known and accepted as a means of making organizations better.

At this point the Army began to recognize that the top leadership in the Army was not doing an effective job of managing its soldiers. Some army officers, with advanced degrees in the behavioral sciences (such as Colonel Ramon Nadal and Brigadier General John Johns, believers and leaders) advocated the use of OD to improve Army leadership.

Two generals in 1969 took command of severely demoralized Army organizations, charged with turning these sorry units around. Major General Phillip Davidson went to Fort Ord in California, while Major General Bernard Rogers was assigned to the 5th Infantry Division at Fort Carson, Colorado. Both employed behavioral science techniques to increase the effectiveness and morale of their commands.

As OD was gaining favor among forward-thinking commanders, many old-line, hard-core senior officers decried it. From their perspective, the Army is managed from the top on down. Those at the bottom are captives to the beliefs and behaviors of those at the top. This was the Army I departed in 1969, when Army leaders were not successful leaders, but only interested in what was best for them. OD, though, does not operate that way. It is a method of evaluating the actual and perceived behavior of an organization, focusing on the human interaction, mostly emanating from the bottom.

Notwithstanding divided opinions on the value of OD in the Army, Fort Ord became the home of a test project to design a program to strengthen the command and increase the quality of life for members of a military organization (after all, soldiers dissatisfied with their job and life as a soldier would not re-enlist). This Field Organizational Development Project began in January 1973 and ended in June 1974. Despite the mixed results, in 1975 the Organizational Effectiveness Training Center at Ord was created to produce Organizational Effectiveness Staff Officers. After completing a 16-week course at the center, these officers (captains and majors) would be assigned to staff positions at Army posts and divisions to assist commanders in the use of OE strategies to effect change. Organizational Effectiveness remained part of the Army for two decades.

Those behavioral scientists in the Army that embraced the tenets of OD and OE (and I was one) envisioned this approach as a way to make the Army a better place to work and live. As a command consultant, OE was one of the most valuable implements in my professional toolbox.

My time with the Human Research Unit had a profound effect on my work as a researcher, which I still use today as a nonfiction writer. I learned how to draft research proposals, and how to word them so they were accepted and financed (by writing the proposal to either answer a question or solve a problem). Many of my OE projects at Bliss required the usage of statistical analysis support. The unit provided access to IBM

1440 and IBM 360/30 computers, and a variety of behavioral science analysis programs. Because of our shared interest in OE, the unit financed two lengthy trips to Fort Ord for me to talk to the people managing the Field Organizational Development Project. This interaction (and my OE projects) resulted in me becoming a writer for the Army Forces Command journal: *The Organizational Effectiveness Forum.*

Ironically, within 90 days of my departure from Beaumont, the Human Research Unit was decommissioned and replaced with a similar research unit, but from a different Army command.

Specialty Training

Part of my fellowship would be devoted to expanding my clinical expertise. Because of my previous training and experience in marital counseling, I wanted professional instruction in sexual counseling (helping married couples who are experiencing sexual incapability). One of the psychologists at Beaumont was trained and certified as a Masters and Johnson sexual therapist. As such, he was qualified to teach me sexual counseling, which he did by providing several weeks of one-on-one lessons and then letting me work with him with some of his patients.

My introduction to clinical hypnosis came during my internship at the Salt Lake City VA Hospital. This was followed during my fellowship by Harold Crasilneck, a psychologist who specialized in hypnotherapy. He spent several days with us, providing clinics and seminars that taught us the basic principles of how to use hypnosis as another clinical treatment therapy. He even used hypnosis on some patients to demonstrate the usefulness of hypnotherapy. I was hooked and wanted more. Later I was able to obtain funding to attend a week-long advanced instructional clinic in Houston, Texas. I became an expert in the use of clinical hypnosis to treat patients. While some individuals may believe hypnosis is hokey, useful only for stage entertainment, believe me, it was a valuable implement in my clinical therapy.

Moving On

In the late spring I received information on my next assignment. I was to be assigned to the U.S. Army Europe (USAREUR) Headquarters in Heidelberg, Germany as the command Drug and Alcohol Abuse Consultant. I did not want this assignment for several reasons. Our troops in Germany at that time had a terrible history of drug-induced malicious behaviors. To go there with my family, we would have to give up one of our vehicles and our family-sized tent trailer, as well as our two family cats.

As an intern at the Salt Lake City VA Hospital, I spent a couple of months on the drug and alcohol ward as the staff psychologist. That was probably the rotation I liked the least during my two years there. The ward houses about 20 beds, in a single, long room. During the warm summer days, we have few patients in the ward. As autumn gets colder, the patients gravitate indoors to the ward, only to depart again as the weather becomes warmer. My rotation was in the winter.

Most of the patients were abusers of alcohol and had Korsakoff Syndrome, a condition of chronic memory deficiency. The signs are difficulty with walking, confusion, and disorientation. The ability for a counselor to effect a change in the patient's drinking (or drug taking) behavior was almost nil. To my way of thinking, counseling drug and alcohol addicts provided no career satisfaction to me, as I rarely encountered positive results.

One day in the ward I watched a patient get out of his bed and wobble down to the open doorway, leading to a hall and the community latrine. He mumbled he had to go to the bathroom. I observed his challenged gait as he ambled to the hall. Stopping in the doorway, he looked confused; glancing around, he'd apparently forgotten why he'd gotten out of bed. Turning around, he searched the room, looking for something. Slowly moving back, his eyes scanned the ward, looking for his bed. He could not remember which one was his. This is my most memorable reminder of my time on the drug and alcohol ward.

I called the Psychology Consultant and voiced my opinion regarding the USAREUR assignment. I explained that this was not a suitable time for my family to move to Germany. Then I played my trump card. I pointed out that in the past eight years I had endured two—not one, but two—unaccompanied foreign tours, both in combat. I emphasized the fact that most Army psychologists had never left the States, and urged them to select someone else.

My argument must have been good, as my orders to Germany were rescinded.

As our year at Beaumont was ending, Anita and I began making plans to move to our next assignment. We had contacted the real estate agent who helped us buy our home in El Paso in August 1973 for $25,760, so when we did leave, he already had a buyer for $28,000. And because he sold us the house, he only took half his sales commission.

The three interns and I were all ready to move on in our professional lives. Jerry would remain at Beaumont as a clinical psychologist. Sam would return to his reserve duty, and Rog decided that seeing people as a clinical psychologist was not in his future. So he switched and became an Army research psychologist concentrating on human factors engineering. I was assigned to the Army hospital at Fort Polk, Louisiana, home of an Infantry Training Center providing both Basic and Advanced infantry training. I had a delay of two weeks to attend my final session of the Command and General Staff College at Fort Leavenworth, Kansas, and then another week to attend the annual American Psychological Association conference, to be held in New Orleans that year.

Our plan was to drive (again, with two cars, one camping trailer, three daughters, and two cats) to Fort Polk, set up Anita and the girls in a hotel, and look for a house. Then I would depart for over three weeks TDY. Anita would get the girls in school and sign all the papers on a house. But during this last endeavor, problems did arise.

PART III

Practicing as
an Army Psychologist
September 1974 to July 1978

7

Fort Polk

20 September 1974 to 30 July 1975

Getting Settled

Our caravan took two days to traverse Texas. On the third day we arrived at Fort Polk, which had an undeserved reputation of being nothing in the middle of nowhere. While created in 1941 as a major maneuvering base for World War II, since the early 1960s, its prime function was to turn civilians into infantrymen to fight in Vietnam. When we arrived in August 1974, it was still a post for Basic Combat Training and Infantry Advanced Individual Training. As such, the majority of military assigned to Polk were recruits, transient people confined to barracks. The few permanent party soldiers were mostly cadre to operate the Army Training Center, plus all the support facilities for the post. One of these support facilities was the hospital, to which I was assigned. With my leave and TDY, I would not report to the hospital for another month.

The main concern was finding a place to live. The post welcoming facility explained that there were no quarters available at Polk, so we had to find a place off base. There were two communities: Leesville, about 10 miles north of Polk; and DeRidder, about 30 miles south. We drove around each town, gathering information and talking to some real estate agents about where to live. The consensus was that DeRidder would be the better place for the family, despite being further away. Each community had a population of around 9000 citizens. Leesville was in Vernon Parish (in Louisiana, a parish is the same as a county in other states), and DeRidder was the seat for Beauregard Parish.

We found a nice real estate broker (who owned her agency). Her husband was a former Army major who left the Army to start his own home construction business. He became a major developer in an area about three miles north of DeRidder, called Green Acres. The neighborhood was by itself, but comprised nice homes, single and two-story buildings. We quickly found a two-story brick- and wood-sided four-bedroom, three-bath home for sale. The owner, a recently retired Army chaplain colonel, needed to sell to move to his retirement home elsewhere. Because Polk didn't have many permanent party personnel, selling a home was not easy, especially a large, more expensive house. We made an offer which was accepted, but then we learned that the laws in Louisiana are not like any other state.

At the entrance to Green Acres is a sort of small shopping mall adjacent to the Green Acre Plaza apartments (some furnished). We moved into one of these apartments. Green Acres was a relatively new subdivision, with many large shade trees, green lawns, and flower beds, inhabited mostly by Army officers and local professional people.

I quickly departed for my last two weeks of Command and General Staff College at the actual school at Fort Leavenworth, Kansas. I finally received my graduation diploma, the termination of five years of correspondence and Army Reserve Schools. It is an accomplishment no Army psychologist, and few Medical Service Corps officers, had achieved. I headed southeast to New Orleans for the APA annual meeting and conference. I was to present a research paper, and had signed up for a two-day seminar on developing and operating a child special education program in a local public school. When the conference was over, I returned to Green Acres, where Anita had our empty house. But legally obtaining the house was not easy. Louisiana is not a common law state.

The Challenging Laws of Louisiana

While the rest of the U.S. follows the concepts of Common Law (based on precedence and judicial interpretation of laws and legislation), Louisiana's Civil Law is based on the legal formats of France and Spain dating back to the 1700s. Decisions in court issues in Louisiana are decided by a judge's subjective opinions. Legal differences are mostly noted in areas of real estate law, trusts, estates, and inheritances. Often Louisiana is said to follow the Napoleonic Code, but that is not true. At any rate, Louisiana Civil Law subordinates women to the control of fathers and husbands. Because of that law, Anita could not sign any legal documents, even though she had my power of attorney.

Before we could purchase the house and obtain the title, I had to sign special legal documents testifying that she was my legal spouse, and therefore I was allowing her to purchase the property in our name. Additionally, I had to certify that I was, in fact, the biological father of our three daughters. Anita was not happy with any aspect of this, but did her part and acquired our home.

Julie (on the left) and friend at home at Fort Polk, 1975 (in DeRidder).

Reporting for Duty

On 20 September I reported for duty at the Fort Polk Army Hospital and met the commander, Colonel William Dwyre. I also met the chief of Professional Services, Colonel George Ford. The hospital had two psychiatrists, one the chief of the hospital Department of Psychiatry, and the other the chief of the Fort Polk Community Mental Health Service (CMHS). Normally the psychologist would be placed under one of the two psychiatrists, but here it got sticky.

The two psychiatrists were recipients of the military Berry Plan for physicians. To recruit physicians for the military, the Secretary of Defense created a plan (named after Dr. Frank Berry, Assistant Secretary of Defense for Health and Medical Affairs) to allow physicians to defer being drafted by completing internships or residency programs.

Interns would enter active duty as a captain. Those who chose to complete their residency would enter as a major, serving two years. Each psychiatrist entered the Army as a Berry Plan physician a year prior, so they had been majors for a year. Army regulations require the boss to outrank those reporting to him or her. In my case, my date of rank as a major was five years earlier than either psychiatrist, so according to the regulations, I could not work for either of them. Colonel Dwyre decided what to do.

My Duties

I would be placed under Colonel Ford and work directly for him. My title would be chief of Psychology Services. Essentially my duties would be to work wherever I thought best in the hospital. This meant that really, I was my own boss, and I had free rein over what to do. I worked out an arrangement of my duties with both colonels.

My job description we created read like this: Provide psychotherapy for military personnel, dependents, and retirees. Administer psychological tests and supervise the CMHS psychodiagnostics services. Direct psychological training to include supervision and teaching civilian counselors, Army counselors, and psychology graduate students in the CMHS. Direct and supervise CMHS community consultation programs for Fort Polk. To conduct, coordinate, and administer clinical psychological research programs to prevent mental illness in the Army. As I said, this allowed me the freedom to do whatever I wanted (and I did not abuse this trust).

Being the chief psychologist (okay, the only psychologist) at a large Infantry Training Center was the best assignment I could ask for. My first order of business was to let the post know my services were available. I devised a short presentation that explained who I was, my background, and what services I offered. In addition to the typical hospital mental health services available, I emphasized my consultation skills in organizational behavior and how I could help commanders experiencing personal difficulties in their units. I made presentations to the various chiefs of the different medical services within the hospital, to the post commander and his staff, and to the Infantry Training Center staff. My infantry background generated interest that resulted in many commanders seeking my advice on large and small behavioral projects. Knowing that a former infantry commander was a counselor in the CMHS, several infantry officers (retired and active duty) requested appointments.

Fort Polk, being an Army Training and Doctrine Command (TRADOC) post, was to undergo a major Army study of combat training, and I was asked to participate. Various hospital service chiefs sought my assistance to improve the efficiency of their services. Even the Officers'

Wives Club asked if I could present a series of seminars on the "Emerging Woman," which came about because of a research project I conducted on Army wives and the woman's liberation movement. This project will be described later.

Moonlighting

The local area was not overburdened with people possessing medical or professional backgrounds. On the other hand, Fort Polk had many officers with the advanced degrees or credentials which were lacking in the local civilian communities. For example, Leesville and DeRidder did not have an overabundance of physicians, so staffing local hospitals with weekend emergency room doctors was a serious challenge. The Army would allow military members to moonlight if their services were lacking in the civilian community. In my case, I was authorized to teach in the Fort Polk branch of a state university providing degree classes on the post. Also, I was allowed to serve (during off duty time) as an educational psychologist to the parish school district.

My time was divided between my clinical patients at CMHS; training and supervising all the psychological testing at CMHS; consulting services; research; and during off-times, moonlighting (teaching at the Polk campus of Northwestern State University of Louisiana in Natchitoches, north of the post and working for the Beauregard Parish school district).

Flight School

During my stay at Polk, I completed numerous research studies and authored papers for publication or conference presentation. Being accepted, I traveled quite a bit, attending professional meetings. The problem in taking these trips is that they took too much time.

Let us say I had a paper presentation to make at a military psychology conference at the U.S. Air Force Academy in Colorado Springs, Colorado, a straight-line distance of 850 miles. To fly there commercially, I must first take a commuter flight from Fort Polk to New Orleans. Then I must fly to the Dallas-Fort Worth airport and connect to another flight to Denver. From Denver I could take another commuter flight to Colorado Springs or drive in a rental car. This travel would take 10 to 12 hours or longer. With all my travel, I was spending a lot of time simply waiting for connecting flights.

Friends of mine who were pilots said I should learn to fly and

Christmas in DeRidder in 1974. From left: Suzi, Julie, and Karen.

transport myself. In many instances it would be quicker and much less hassle. I contacted the Fort Polk Flying Club to find out what it would take to become a pilot. What I was told fascinated me.

With a home to live in, and the girls in school, Anita began to set up our house for my three-year tour as I began my first job as a solo Army psychologist. Being back at an Infantry post was exciting and fulfilling, allowing me free rein to perhaps institute changes to the system which drove me out of the Army five years previously.

Yet this was my first time working alone, with no senior psychologist monitoring or mentoring me. How would I do? What would I do? Well, I would soon find out.

8

Clinical Support
and Research Studies

Project OSUT

Shortly after my arrival at Fort Polk, I received a phone call from the office of Major General Charles Spragins, commander of Polk. I was asked to attend a meeting at the general's office that afternoon. Upon showing up, I noticed that some of the officers also at the meeting wore, on their left sleeve, the patch signifying they were assigned to a new command, TRADOC (U.S. Army Training and Doctrine Command, directed by a four-star general). Because Fort Polk was an Army training base, it was part of TRADOC. The meeting was to discuss my participation in a major TRADOC study concerning basic and advanced individual training.

When the war in Vietnam ended, the Army was tattered and worn, a demoralized organization lacking in insightful leadership. It badly required fixing. By the early 1970s the Army realized massive changes were necessary to recreate an army disciplined and strong enough to fight the next war. The challenges were monumental. As an all-volunteer force, this institution must adapt to recruiting new soldiers and retaining them. It needed to redo the leadership education of NCOs and officers. It had to open more positions for women. Essentially the entire system, from recruiting men and women, to providing sufficient attractions and motivation to retain them, through retirement, needed to be transformed. To accept and master this challenge, General William DePuy stepped up.

In 1973, Army Chief of Staff General Creighton Abrams (who commanded the Military Assistance Command, Vietnam during my last tour as a combat advisor) recognized the need to reorganize the Army, starting at the very beginning with the training and education of its soldiers and officers. Thus, he established the Training and Doctrine command (TRADOC).

On 1 July 1973, General DePuy became TRADOC's first commander.

Its mission was to manage Army training, create operational doctrine, and oversee Army branch schools and posts designated for training. DePuy was an intelligent, innovative, and decisive officer, a highly decorated hero of World War II and Vietnam (where he was noted for firing many of his division officers for poor leadership). During World War II he rose from second lieutenant to lieutenant colonel in less than five years. He became the front-runner in restructuring the Army after Vietnam.

General DePuy had a clear-cut concept of Army training. He stated that improved training was a top priority to fix a broken Army. It must begin with the initial entry training for our recruits, then continue to units, NCOs and officers. It must be efficient and effective. Currently, Fort Polk was primarily an Infantry Training Center providing eight weeks of Basic Combat Training (BCT) to turn a civilian into a soldier, and all recruits were now volunteers, not draftees. Additionally, Polk provided an additional eight weeks of infantry training (after basic) called Advanced Individual Training (AIT). Polk, by the way, trained more soldiers for Vietnam than any other Army base.

Currently, civilians who had enlisted arrived at a basic training base, and then were processed into the Army, which could take several days. After processing, they would be assigned to a BCT company for eight weeks, then out-processed and individually assigned to other AIT companies, often at another post. They would undergo orientation again, then eight weeks of AIT, then go to their regular assignment. TRADOC calculated that this entire process could last as long as five months, just for four months of training. Additionally, they thought that more wasted time was due to the time it took for the individuals to form into a cohesive group twice, at the beginning of both BCT and AIT.

The meeting at Fort Polk was conducted by the TRADOC officers. General DePuy wanted to reduce the wasted time spent in BCT and AIT, so a study was created to evaluate a new means of combining BCT and AIT. TRADOC had two concerns: first, could BCT and AIT be combined, and in 12 weeks prove to be just as effective as two separate eight-week courses? Second, it was assumed that much time was spent in generating the cohesiveness of a group of soldiers for BCT, then scattering them to other units for AIT and undergoing the same process again to form another cohesive company. If BCT and AIT were provided in the same company by their same drill instructors, could the time wasted by two separate unit integrations be eliminated?

TRADOC needed a behavioral scientist to create a scientific study to measure cohesiveness in a group relative to productivity. The study should develop a means to calculate how long it took a collection of individuals to form into a productive organization, together dedicated to achieving a common goal (i.e., BCT or AIT). TRADOC wanted to demonstrate how much time clearly and unequivocally was wasted by having a separate BCT and AIT.

Upon arriving at Polk, I made known my availability for command consultation, and with my infantry experience, it paid off. Because of my background and the fact that I was the only psychologist at Fort Polk, I was asked if I could create a program to evaluate cohesiveness in a group of soldiers. I responded: "Yes."

The new training concept was to be called OSUT or one station unit training. Test OSUT companies would be created and trained. For several months, the new OSUT units would be followed, measured, evaluated, and tested to see how cohesiveness affected the OSUT companies and how effective their training was. Additionally, the same measurement processes were applied to regular BCT and AIT companies. Thus, one group of recruits would have 12 weeks of combined BCT and AIT, while other recruits would experience the normal eight weeks of BCT and then a separate eight-week AIT. Of course, the final scores of BCT and AIT in both the two separate eight-week and the single 12-week programs would be tabulated and compared to determine if the combined 12-week BCT/AIT could produce the same training results as the two separate programs totaling 16 weeks of training.

I explained that we could employ Organizational Effectiveness (Organizational Development) techniques to measure group behaviors relative to the two concepts of training. Using short organizational surveys completed by the recruits every couple of days, as well as observations and sample recruit interviews, we were able to determine how unified the members of the unit were. Using these measurements, we documented how fragmented this group of recruits was when they first joined their BCT or AIT company. Over the first several days we could clearly see how the uncoordinated, individual struggles transitioned into the group working in a more systematic, harmonized fashion. Also, as they melded into a synchronized faction, their training became easier, and accomplishments increased.

Now all the OD training I received at William Beaumont would be employed in a "real world" situation. I had the tools and knowledge to make this work.

The TRADOC team was large. It consisted of me, several enlisted men to do the testing and collect the data, several training experts, other administrative types, and a unique officer. He was an Army helicopter pilot, but also an expert with computers and computer technology. He was provided access to a large computer center located at Fort Hood, Texas. There he was given a team with the ability to take our raw data, transfer it to punch cards, analyze it, and create the final reports. To make this work efficiently, he was personally assigned a helicopter so he could quickly move between Polk and Hood, taking our collected information one way and immediately return with the results. I considered this amazing.

I was able to show how long it took a group of recruits at the beginning of both BCT and AIT to become a functional group of men, as opposed to a collection of individuals, each with their own singular behaviors. As predicted, by scattering the BCT graduates into different AIT companies, organizational cohesiveness vanished, and building it had to begin all over again. The OSUT training cycle could be completed in 12 weeks instead of 16. The 12-week combined cycle yielded the same training results as the two eight-week cycles. The bean counters were able to use this information to set a price tag on the dollars saved. This project took several months, but the accumulated data clearly showed that combining the separate BCT and AIT training cycles would save the Army seven million dollars each year and require fewer training posts.

In late spring of 1975, the Fort Polk team was flown to TRADOC headquarters at Fort Monroe, Virginia. We made our presentations to General DePuy, his staff, and other generals from the Department of the Army. Our research was accepted, approved, and packaged, and the documentation presented to Congress (because Congress controls budgets).

The final proposal indicated how the OSUT plan would work. Overall, fewer recruits would be trained due to the end of the Vietnam War and downsizing of the Army. I had heard that there was some political opposition to the OSUT plan, because consolidation of BCT and AIT could render some smaller Army training bases unnecessary and possibly cause them to be closed.

In 1977, though, OSUT became an accepted part of entry training, employed mostly for soldiers being trained for the combat arms to obtain their basic and advanced individual training in one unit at the same location.

Clinical Practice

One of my first visits was to the Provost Marshall's office. Part of my advanced hypnosis training involved using this skill to assist a person in recalling forgotten events or situations. Clinical psychologists have been using hypnosis in police work for some time. Used often in criminal investigations, a forensic psychologist using clinical hypnosis can help a victim or witness recall events or situations he or she may have participated in or witnessed, but is now blocking or forgetting. As a former police officer, I offered my services to the military police.

Hypnosis is a much-misunderstood procedure. Only about 10 percent of the population are exceptionally good subjects. To be a good hypnotic subject, one must have a purpose or motivation to be hypnotized. Once hypnotized, a subject will not reveal secrets or do things they would not ordinarily do. Hypnosis is not a procedure to force someone to do things in opposition to their values or beliefs. Considerable medical research has demonstrated how clinical hypnosis has successfully mediated pain management, enhanced trauma reduction, restored memory lapses, and aided therapeutic relaxation.

Clinical hypnosis is a process used to alter behaviors, increase learning, overcome anxiety, lessen addictions, or suppress pain. It is a means of allowing the subject to reduce or eliminate their peripheral awareness and attain a state of focused attention. The subject can then relax their brain and concentrate on specific instructions or suggestions. When the subject focuses on specific tasks, behaviors or mental capacities may be increased or diminished. The following of any induced suggestions must be accepted by a subject who is motivated to change.

How is one hypnotized? In concept it is easy, but it requires quite a bit of training and supervised practice. Initially the clinician should explain to the subject exactly what will be done and the expected goals or outcomes of hypnotherapy. If the subject agrees to be hypnotized, the next step is tests of suggestibility or susceptibility. This is a process to discover how well a person may be hypnotized. Here is what I preferred.

First, a person should get into a comfortable, restful position. He or she is asked to relax, close their eyes, and clasp their fingers together. The clinician commences to quiet the subject, to ease their breathing, to encourage them to feel good. The subject is then told that their fingers are locked together and as hard as they try, they cannot pull their fingers/ hands apart. Encouraged to pull their fingers apart, the clinician suggests they will not come apart. Those people whose hands immediately fly apart are most likely not good candidates for hypnosis. The longer the subject struggles to separate their hands, the more likely they are to be hypnotized. There are many other tests to determine if a subject is a suitable candidate for hypnotherapy.

If the subject is motivated to try hypnosis, the clinician has the person visually and mentally focus deeply on something. Some use a small crystal ball on a necklace chain. I used the person's thumbnail. I would ask them to relax and suggest they are getting sleepy, and their eyelids are getting heavy and want to close, while visually focused on one of their thumbnails. Shortly, this induces a trance-like state (resembling sleep), and the suggestions begin.

When the session is over the clinician slowly brings the person out of the hypnotic state by saying, "I will count backwards from five and when I say one, you will wake up, refreshed, and feeling great." Then I begin the countdown.

The Rape Victim

Shortly after I arrived at Polk, a Criminal Investigation Division Special Agent contacted me, asking if I could help him with a rape case. A young, enlisted female had been drinking with others and somehow taken into a vacant barracks building and sexually assaulted. She reported the rape, but told the investigator that she could not remember much of what happened. In the barracks was insufficient evidence to help solve the crime. Frustrated, the CID agent asked if I could use hypnosis to help the victim recall anything. I said we could try.

The CID agent and I met in my clinic office with the rape victim, and we covered what we wanted to do and why. I explained that under hypnosis, she might be able to remember more, so she agreed. The susceptible test suggested she would be a good subject. Getting her into a trance was not difficult, but that is as far as it went. She either would not or could not respond to my suggestions. She did nothing. Bringing her out of the trance, I realized what had happened. She was attacked and assaulted by an unknown male. That was traumatic for her. Now another strange male was attempting to take control of her again, so her body and mind resisted. While she was suitable for hypnosis, in this case she would not allow herself to respond when hypnotized.

That was the first time I used hypnosis by myself with another person, and it did not go well. Since then, I have used clinical hypnosis successfully multiple times; this was my only failure.

The Conflicted Recruit

Using hypnosis can often bring about behaviors that shed light on psychological problems. One such case involved a recruit undergoing BCT. Serving in the Army was a family heritage. Every male, after graduating from high school, enlisted. Family lore showed that every man was proud to have served and thoroughly enjoyed the service.

This family member enlisted, and during a BCT march slipped off the edge of the pavement, injuring his ankle such that he couldn't walk. X-rays revealed no fractures, so he was placed on quarters (bed rest, no PT, etc.) for a week. At the end of a week, he still could not walk. He was examined for several days and then he was referred to me by an orthopedic physician because medical examinations showed he no longer had any physical injuries. The doctor believed the recruit's inability to walk must be a psychosomatic problem.

Under hypnosis I discovered the problem. In a trance he was able to walk without difficulty, confirming the physician's diagnosis. I learned that he felt responsible for upholding the family military traditions, while at the same time, he hated the Army.

Instead of returning home, humiliated because he was a quitter or a coward, his unconscious mind and body took charge. A simple, minor sprain became the honorable way to get physically discharged for something that happened that was not his fault. He was not a malingerer; his body was unconsciously disallowing him to walk. This way he could depart the Army and at home be seen as a victim of an accident instead of as a quitter.

I explained this condition to the recruit and discussed this with his company commander. The man acknowledged understanding what was happening. What became of the recruit was an administrative issue, not a medical one.

Female Spouses and the Women's Liberation Movement[1]

As my availability became more known, I began to see more infantry NCOs, captains, and majors, recently returned from a tour in Vietnam, who were encountering marital difficulties.

The wife's complaints centered around feelings of frustration, guilt, confusion about her emotions, and hopelessness. The husband reported not understanding his wife after a year of separation as he attempted to return to the home life he left, 12 months previously. The period of post-separation readjustment, instead of a joyous reunion, became a time of distance, conflicts, and opposing thoughts of how their lives should be.

During the time apart, the husband was almost totally focused on his military mission, while the wife became the head of the household, making all decisions to manage the family. The husband's expectations were to return to what once was, but is no more. The year of independence for the wife is expected to cease by the husband, yet not by the wife. Added to this mix was that, by the 1970s, times were also changing for women's roles.

The military (especially the new all-volunteer Army) now has expanded roles for females that include commanding mostly male units and piloting aircraft, and on 7 October 1975, Congress approved Public Law 94–106, requiring the military branches to allow women to attend their academies.

Traditionally the role of the military spouse has been a passive, reactive one. The military member does what he is told by the military and goes when and where he is told. It has been up to the wife to react to this change and make the transition quick and smooth for the entire family.

During the husband's overseas tour, she now is in charge of her life and of their children. Essentially, she is emancipated from reacting to the demands of the military, which are placed upon her husband. A wife might take a part- or full-time job during the husband's absence. Additionally, the emergence of the women's liberation movement reinforced what the geographically single military spouses experienced; thus they received positive feedback on their new-found freedom.

The returning husband (especially after a year of combat) is not the same husband who left a year before. And most especially the wife is no longer the person he left behind. So now we have two people expecting to return to an existence that is no longer viable.

This phenomenon was most noted upon the return of the American Vietnam prisoners of war in early 1973 (see Chapter 11, Operation Homecoming). A part of the POW's ability to survive was to hold as true an emotionally and intellectually idealized concept of his wife and family. Upon his release from a captivity of several years, the reunion was of two totally different people. Often the male's expectation of his role in the marriage was no longer valid. The husband finds his wife's success at managing the family and her reluctance to return control to her spouse such that he perceives himself as "left out" and no longer an essential element in the marriage and family. Within a few months of being repatriated, several service members were getting divorced, as the expected reunion of two loving spouses was more like two strangers meeting and no longer being compatible.

Consider, for example, Sara and Ralph. They married when Sara graduated from high school. Ralph, six years older and a sergeant in the Army National Guard, went on active duty shortly after marrying. Now she is a 30-year-old mother of two and he is a 36-year-old staff sergeant, recently returned from an unaccompanied tour in Korea. In the mid–60s, he served a tour in Vietnam. About 12–16 months after his Korean tour ended, she reported increased feelings of depression and a growing dissatisfaction with her life. While Sara refused to accept her mental state, I did see Ralph who was seeking professional help. Eventually Sara was persuaded to recognize her feelings and to join her husband in therapy.

The treatment consisted of helping them to realize what was happening and why. This involved many sessions exploring their concepts of their roles in the marriage and what they expected of each other. As the sessions continued, it became clear that compromise was necessary for the marriage to survive.

An initial goal was for Sara to express her strengths and self-described weaknesses. Upon Ralph's return she resumed her previous position in the family dynamics and, by giving up her freedom, became depressed, questioning her self-worth. She had spent her entire adult life raising a family, while her husband had a career and went to different places (although some would not count tours in Vietnam or Korea as inviting or pleasant). Her impression of herself was low.

A battery of psychological instruments was completed by Sara (IQ tests, projective tests, vocational interest and aptitude inventories, and personality tests). The tests revealed she was quite intelligent, had an outgoing personality, and had an interest and aptitude for management and organization (which she had clearly demonstrated by managing the household and raising their children). She and Ralph recognized what was going on in their lives and what each of them needed to achieve their own self-worth. Together they came to realize that their pre–Korea roles and expectations were harming their marriage. Sara had the ability to function successfully outside the household, and Ralph had to accept that fact.

At this time both children were in school, so Sara was able to become employed at a local auto dealership as a receptionist and assistant office manager (which she excelled at). While this transformation was not an overnight achievement, after several months of counseling and testing, the couple became more aware of who each of them was, and how to accommodate each other's desires and what was necessary to enhance both their own and their partner's self-worth.

This is just one illustration of assisting couples, via counseling and psychological testing, to repair their marriages. Achieving marital harmony was just as satisfying for me as it was for the couples in therapy.

The Reluctant Recruit

One afternoon I received a call from the lieutenant colonel who commanded the Training Center Reception Station. He called to describe an incident he did not know how to handle, asking for my help.

The Reception Station is where all new recruits enter the Army. Being delivered by bus, they are deposited in front of the station and immediately come under the control of drill sergeants. They are quartered in barracks, and receive haircuts, uniforms, tests for future training and assignments, and their initial indoctrination into becoming a soldier. When enough recruits are accumulated and processed, they are assigned to a BCT company to begin their eight-week journey of metamorphosing from civilian to soldier.

Quite simply, the station was processing a recruit (well over six feet tall, weighing about 220 pounds, a former high school football lineman) who went crazy. He began to destroy the testing area and then locked himself in an office, refusing to come out. This is when I was called. The colonel's original thought was to call the MPs and have the recruit subdued and arrested. Then he realized this guy was mentally unstable rather than vicious and destructive.

Talking through the door, I explained to the recruit that the colonel was concerned and had asked me to see what was wrong, and what we could do. He let me in, and sat on a desk while I took a chair. His thought patterns were disorganized, his speech slurred, his behavior jumpy and uncoordinated. I realized he was experiencing a psychotic break, most likely initiated by the controlling in-processing requirements, and the strict regime he was being forced to endure.

I asked him what he wanted; he said that he wanted to go home. I asked what he wanted us to do right now, and he responded that he wanted to be left alone. I left and found the colonel. I suggested the recruit be left in the office in which he now resided, and to bring in a cot and a TV set. Make him as comfortable as possible and leave him alone. I explained what was happening and why. I obtained information on his parents and suggested the colonel out-process the recruit as fast as possible, and I would prepare the papers certifying him as psychologically unfit for service. Returning to my office I contacted his parents, learned that this was not his first psychotic incident, and received the contact information for a mental health service where he lived.

Next, I contacted the service, explained what was going on, and arranged for him to be transferred from the Army to their unit. I provided all this information to the colonel, along with the psychologically unfit documents, and left the return home transportation issues for the colonel to resolve. I told the recruit what we had done and that, in a day or two, he would return home. As long as he had his bed, TV, and food, he did not complain or cause any more trouble.

Consultation

Most of my consultations were with administrative or medical service units. The assistance provided mainly involved team building to improve the services offered by the organization I was consulting with.

Initially I would meet with the chief of the unit (typically a full colonel or a lieutenant colonel). Most members were enlisted soldiers, with some officers and NCO supervisors. The first step was to interview each member of the unit to solicit their perceptions on what was going well, and the unit's shortcomings. Then I would hold separate group discussions (officers, NCOs and enlisted) to obtain more data on collective group perceptions of how well the unit was functioning.

With a consolidation of this information, a plan (with the unit chief) was created to capitalize on the unit's strengths and to improve the weak areas. Team building exercises, sessions on improving communication skills, and feedback meetings with the unit members allowed them to gain insights into more productive behaviors. The results were improved unit effectiveness and enhanced patient or client interaction.

This kind of work was both productive and enjoyable. I delighted in being able to use my skills as a behavioral scientist as well as those of a former combat soldier to assist in the generation of improved performance in the military and medical units consulting with me. To me, this was not work, but fun.

I was very much able to assist in changing the Army from what it used to be (which was the reason for me leaving in 1969) into an organization once more concerned with its mission and its soldiers.

Research

As previously mentioned, I had a keen interest in the adjustment of the Vietnam vets as well as in continuing my investigations into why some people are unable to become productive soldiers. Fort Polk was the perfect place to conduct more research in this area of interest. With the OSUT project I had interacted with several BCT commanders, so I was able to arrange to collect demographic data from those recruits who would graduate from BCT. At the same time, all soldiers who were seen by their training cadre as not capable of becoming soldiers for mental, motivational, or disciplinary reasons, or attitude problems, had to be evaluated by Community Mental Health Service personnel and recommended for either retention or release from the Army.

With the availability of these two populations I needed (those men who became soldiers and those who failed), I developed a major research project to determine if demographic differences did exist in these two groups of recruits.

One sergeant, Gary Heffner, a former artillery soldier, currently a CMHS mental health counselor, contributed greatly to this project. With his eagerness to learn, I was able to teach him how to administer several psychological tests. Unfortunately, the Army decided he was needed more as an artilleryman, so he was changed back to his former MOS, sent to the Fort Sill Artillery School, and promoted to staff sergeant. No longer happy, he left the Army, returned to school, and became a master's level counselor. In his 50s, he joined the National Guard, and volunteered to go to Iraq in 2006, when American troops were fighting there. While there, we emailed back and forth, comparing Iraq to Vietnam.[2]

Those Who Make It and Those Who Fail[3]

The argument still existed: did service in Vietnam render vets unable to adjust when returning to civilian life? Some behavioral scientists claim "yes" and present mostly anecdotal data to support their contentions. Other behavioral scientists, who have conducted scientifically controlled research, say "no." This dispute continued.

The second part of my research on the Salt Lake City Army veterans (see Chapter 4) suggested that those soldiers who encountered difficulty upon being separated had experienced adjustment problems even before military service. To me, this suggests that many soldiers with post-service adjustment problems entered the Army with these problems already a part of their lives; military service was not to blame.

At Polk, I created a demographic form (requesting more information than I asked for from my Salt Lake vets) which provided a detailed background history of each recruit in the study, comparing those who graduated versus those who failed.

The forms were administered by several enlisted mental health counselors from the CMHS. Between May and August 1975, data was collected from 75 recruits who were recommended for immediate discharge from the Army. Between July and November 1975, 1489 recruits were questioned (again with mental health counselors administering the forms) in their seventh (next to last) week of BCT. This group comprised the "successful" soldiers. Clear differences in the two populations were noted.

The unsuccessful group had less education, a larger high school drop-out rate (when their education ended in the tenth grade, they were a year older than their classmates), fewer single males yet a higher percentage of divorces and multiple marriages, and a spotty work history. They had a more disrupted family life with almost two thirds (61 percent) without one or both parents. This group indicated almost one fifth (19 percent) had a pre-service psychiatric history and 43 percent of family members had received psychiatric treatment.

Seventy percent of the CMHC recommendations for discharge were for immaturity, maladjustment/anxiety/stress, and character behavior disorders. Most problems were noted during the first two weeks of training.

The background of both the unsuccessful soldier and his family was highly indicative of possessing poor adjustment skills or coping resources. Families failed, marriages broke down, and schooling was seen as non-productive, thus ceasing early, so life in the Army was no different. This study just replicated my earlier research findings. Army service did not produce adjustment problems after service. Many soldiers entered the service with a family history of poor coping skills which remained present while in the Army and after discharge.

Special Education Program for Beauregard Parish School District

Moonlighting in the off-post civilian world offered two advantages: extra money, and the opportunity to expand one's professional experiences. Additionally, the Army encouraged this. It allowed the local community to see what Army professionals could do and provided expertise to the civilians they did not possess. In the fall of 1974, shortly after I arrived at Polk, Northwestern State University contacted me. Learning that Polk had a PhD psychologist onboard, they asked if I would teach a graduate introductory behavioral management class in the spring for their MBA degree program. I agreed and was appointed adjunct professor of psychology in the Department of Behavioral Sciences.

Anita was considering getting her MBA, so she began processing the application to enter the program. Looking over the first class offered, she noted it was the one I would teach. That ended her interest in returning to school.

Soon after I was settled in at Polk, I contacted the parish school district admin offices. Explaining my experience as a school psychometrist in Arizona and my PhD-level courses in child and educational psychology, I inquired about the need for my services as a school psychologist. I was told no. The school district had a contract with some education professors at McNeese State University, some 54 miles south in Lake Charles.

As I was preparing to leave, somewhat dejected, I was asked to visit another office to see a man named Nathan Lewis, the Director of Curriculum. A big and gregarious man with short, thinning sandy hair, wearing glasses, he gave me a warm welcome, reinforced by his down-home soft Southern accent. Nathan quizzed me on my family, background (he had served in the Army as a first lieutenant during the Korean War), and my education and skills as an educational psychologist. After apparently accepting me as an educated person and a friendly guy, he cut to the chase.

The Beauregard school district was in desperate need of a comprehensive special education program for kids at the lower elementary school level. He continued to say that they had the funds but did not have anyone who could develop such a program. He then asked if I could do that. I told Nathan about the course I just took in developing a special education program. The course covered what was needed, how to set it up, and most importantly, what resources were needed and where to get them. Over the next few weeks, Nathan and I created a training program designed to put together a district-wide special ed program.

Nathan and I went over personnel needs and costs and put together a budget. The program would begin in January 1975. We needed a teacher to supervise the entire program, then teachers to conduct the testing, and then aides to work with the special ed students. Nathan rounded up applicants and together we interviewed them. By late fall we had the entire team selected. I then began training them to cover what the program would be, what it would do, and the specific duties of each team member. By the time the January training began, each team member had an incredibly good concept of what the district special education program would look like.

The plan was to create at the district level a team capable of evaluating children and then creating a school class program to meet their needs. Each elementary school would appoint a teacher as a special ed professional, trained to detect students who might benefit from a special ed program and monitor the program within each school.

The training went very well and by the end of the school year (in May 1975) we had a well-trained cadre of special educational individuals, ready to begin their new jobs. The 1974–75 school year had been devoted to selecting and training a team. During the 1975–76 (September to June) school year we would implement the program for its initial year and evaluate it closely to see where improvements could be made.

For the first year I would teach one afternoon a week and also hold evening and weekend classes. When we would have a week-long intensive training session, I would take leave. For the second year my time would be reduced to half a day each week, but also a couple of week-long education sessions. For the third year I would mostly monitor the progress and meet with the team for one day each month. Of course, throughout the three-year program I was always available for issues or problems that might arise. All my teaching and consultation duties for the second and third years of this parish program were conducted during leave time.

This program was seen as so successful that it became a prototype for similar programs in other parishes. It also won an award provided by the Louisiana State Board of Elementary and Secondary Education.

Through this program Anita and I met many wonderful local people and became a part of the DeRidder community. Several families we met became lifetime friends who remain in contact.

Learning to Fly

Encouraged by my pilot friends, I had called the Fort Polk Flying Club and inquired what it took to become a pilot. While the club was managed by military members, it did have a full-time civilian flight instructor: Steven Willoughby, a young man who did all the flight instructing for the club. The club had a couple of well-used, 1960s era, two-seat small single-engine trainers: Cessna 150s. The club also had a couple of larger, used, four-seat single-engine planes: Cessna 172s. Finally, it had an old surplus Army T-41, which was a souped-up military version of the 172, and another Army surplus plane, a six-seat DeHavilland DHC-2 Beaver. The Beaver is a high-wing STOL (short take-off and landing) plane with a 450 hp radial engine. Some say the Beaver is the best bush plane ever built because of its carrying capacity, big engine, and ability to get in and out of rough, short, wilderness dirt strips. Both ex-Army aircraft still had much of the Army radio and navigation equipment aboard.

The procedure for getting a Private Pilot Certificate was explained to me. I needed the ground school to learn the theory of flight, FAA rules and regulations, weather, aviation safety, navigation, and flight techniques. At the end of the ground school, one must take an FAA multi-choice test. The student pilot must also complete some 40 to 80 hours of in-flight training in taking off, cruising, and landing an airplane, plus how to handle in-flight emergencies. When the instructor certifies the student as competent to become certified, the student pilot must take an oral and flight exam conducted by a pilot examiner. To fly the plane wet (this means the rental cost also includes the fuel cost), the 150 rate is $5 an hour, with the instructor also getting $5 an hour. In 2022 a Cessna 150 rents wet from a flying club for $125 to $145 an hour, with an instructor charging $50 to $60 an hour.

On 27 June 1975, I took my first flight, spending one hour and eighteen minutes in the air. On 19 July after receiving 20 hours of flight instruction, I flew my first solo flight. I would arrive at the club at sun-up to fly, and fly after work in the early evenings. For ground school I took a weekend Private Pilot ground school course in Houston, Texas. We were mailed the course materials before the class and expected to know all of it.

We would spend 10 hours each day in class and Sunday night, we took the written FAA exam. My score was around 90.

On 26 August, with 47.1 flight hours I was found qualified to take my FAA Private Pilot flight exam. Unfortunately, that never happened, because I was transferred to another post.

Moving ... Again

Most of the professional medical officers at Polk hated their assignment. Polk was located in the country, between two small towns that were forty miles apart. Medical schools and graduate schools are usually in metropolitan cities with people, restaurants, theaters and shows, night clubs and night life, cultural events, sports, and much more. Young, single, and newly married professionals sorely missed the action and bright lights of the cities. Houston was 185 miles away, and New Orleans 223. So, for many of my colleagues, being stationed at Polk was a depressing time of their lives.

On the other hand, Anita and I found the small-town atmosphere inviting. We made several local friends and socialized with them. Career-wise I was doing everything I wanted. Anita was also busy with a multitude of volunteer activities. A three-year tour at Polk was viewed as existing in a paradise. I grew up in rural Connecticut, spending much of my time camping, hunting, and fishing. I still enjoyed camping and fishing, activities which were readily available in Louisiana. We settled in to enjoy a long assignment here.

In the middle of the summer of 1975, I received a phone call from Dick Hartzell, now the Psychology Consultant to the office of the Army Surgeon General, working in the Pentagon. After exchanging pleasantries, he asked, "Bob, how would you like to move to San Antonio?" He explained that about two and a half years ago, a new two-star command was created: the Health Services Command (HSC), which controls most Army medical facilities and personnel in the Continental U.S., Alaska, Hawaii, and the Canal Zone (Panama). This command comes under the Army Chief of Staff in a move to relieve the Surgeon General from the task of managing all medical facilities to focus on major health and medical issues in the Army. The command is headquartered at Fort Sam Houston in San Antonio, Texas, and a new position had just been created on the command staff: Psychology Consultant. Dick said this position would be a big step up in my career and he would like me to occupy that position. I asked a few more questions and said I would need to talk to Anita. He said I should plan to report to HSC in September.

I told Anita and the kids about the new job and the required move to San Antonio. Everyone's feelings were mixed. We really loved living in DeRidder, but the idea of moving to San Antonio seemed exciting, so while we would surely miss Polk, we looked forward to a different assignment and a new home.

Moving required quite a bit of work. I had to complete my research project and there would be no immediate replacement for me. I arranged with Nathan Lewis to come back to continue with the special education program by commuting from San Antonio, 380 miles away.

We found ourselves in an extremely unusual situation. During my almost-year at Polk, it was undergoing a major transition. In October 1974, some advance cadre for a new division began to move to Polk to determine what was needed to sustain a division. The planned activation of the 5th Infantry Division (mechanized) was scheduled for September 1975, a month after I was to move. The transition from an Infantry training post to a division post was to take place over the next several months. By spring 1976, the training center was to be gone.

This meant permanent party soldiers from privates to generals would need a home for their families. Polk lacked these facilities, so most families had to seek off-post housing. By late summer 1975, local real estate became a sellers' market. Purchasing our home in September 1974 for $33,500, it sold, 11 months later, for $42,000 after being for sale only a few days.

Again, we made the trek in a two-car caravan, tent trailer, three daughters and two cats. The assignment would be totally different. No more patients. No more command consultation. Whatever my new role would be, I had never served on a general's staff before, this was all new to me. What would my role be, and what would I do?

9

Health Services Command Psychology Consultant

New Assignment

Orders to Fort Sam Houston did not indicate a job or position but only directed me to the USA Health Services Command (HSC) on 15 September 1975. Special instructions required proceeding to the Family Housing Referral Office before making arrangements for renting, leasing, or purchasing any off-post housing.

Upon arriving at Fort Sam, the Housing Office explained that no on-post housing for my rank was available. I could be put on a waiting list, maybe moving into a government home in one year. Suggesting I seek off-post housing, the office authorized me to do so. Which is what I did.

Anita and I located a nice, small, furnished apartment near the post and enrolled all kids in on-post schools, where they remained for the fall term, while Anita and I began our search for a suitable house adjacent to Fort Sam. First, though, I had to report in as the new HSC Psychology Consultant for CONUS (the continental U.S., the lower 48 states).

Army Psychology Consultants

The Army has psychology consultants at various levels. The top one is located on the staff of the Army Surgeon General at the Pentagon (OTSG, Office of the Surgeon General). There is also a psych consultant for the Army in Europe, and in 1975 the new position for CONUS was created at HSC.

The Army has long known the importance of having advisors with broad military experience as well as expertise in their specialty. For example, when I returned to active duty as a graduate student, the OTSG

Psychology Consultant was a World War II aviator. When he retired, his replacement, Lieutenant Colonel Dick Hartzell, was a former Naval line officer. As the military shifted to include more professionals with social sciences expertise, the need for a broad military background did not diminish. That is one reason I was picked by Dick Hartzell as the best person to fill the new psychology consultant position.

In the 1970s, the background of Army clinical psychologists was changing. Previously, most psychologists came from college and graduate school to become psychologists in the Army, only to leave after completing their initial commitment. Therefore, most clinicians were captains. Now, though, as several former combat officers from Vietnam were obtaining doctoral degrees (thanks to the Army graduate program), more were coming in as majors. I was one of this group, but a senior major.

My background in the Army was quite varied (and I was also a graduate of the Army Command and General Staff School). As a clinical psychologist, I excelled in command consultation, served in both hospital and mental health clinics, and possessed a lengthy résumé of presented and published research.

Julie, Karen, and Suzi in San Antonio when Bob received his pilot certificate in 1975.

My experience in practicing counseling and psychology was about five years. But I had years of tradecraft as an infantry soldier; I knew what it took to succeed in combat. The professional medical consultant roles at Health Services Command included multiple and varied capacities. They monitored what the personnel within their areas of expertise in HSC accomplished, provided professional training, and served as the staff experts in their medical areas concerning issues or problems HSC encountered throughout its Command.

San Antonio, Texas

My last six years in the Army were spent in San Antonio. These were, by far, the best years of my military career. The entire family thoroughly enjoyed living in the city, with fond memories remaining today. San Antonio, the tenth largest city in the U.S., had just under one million people (48 percent Caucasian and 45 percent Hispanic), spread over 450 square miles.

San Antonio also had a unique situation called silk-stocking areas (also called silk stocking cities or districts). The term "silk-stocking" means aristocratic or wealthy. In the 1920s, prominent and affluent residents of the city desired to escape the hustle and bustle of the city (and the summer heat). They bought rural land a few miles north of the city (and 150 to 200 feet higher than downtown). This rolling, hilly, and forested land developed into separate enclaves of residents, becoming small, incorporated cities by the 1930s. Over time, as San Antonio grew, these silk-stocking areas became enclosed by the city.

The Military in San Antonio

Known as a military city, San Antonio is surrounded by four Air Force bases, one Army base and one outlying Army maneuver area. The oldest military post is Fort Sam Houston, created in 1876 as an extension of the Army fort in downtown San Antonio. Originally the post consisted of a large native limestone quadrangle with an 87-foot-tall watchtower. After World War II, it became the Army's primary medical training facility, known as the home of Army medicine. When I arrived at Fort Sam, the post had some 900 buildings registered as National Historic Landmarks, being the largest collection of ancient military post structures.

In 2010, due to the Base Realignment Act, the Department of Defense consolidated Fort Sam, Lackland and Randolph USAF bases, and the Army training facility, Camp Bullis, into Joint Base San Antonio, the single largest DOD installation. Kelly and Brooks AF bases were abandoned. This new command came under USAF authority.

Fort Sam Houston

Through the center of the post is a long (well over a mile), dog-legged parade field named after General Arthur MacArthur (five-star General Douglas MacArthur's father). By the reviewing stand (where generals and dignitaries sat for viewing troops marching by) is a stone monument.

Bob petting a deer in the Fort Sam Houston Quadrangle, approximately 1978.

Inscribed into it is the information that this field was the site where the U.S. Air Force was born. First Lieutenant Benjamin Foulois received orders to take the Army's first (and only) airplane to Fort Sam Houston and teach himself to fly, which he did. He remarked later that on his first solo flight he managed to take off in a plane, fly it, and crash it, all on the same day.

As a captain at Fort Sam, he formed the U.S. Army 1st Aero Squadron, which chased Pancho Villa in Mexico after he killed 18 soldiers and civilians when he raided Columbus, New Mexico, in March 1916. This was the first combined aircraft-supported ground operation for the Army. Foulois rose to become a major general and, from 1931 to 1935, the chief of the Air Corps.

The day I read the inscription, I recalled that when I went to high school in Washington, Connecticut, some kids in my school were named Foulois, who once had mentioned their grandfather was a soldier. That night I looked further into Benjamin Foulois and discovered he grew up in Washington, Connecticut; went into the Army; and was buried in Washington after he died in 1967. My classmates were his grandchildren. He was the father of the U.S. Air Force and his grandchildren only saw him as "in the Army."

Fort Sam Houston parade float showing replica of the Army's first airplane, 1980.

Fort Sam is one of the nicest posts to which I have been assigned. On the north and west side of MacArthur Field are historic quarters for officers, which are fine-looking historical homes. On the east and south sides are more historic headquarters buildings and barracks. The quadrangle (the original Fort Sam) is about two large blocks south of the west end of the parade grounds. Brooke Army Medical Center is located at the north end of the field. Health Services Command headquarters is on the east side of the dogleg, on Stanley Road.

On 28 September 1975 I was officially the Psychology Consultant to HSC, a lonely major among a collection of lieutenant and full colonels. With the girls in schools on post, Anita and I started to find and buy a house, focusing on Terrell Hills, adjacent to Fort Sam.

Terrell Hills

Forty-eight hundred residents populated the 1.6 square miles of this silk-stocking city, named after the doctor who first developed the area. A unique set-up, inside the city were no commercial businesses, only residents.

Anita and I decided to confine our search to Terrell Hills for two reasons. First, it had a deserved reputation as a very desirable neighborhood in which to raise a family; and second, the south boundary met with the northeast boundary of Fort Sam. Getting to work would keep me on small streets with little traffic, allowing direct access to Fort Sam via a seldom-used back gate.

We were shown a smaller single-story board and batten home, owned by a physician who recently terminated his Army duty and had moved his family out of state. He needed to sell, and right now. The house was at 904 Canterbury Hill Street on the east side of the small city. Across the street was Saint David's Episcopal Church with a large, grass-covered, sloping park that was shaded by large, leafy trees. The park served as an ideal (and safe) place for kids to play, which the church did not mind.

The house was about 2000 square feet consisting of three bedrooms, a full bath, kitchen, dining room and formal living room (with a see-through fireplace). A large family room had been added, sometime in the past. Since the house was smaller than we wanted, we consulted a home construction company, which confirmed that a wing with a den, a large master bedroom, and a bathroom could be added to the existing home for $8400. We bought the house in November and signed a contract for the addition. The house before construction cost $51,500, a real bargain. The add-on was completed in December, and we moved in. Two girls remained in the Fort Sam schools throughout the academic year, entering local schools in the fall of 1976. Suzi switched schools before the year ended.

Health Services Command

The final orders assigning me to HSC as the Consultant to the Deputy Chief of Staff, Professional Activities, in the specialty of psychology, became effective 15 September 1975. This activity was staffed with many professionals covering all fields within Army medicine.

The mission of this new command was readiness to support an Army committed to combat. This mobilization preparedness was achieved by providing total health care and services to support the Army in peacetime. The range of health care services included hospitalization; outpatient care; dental, optometric, veterinary, and nursing care; physical and occupational therapy; and dietetic services.

HSC developed doctrine, concepts, and systems for the Army Medical Department of the future. This was accomplished by providing professional education and training for Army medical personnel. The peacetime Army and its health care people and facilities must always be prepared for wartime mobilization. Additionally, preparing for deployment depends on America's soldiers being healthy and ready for combat, which is a major responsibility of HSC. HSC also assumed training responsibility for the medical assets of the Army Reserve and Army National Guard to insure their readiness to augment medical and training staff if activated.

Each consultant was a senior member within his specialty. Their job was to serve as the commander's medical expert in their area. They were required to remain current with whatever is happening in their discipline, to advise the commander or other staff members when advances in their sphere occurred, and to monitor the activities of their colleagues within the practicing facilities of HSC. As leaders in their area of expertise, the consultants were often asked to present seminars or provide teaching sessions in the medical centers or hospitals. Additionally, the consultants were expected to liaise with their counterparts in other branches of the military. Representing HSC by attending professional conferences and presenting papers was encouraged. If questions, issues, or concerns in their area of expertise came before HSC, the consultant briefed the commander and presented recommendations.

The Health Services Command headquarters was imposing. With its red tile roof, large windows, and an impressive double-glassed front door, the building echoed several others lining the street. The offices for the medical consultants were on an upper floor. Each of us had a grey metal desk and chair, telephone, shared grey metal file cabinet, and another chair beside each desk. Administrative assistants and secretaries shared our office space. The room was open, but dividers separated us, allowing for a degree of privacy. Our boss was a physician, a colonel, the Deputy Chief of Staff for Professional Activities. For my officer efficiency report, two physician consultants, both colonels, were assigned as my rater and endorser.

The HSC commander was Major General Spurgeon Neel Jr, the most decorated Army physician and father of aviation medicine. With a round face and short crew cut, he was the Army's first aviation medicine officer, who created the Army medical evacuation system (call sign Dust Off) using helicopters. Having served with the 82nd Airborne Division, he was jump qualified and an expert on paratrooper medicine. General Neel had served in three wars: World War II, Korea, and twice in Vietnam.

HSC consisted of eight Army medical centers across the U.S.; 29 Army hospitals; 38 dental facilities; six specialty facilities; and the Academy of Health Sciences, an educational institute providing medical training for enlisted personnel and medical-related training for officers (it is not a medical school) as well as advanced degree programs. CONUS was divided into seven medical regions, each the responsibility of a regional medical center. For example, Letterman Army Medical Center in San Francisco served California and Nevada while Brooke Army Medical Center at Fort Sam Houston served central and east Texas, Louisiana, Oklahoma, and Arkansas. Other medical centers served the states around them. The exception was Tripler Medical Center in Hawaii, which had no medical region.

Within the command were 66 clinical psychologists and 55 Civil Service government psychologists, for whom I served as their career program manager. I would monitor their career progression, discuss with them their professional goals, and offer suggestions on what they could do to enhance their promotions, upgrades, or job changes.

Because of the HSC commitment to the reserve and Guard medical personnel and facilities, I was able to specify, by name, Guard or reserve psychologists and enlisted counselors to be assigned to me for their two weeks of active duty. They would serve under me, performing clinical or research duties. This was a proposition where everyone benefited.

My Job

As the psychology consultant, I was expected to carry out consultation visits to the HSC medical facilities throughout the nation, serve as a career advisor to all HSC psychologists, present professional training and seminars as requested, assist in staff studies, and offer advice regarding professional issues related to psychology. This required considerable travel because HSC facilities were scattered all over CONUS, Hawaii, Alaska, and the Canal Zone. In practice, though, I never visited an HSC facility outside of CONUS. Additionally, as the commander's psychology expert, if any issues, concerns, or questions arose in my area of expertise, I was expected to research the issue and prepare a recommendation (a response) for the HSC commander.

Primarily my job consisted of two responsibilities: visiting HSC medical facilities across America to observe and offer (if necessary) suggestions to improve performance (such as presenting training seminars or classes) or enhance career potential. As such, much of my time was spent traveling, as I would call on medical facilities three or four times each month. Additionally, I needed to be prepared to respond to any requests or questions presented to me by command.

During my facility visits, I would meet with the hospital commander and inquire how I could be of assistance to his unit. Most of the time my question would be referred to his staff psychologist, but occasionally he would mention a need he had in the mental health field and request help in that area. Often that problem could be solved with me providing additional training to the mental health officers and their enlisted counselors. The officers could be psychologists, psychiatric nurses, social workers, or psychiatrists. For example, an installation's personnel might have noted an increase in military dependent children reporting educational issues and the medical facility needed to be able to detect, identify, evaluate, and produce proper treatment programs for them. I might then spend several days training the mental health staff in child educational evaluation instruments, testing protocol, resources needed or locally available, and ways to develop appropriate therapy options.

All visits terminated with a written report for the HSC commander (which I believed was often filed without being read by anyone) detailing who was visited, when, and why. Most were routine trips to see how the psychologist (and the mental health staff) were doing, to offer any assistance needed and to become acquainted with another HSC psychologist. The HSC commander expected his consultants to keep abreast of all happenings and all military personnel within their specialty, and to apprise the commander if anything required his attention. If not, the consultant worked independently, keeping informed, contacting the commander only if his attention was necessary.

Another area of my responsibility, requested by HSC, was to emphasize more command consultation by mental health professionals. Few Army psychologists had any military experience beyond their time as a medical officer. Going to combat arms commanders and trying to convince them the psychologist could help them manage their people appeared daunting to most psychologists. In their clinics, they were in charge; they were in command. Moving into the arena of the "real" Army and interacting with aggressive company or battalion commanders could be difficult because few commanders would acknowledge they had people problems they could not resolve. This situation led to my creation of an effective command consultant program that included the training to implement it.

HSC Programs

At the time of my appointment to HSC, all clinical psychologists in CONUS were loosely connected, professionally, to the OTSG Psychology Consultant. While all were in facilities within HSC, there was no formal structure between the Army hospitals and the Army Medical Center serving the hospitals. Yes, there was the military chain of command but almost always, those in their chain of command were physicians, not psychologists. Often professional or career concerns came forth in which only the Psych Consultant at OTSG could appropriately respond. This could be a time-consuming and occasionally awkward process.

I established medical region psychology consultants (the senior psychologist at the medical center). Thus, requests for assistance and guidance would go from the psychologist at the hospital to the medical center regional psych consultant to me. Instead of liaison and communications being piecemeal, they were now coordinated and structured, providing continuity and consistency. The psychology consultant for the Surgeon General was my contact up the chain of command. This regional consultation and liaison system was also replicated in Europe.

Another accomplishment was in changing who serves as the chief of Army installation Mental Hygiene Consultation Services (the Army's mental health clinic for soldiers). On 20 May 1976, a new regulation (AR 10–1) changed the name to Community Mental Health Activity (later called Community Mental Health Service) and authorized the commander of the hospital or medical center to appoint any behavioral scientist officer as the chief. Previously the chief had to be a psychiatrist but now could be a psychologist or social worker. In 1976, two psychologists became CMHS chiefs.

My research to evaluate the human factors elements of basic and advanced Army training at Fort Polk for TRADOC (Army Training and Doctrine Command) was seen as so successful it was used for implementation at all six major TRADOC Army Training Centers. I was asked to assist in the design of a comprehensive plan to help conduct another similar study at the Fort Sill, Oklahoma, training center. Reports of my research were specifically prepared for TRADOC to assist in their preparation for a congressional review of Army training methods.

The careers of civilian psychologists working at HSC hospitals or medical centers came under the purview of a review board, its members selected by me using both civilian and Army HSC psychologists.

HSC Consultation Services

Occasionally an HSC medical center or hospital would propose a question or present a psychology project, referred to me, in which I would become involved either as a helper or as an onlooker. Sometimes my role would be limited to that of observing what is taking place, or contacting the psychologist involved to learn what he or she was doing so I could brief the HSC command. One example was Delta Force.

Delta Force

On 21 November 1977, the 1st Special Forces Operational Detachment-Delta (Delta Force) was created as a national organization to counter terrorism. Located at Fort Bragg, North Carolina, it was commanded by the founder, Colonel Charlie Beckwith, a Vietnam Special Forces officer. Delta was to be the supreme national counterterrorist force, thus requiring the best of the best soldiers.

To acquire these men, Delta had an extremely rigorous selection process. Lasting several weeks, it included a variety of tests of physical endurance, military knowledge, and escape and evasion cross country navigation techniques. Also part of the selection process were numerous pen and paper psychological tests.

Basically, Delta needed men who were NCOs, physically superior, able to successfully work as part of a team, yet possessed the ability to function alone if necessary. The candidate's background would offer evidence if the individual was a team player. The grueling physical aspects of the selection process would reveal their bodily stamina, and the psychological tests would disclose their personality characteristics. The selection process for the initial group of Delta men was so difficult that less than 10 percent of the 163 that applied were accepted.

My background when an Infantry officer included two combat tours in Vietnam as an unconventional warfare specialist (I graduated from the Army Special Warfare School at Fort Bragg). On my second tour I participated in several special operations raids, so was aware of the experiences and training necessary for Delta Force operators. Also, I knew from first-hand experience the need to be in excellent physical condition to survive prolonged combat missions.

With my special ops background, the use of a psychologist for Delta selections interested me. I arranged to meet the Delta unit psychologist at a national psychology conference. We planned to meet in our hotel lobby, and I would accompany him to his room where he would explain his job and what he was doing. At the appointed time we met, and I was shocked.

Before me were three scraggly men. One was a captain, the psychologist I was to meet. All three had long, unkempt hair, unshaven faces, and clothes that were not the newest or finest garb. In no way were these men soldiers. But they were. Delta Force members did not want to be identified as military, which they did not resemble. The psychologist's two companions were Delta officers also involved in the selection process.

In his room the psychologist explained the reasoning for the continued testing for the candidates, and described the tests used. He explained that the testing showed personality traits which could be compared to what Delta wanted. The tests were not the only evaluation means of selecting a candidate for Delta, but one of many snippets of a candidate's behavior and physical strength matched against the requirements for Delta

Force personnel. As I left, I thought that being a Delta Force psychologist must be a most interesting job for a military psychologist, one I would certainly enjoy.

At other times, I became very much involved in a psychological need of another part of the Army. Typically, someone or some Army institution or facility would request assistance from HSC, and if it involved psychology, it was directed to me.

Sometimes these requests required my actual hands-on participation. I would examine the problem and then inform the psychologist in the situation about what could or should be done. An instance of a "helper" request was the leaking nerve agent.

Leaking Nerve Agent

HSC command became involved in health issues regarding an Army arsenal in a western state. The arsenal was used to store containers of a nerve agent, which had apparently cracked, so some of the liquid had leaked out. Some workers had been near the contaminated area and believed they had suffered ill effects. Some claimed a lessening of their memory and other mental aspects of their functioning. I was asked if there was any way to determine loss of intellectual performance. I said probably yes.

A medical team was assigned to determine if any of the arsenal employees experienced any loss of physical, mental, or behavioral abilities. I requested a psychologist be a part of the team, and that was done.

The chief of the psychology service at the medical center in charge of the Army medical region where the arsenal was located joined the team. My proposed solution suggested what should be done. The psychologist would collect from any sources such as psych tests, school test records, and any other available intellectual functioning evaluations done previously on the workers.

This information would form a baseline of past intellectual performance. Next the workers should be evaluated with I.Q. tests as well as a neuropsychology battery to determine current intellectual functioning. The two could be compared to establish if any loss of functioning had occurred. The testing was done, but I never heard whether there was any loss of mental capacity due to exposure to the nerve agent. Because the arsenal was not an HSC facility it was not under our command. I received no feedback; therefore, I presumed there was no brain damage.

West Point and Women Cadets

Another time, two requests were passed on to me simultaneously. One came from the HSC command and the other came from the OTSG Psychology Consultant. The first originated from the mental health unit at Keller Army Hospital at the U.S. Military Academy at West Point. The second request ended up being a solution to the first.

On 7 July 1976, West Point entered its first class of women cadets, thanks to Public Law 94–106, signed by President Gerald Ford. One hundred nineteen females entered the Academy but only 62 graduated in 1980. Like most male-only colleges allowing women students, West Point encountered its difficulties. Aside from animosity by some male cadets and alumni, uniforms were ill-fitting, and the PT exercises were designed for the male cadets, creating physical problems for females. West Point had reached out to HSC for help finding a female counselor (a PhD counseling or clinical psychologist) to work with the new women cadets as the school transitioned to a coed institution.

Each military academy used a different approach to integrating women into its cadet environment. West Point wanted to know what problems other male institutions encountered introducing females into the student body. Dartmouth College had matriculated women students in 1972, so West Point worked with Dartmouth to learn what problems occurred and how the school handled them. That connection fascinated me because Dartmouth, West Point, and I have our own interesting connections.

Sylvanus Thayer graduated from Dartmouth as valedictorian in 1807. He never gave the valedictorian speech because he immediately entered West Point to become an Army officer, graduated, and was commissioned a second lieutenant as an engineer. In 1817 he was appointed superintendent of West Point, and over the next 16 years changed the academics and institution into the premier school it is today. Thayer is known as "the father of West Point." Thus, he was Dartmouth's first contribution to West Point.

While a Dartmouth freshman, I applied for and received a congressional appointment to West Point. A conflict in the timing of physical exams for West Point and my year-end freshman finals resulted in me turning down the appointment. Fifty-eight years later in 2014, my granddaughter graduated from West Point (I commissioned her), continuing the connection between West Point, my alma mater, and me.

While Keller Army Hospital requested a female psychologist, the OTSG Psychology Consultant, Lieutenant Colonel Dick Hartzell, contacted me to check something out. An Army recruiter in eastern Texas had contacted him about a woman who recently earned her PhD in psychology from Texas A & M and wanted to enlist in the Army (as a private). The recruiter knew that psychologists in the Army were officers, so he contacted Colonel Hartzell about Teresa Rhone. Hartzell asked me to interview her to see if she could be an Army psychologist.

Ms. Rhone came to HSC where I inquired about her background and what she wanted. Her grades were fine, her practical experience in counseling impressive, and just as important, she had spent several years at Texas A & M, which has a 2000-member Corps of Cadets where ROTC students wear uniforms every day. The school is entwined with the cadets because of the cadets' headquarters, a quadrangle; their band; and several other of their activities encompassing the campus. She was the ideal candidate to serve as the first female counselor at West Point.

I approached her about being commissioned and attending the Basic Officers' Course (an introduction to serving as an Army officer) of the Medical Service Corps (the medical branch psychologists belong to). Upon completion, she would be assigned to the Military Academy. She agreed and, after the basic course, served proudly as a counselor at West Point.

Other Duties

While I did not do any research at HSC, I did author papers based on previous research completed and made several presentations of these papers. I represented HSC by attending various military seminars and conferences involving psychology. I began teaching at Webster College during off-duty time and, as the HSC Psychology Consultant, received appointments at local medical institutions as adjunct faculty to present seminars on community psychology.

A major emphasis by HSC was to get medical people in the field where the troops were. This led to seminars, lectures, and conference presentations on command consultation, and for civilians on community psychology.

Psychology as a professional field was changing. Psychologists were expanding into many other areas regarding behavioral science. As the psychology consultant, I needed to become familiar with them and consider how the Army should interact or become involved. As the senior representative for all Army psychologists in HSC, I explored innovations in psychology, prepared briefing papers, and created recommendations seeking approval for further training for behavioral scientists in our profession.

Independently, clinical psychologists and the commanders of their medical facility investigated the possibility of creating various fellowship programs to expand educational opportunities for other Army psychologists. Fellowship programs were created, and permission sought for HSC to approve them. My recommendations supported these requests. Within the next few years, several options for advanced training became available. The following post-doctoral programs for Army psychologists were authorized.

The Fellowship in Clinical Child Psychology, a one-year program conducted at Madigan Medical Center in Tacoma, Washington, provided an intense year of supervised training in clinical work with children, adolescents, and families.

Madigan and William Beaumont (at El Paso, Texas) initiated a post-doctoral fellowship in clinical neuropsychology. This one-year program was accomplished in three ways: academic study, clinical-practical experience, and research. Areas studied included neuroanatomy, neurophysiology, neuropathology, neurosurgery, neurology, and the Halstead Reitan and Reitan-Indiana neuropsychological batteries. Fellows were trained in the usage, scoring, and formulation of appropriate treatment recommendations.

William Beaumont also crafted a one-year post-doc in community mental health, like the program created for me in 1973. The curriculum and practical experience consisted of organizational effectiveness, rape crisis treatment, military unit consultation and the development of intervention strategies to resolve command problems.

A new interest (and demand) by psychologists (both military and civilian) working in clinical settings was the authorization to prescribe psychotropic medicine to certain patients. My personal feeling is that if psychologists wanted to hand out pills, they should have gone to medical school. But my job was not to dictate, but to evaluate trends and provide recommendations. As HSC Psychology Consultant, I supported this request. This program did not begin until a decade after I retired.

In 1991 this three-year program became available as the Department of Defense Pharmacology Demonstration Project. Designed for qualified psychologists from any military branch, the academic education was at the Uniformed Services University of the Health Sciences at Bethesda, Maryland, with practical training at Walter Reed Army Medical Center and an Air Force base. After successful completion, a psychologist would be authorized to write psychotropic prescriptions. Due to budget constraints, the program was terminated in 1997. Ironically, one of the 10 graduates, a now-retired USAF psychologist, is in private practice in Las Cruces, New Mexico, where I live. New Mexico, in 2002, was the first state to allow certified psychologists to prescribe psychotropic medication.

Too Many Consultants and Counselors

In the mid–1970s, the Army was experiencing various degrees of turmoil. The draft was long gone. The Vietnam War was over. The Vietnam-era Army was too large for peacetime duty, so reductions were necessary. One study conducted determined the Army had too many soldiers assigned full-time duty as a consultant or counselor. There were medical consultants, education counselors, enlistment counselors, re-up counselors, religious counselors, legal consultants, Army branch consultants, and the list goes on. A decision was made in the Army medical areas that most professional activities consultants would become dual-hatted. Most would be reassigned to a clinical (or teaching) position commensurate with their rank and professional expertise yet retain the consultant position as an extra duty.

For me, that meant moving again to return to practicing psychology. Fortunately, the chief of the Psychology Service at Brooke Army Medical Center had just departed, so the position was vacant. I elected to fill that slot and work just a few blocks away.

Moving Up the Street

Departing my full-time job (for less than a year) as the HSC Psychology Consultant, I received my third Army Commendation Medal for meritorious service for my exceptional competence and distinguished record of achievement during this assignment (that's what the citation said, not my evaluation of myself). You know, I really should not have refused that third Bronze Star for an ARCOM.

My feelings about being reassigned were ambiguous. Being released from the prestigious job as a full-time member of a two-star staff hurt. On the other hand, returning to once again being a practitioner was exciting. Also, becoming the chief of a

Bob receiving his third Army Commendation Medal as the HSC Psychology Consultant (U.S. Army photo, 1976).

service at a major medical center was far from shabby. Besides, Anita was incredibly happy. This move meant at least three more years in San Antonio, which the whole family loved. Also, this new assignment meant less traveling for HSC, which my family liked.

My last job in the Army when I left active duty in 1969 had me commanding a combat advisor team; before that, I was a company commander, and before that, I commanded another combat advisor team. My Infantry background had composed over half my career as an officer in charge of groups of men. Over the past seven years, as a reserve officer or an Army psychologist, I had not commanded anyone but me. Now I would once again oversee an organization of over a dozen men and women: officers, civilians, graduate students, and enlisted staff. I was eagerly looking forward to my future in my next move as an Army psychologist.

PART IV

Return to Practicing Psychology
July 1976 to September 1981

10

Psychology Service at Brooke Army Medical Center

Department of Psychiatry

Brooke Army Medical Center (BAMC, pronounced "bam cee") was a 600-bed medical center consisting of three major hospital complexes and 12 separate outpatient facilities. The main hospital building was a massive (210,000 square feet), six story (plus a penthouse) structure built in 1937. At the north end of MacArthur Parade Field, the entrance was imposing, with gigantic entrance doors. BAMC facilities and clinics were scattered around Fort Sam, although most offices were not far from the main hospital.

Within the medical center was the Department of Psychiatry (in a separate building, not in the main building), one of the numerous medical departments found in most hospitals. This department was like an independent psychiatric facility, with a separate Community Mental Health Service (CMHS) located within the troop area. The department consisted of four distinct services: psychiatric outpatient (where patients are seen in a clinic, staffed by the chief, a medical officer psychiatrist lieutenant colonel, three psychiatrists, some psychiatric nurses, and enlisted medical personnel); a psychiatric inpatient hospital (staffed by a colonel psychiatrist, nurses, and hospital medics); psychology service; and the CMHS (staffed by a lieutenant colonel psychiatrist and several other officer and enlisted mental health professionals).

On 10 September 1976, I reported to Colonel Otto Schreiber, chief of the Department of Psychiatry. A tall slim man, with thinning sandy-colored hair and wire-rimmed glasses, he was open, friendly, and one of the best bosses I ever had. We sat in his office while he discussed his department and the role psychology played in it. While the Psychology Service supports all other services within Psychiatry with psychological testing and counseling, Dr. Schreiber also explained that the service operated independently. The chief of Psychology was in charge; a psychiatrist did not run the show. I reported directly to him, and together we decided what psychology would do. I concurred that was how I would like to work with him. He said the only continuous, mandatory requirement was a weekly morning briefing where the service chiefs met to update everyone on what was being done in their specialty. He then took me to the Psychology Service (on the first floor of the Psychiatry building) and introduced me to the staff.

Psychology Service

The facilities of the Psychology Service occupied most of the first floor of the building. The door to our clinic opened into a large waiting area with the receptionist/secretary's desk to the left of the entrance. All around the reception area were numerous small offices, one for each psychologist and one for each enlisted counselor. In another area were psychological testing rooms and offices for our graduate student interns.

My staff included one civilian secretary; four permanent captain psychologists; two other Army psychologists assigned temporarily until the Army decided what to do with them; several enlisted mental health counselors (staff sergeant, sergeants, and specialist four); and two to four psychology master's-level graduate student interns from three local universities: St. Mary's, Our Lady of the Lake, and Trinity. While most were psychology students, social work students were trained occasionally.

We could provide any psychological test available (I.Q., personality, educational, vocational, and aptitude, as well as a full neuropsychological battery). All the psychologists had extensive experience conducting psychiatric patient interviews to evaluate psychotic behaviors. The Service was responsible for all psychological evaluations, treatment, consultation, and research provided to Psychiatry and BAMC. We did individual, couples, and group counseling; provided assistance to the BAMC Adolescent Medicine Clinic; and conducted hypnotherapy sessions for dental patients, as well as hypnotherapy and pain management for oncology and burn unit patients. The service conducted classes for other medical services within BAMC and participated in major BAMC patient and research programs.

Our patients consisted mostly of older NCOs, officers (who could use the CMHS, but elected not to because most of the CMHS patients were younger enlisted), and retired military and dependents (retirees and dependents were not seen by CMHS). We would also evaluate and treat patients throughout BAMC, mostly in psychiatry wards, oncology, and the burn unit. Additionally, psychologists evaluated rehabilitation patients and worked with the physical and occupational therapy teams to discuss patient limitations (after an accident or physical event such as a stroke) and helped create treatment plans for patients. Because often patients in rehab had serious disabilities, we also counseled family members, helping them to adjust to the sudden limitations of their loved one.

My office was a very small corner room (it had two windows) just behind our secretary's desk. Long and narrow, it held a short bookcase, a small table, a metal desk, a chair, and a filing cabinet. Beside my desk were two wooden chairs for clients, patients, or guests.

I was looking forward to practicing psychology again.

Clinical Practice

Going into a Windshield

One day Warrant Officer Alvin Benson saw me by appointment to discuss a problem he and his wife (Betty) suffered from. A few months ago, Alvin and Betty spent the weekend at Corpus Christi, on the Gulf of Mexico, some 145 miles southeast of Fort Sam. As they headed for home on Sunday afternoon, it was raining hard with slippery roads. Interstate 15 was slick and traffic most likely exceeded safe driving conditions. Alvin, driving, was reluctant to slow down and hinder traffic. Suddenly, the semi in front began to jackknife, its trailer swinging sideways, almost stopping. Slamming on his brakes, Alvin tried to avoid the vehicle to his front but failed. The impact threw both Alvin and Betty into their windshield, resulting in surgery and weeks of recuperation and rehabilitation.

Physically they had recovered, but mentally they were a wreck; neither could drive again. Approaching a car and sitting in it brought severe bouts of anxiety, fear, and depression. Shaking, crying, and unable to do anything in a car, they were desperate for help as they were suffering from PTSD (post-traumatic stress disorder).

Initially I saw Alvin as he described what happened and what happens physically and mentally every time he tries to drive. He said his wife felt the same way. Together they described their fear of driving and how it was causing considerable difficulty for them for getting to work, shopping, or just going somewhere. They were unable to function inside a car, and it was destroying their lives.

I explained what I thought would help: clinical hypnotherapy. I described what I would do: use hypnosis to remove the bad thoughts they had recalling the crash, the injuries and the suffering and pain, replacing them with images of their own personal peace and tranquility. I would see each one separately, but first test each one for hypnosis susceptibility.

I then began seeing them individually. They both proved to be excellent hypnosis subjects.

The plan was, by using hypnosis, to first elicit images that each found very soothing, peaceful, calming. For some, it is visualizing (under hypnosis) lying down on a beach at a lake or the seashore; for others, it is hiking through a field or on a mountain trail; or napping in a hammock; or whatever calms them down, bringing a relaxing, restful feeling.

For both Bensons, the most epic and fearful second of their accident was the imminent shock of going into the windshield. For him, the peaceful event was stopping after a hard, sweaty hike, coming across a lovely meadow, lying down in the sun, resting, and going to sleep. For her, it was relaxing on the sandy shore of a lake next to a cabin her family owned. Under hypnosis, I could bring each to their own calming image and achieve total relaxation.

Next, I said I would hypnotize them (each in separate sessions) and I would describe their accident in detail. As each became fearful, anxious, scared, and uncomfortable, they would raise their finger. As I began to describe what happened, quickly the finger moved upward, and I stopped discussing the accident and immediately began describing their safe, peaceful place. As the image in their mind swung from a fearful image to a relaxing one, they became calm again, no longer twitching and jerking uncomfortably in their seat. Instead, they exhibited slower breathing, relaxed, and seemed to be in a peaceful slumber.

Lieutenant Colonel Bob Worthington, Army psychologist (U.S. Army photo, 1976).

The idea was to describe the accident each session (we met twice a week), and each time move a little closer to being thrown into the windshield before raising the finger. After a few weeks, we achieved this; I could describe the accident without the finger coming up. I taught the couple how to create a mental image of their peaceful scene whenever an anxiety arose because of recalling the accident. Soon they could do this on their own, without any assistance from me. A couple of weeks after our final session with both together, Alvin came by my office. He was now driving to work with no anxiety and his wife was beginning to drive a little without fear.

These patients ended up in my success column.

The Sergeant Who Threatened to Hold a Press Conference

One morning around 6:30 I received a call from the commanding general of BAMC. He said he had a problem and needed me to investigate it. Apparently a staff sergeant, an infantryman from Fort Hood, Texas (about 145 miles north of Fort Sam), threatened to hold a press conference on the front steps of BAMC unless he was treated properly at BAMC. I asked why I should explore this situation. The general said that some of his staff believed the sergeant was crazy, so I should determine if that was true. He said he would arrange for the soldier to be in my office at 7:30. I asked why people thought the sergeant was crazy, and the commander said he was making all sorts of crazy claims, such as that he was injured in the back (but a neurologist said he was okay), and he claimed he was a millionaire and deserved better. The sergeant said if he did not get proper medical care, he was going to tell the world how bad BAMC was.

At 7:30 a.m. the sergeant was waiting for me outside my office, so we went inside. I explained that the general asked me to talk to the sergeant about his problem. The sergeant looked around, realizing he was in the Psychology Service. Looking at me, he said that testing him was a waste of time. His father was the top psychologist in the Air Force, so he became a guinea pig for all the psych tests available. He claimed he had taken every test.

Asking the sergeant to tell me what had happened, I indicated I would try to help him. He began his story, but an abbreviated one. He said he hurt his back in Vietnam and it was acting up again. He saw a doctor in the Army hospital at Fort Hood, who referred him to the Neurology Service at BAMC. When he arrived, he had to wait a long, long time to be seen. Finally, he was seen by a doctor who rushed through the exam. While checking his back, the doctor was eating a Twinkie, spilling crumbs on the sergeant's back. The doctor said he couldn't find anything wrong. Incensed, the sergeant left, intending to do something about that. Therefore, he threatened to hold a press conference.

When I asked about his father, he said he retired and was now a professor at St. Mary's University. Regarding his being a millionaire, he said he owned some land in the city that was valuable. Leading him to our waiting area, I said I would return. I called the Psychology Department chair at St. Mary's and inquired if they had a professor, a retired Air Force officer, giving the sergeant's last name. She said "no," so I asked her if she could see if there was any professor at St. Mary's with that name. A few minutes later she said there was no faculty member with that name. I was now thinking that the general was right, and the sergeant was conning all of us.

Returning to the sergeant, I explained there was no professor at St. Mary's with his name. The sergeant, looking at me, apologized. His father was actually his stepfather, as his biological father had died. His mother had remarried the colonel, but the sergeant kept his real father's name. Again, back to the phone and St. Mary's. There was no psychology professor at the university with the name the sergeant gave me. Being conned again? But I was told that there was a professor in the school of business with that name. I was able to connect with him.

I explained why I was calling, to verify some facts the sergeant provided. Yes, the sergeant was his stepson. The professor was a retired colonel and a senior clinical psychologist in the Air Force. Toward the end of his career, he became very much involved in biostatistics and was hired as a statistics professor in the business school.

Yes, his stepson had a bad back; it was seriously injured in Vietnam when he fell out of the back of a truck, requiring hospitalization (but being in a combat area, the handwritten records became lost). Yes, he was a paper millionaire. His mother was a top real estate agent who had invested all his Army pay while in Vietnam (being single, he had multiple tours) in raw land real estate outside the city limits, north of San Antonio. Today, over a decade later, his property was now inside the city limits and very, very valuable. So, everything the sergeant said was true.

Calling the general, I explained everything I had learned. I suggested that the sergeant be seen again by neurology, but by another doctor. The general said to tell the sergeant to report to the chief of Neurology Service, who would take care of him personally. I told the sergeant and off he went, much happier now than when I first met him.

Some days I was a clinician; others, a detective.

Coffee Crazy

One day our service was asked to evaluate a psychotic female, just admitted to the psychiatric ward as an inpatient. I said I would do the evaluation. The woman was in her early 50s, the wife of a retired soldier. Her husband explained that over the past few days she seemed dazed, talking nonsense, and doing weird things, unlike her. He also noted she had problems sleeping at night and appeared unduly fatigued. Finally, her behavior early that afternoon became so bizarre that her husband brought her to the BAMC emergency room.

Her intake evaluation reported her symptoms: delusions, hallucinations, rambling speech, irritability, agitation and hostility at being in the ER, nervousness, and anxiety. The on-call ER psychiatrist diagnosed her as psychotic, exhibiting mental disturbances, and out of touch with reality. She was admitted to the psychiatric ward in the Department of Psychiatry. Her behavior when I visited her late that afternoon was no different. I could observe, but any meaningful conversation was impossible.

The next morning, I visited her again. While she was still in a psychotic state, her frantic posturing and rambling dialogue were less so. It seemed like her psychiatric condition was slowly decreasing. I again spoke to her husband regarding what she did at home, looking for some clues causing her psychotic break.

He described her normal daily routine: wake up, walk to the bathroom, go into the kitchen, and make coffee. Obtaining the morning paper, she would drink her coffee and read. Next was breakfast and another cup of coffee. After cleaning up, she would shower, dress, and move to her hobby room. Work there, get lunch, clean up, and return to her hobbies. At the end of the afternoon, she would prepare supper, clean up, watch TV, or read until bedtime. Sometimes her daily activities would change if she went shopping. I inquired about other personal habits such as smoking (no); drinking alcohol (very little); drugs (no); eating (good variety of foods, not much as she was slender); or other habits she pursued (nothing out of the ordinary for her). He said there was no history of any psychotic behavior in her family history nor any recent stresses he saw.

The big question was, what caused her psychotic break?

I returned to her ward on the third day of her admittance. Her delusional behaviors and her hallucinations had lessened considerably. Her rambling and incoherent speech was almost totally gone, but she was irritable, anxious, and complained of being unable to sleep, having a headache, and feeling nauseated. Her symptoms and behavior closely resembled that of an addict encountering withdrawal pains. She was confused, but more coherent and more aware of her condition and where she was.

The ward psychiatrist and I were totally clueless regarding what happened to her or why. Both of us spoke to her husband again, frantically seeking some indication of what happened to her. He reiterated her "normal" existence as he recited her daily behaviors. Both the psychiatrist and I noted one part of her daily existence which we both viewed as not normal. When she got up in the morning, she had a cup of coffee, another reading the paper, another at breakfast, another while getting dressed, a couple more during the morning, one at lunch, and more during the day. Both of us recognized her consumption of ten to twelve (or more) cups of coffee seemed excessive. We knew that a normal intake of coffee (caffeine) was a stimulant intensifying the central nervous system, leading to feelings of well-being, energy, alertness, and relief of fatigue. Yet her symptoms were the opposite.

Together the psychiatrist and I began our research, reading medical journals and talking to pharmacologists and nutritionists. What we learned is that a low dosage of caffeine leads to stimulation, while an overdose leads to psychosis. Our research led us to conclude her psychiatric condition was because of her consuming too much caffeine. We further concluded that her time in the hospital with very limited coffee brought forth withdrawal symptoms, which were most prominent during her first two days after admittance. A week later she was discharged from the hospital, symptom-free.

At this time, caffeine addiction and the psychotic consequences were unknown in psychiatry. But as Americans consumed greater quantities of caffeine-laden substances (coffee, tea, sodas and energy drinks, chocolates, cold remedies, and weight-loss aids), it became recognized as a health issue. By the mid–1990s, caffeine overdose and withdrawal had become recognized psychiatric disorders.

The Little Secret Base

Receiving a call from the BAMC Chief of Professional Services, my presence was requested for a meeting with two U.S. Air Force officers. I met with them.

A colonel and a major were in Colonel Ognibene's office. The two Air Force officers were from a classified base located inside another, larger Air Force base in San Antonio. The mission of the secret base was to collect intelligence information and pass it on to analysts located elsewhere. The base experienced a personnel issue which required psychological help, but no local Air Force psychologist had a high enough security clearance to enter the base. Because of my Infantry background (and classified training as a nuclear weapons employment officer) I possessed a top-secret clearance and could work in the secret base. I inquired about the problem, and it was presented to me.

The base is very small, with several dozen Air Force personnel, and part of a much larger intelligence organization. The secret base comprised various small work groups, with people doing different things. One section consisted of a couple dozen men and women, officers and enlisted. This unit had a captain in charge and several senior Air Force NCOs, with mostly enlisted airmen and women. The main workload included the use of military computers, collecting information which was sent elsewhere. The work environment was made up of individual cubicles or workstations. While the younger enlisted gathered data, their work was closely supervised by the senior NCOs.

The performance of one young, enlisted female began to decrease in quality. She appeared fearful and depressed. One of the NCOs, noting her unusual behavior, tried to talk to her but got nowhere. She was taken to the captain, who also could not elicit any reason for her work conduct, but clearly recognized she needed help. For this reason, the colonel (the secret base commander) wanted a counselor or psychologist with a high enough security clearance to come to the base to learn what was happening to or with the young woman. I was the only military mental health professional (in San Antonio) with the requisite clearance to enter the base.

The colonel handled the paperwork necessary to allow me to get on the base. I drove there a few days later. Going to the captain's office, I introduced myself and we moved to an empty office. The captain explained in more detail what his unit did. The collection of data required intelligent and educated people. All had to be bilingual at least. Some had spent a year attending a military language school (in 1965 I studied Vietnamese at the Defense Language Institute at the Presidio of Monterey in California, and upon graduation the University of California granted me two years of credit for Vietnamese), yet many already were bilingual. Their work required total focus and concentration, all day long, which could be very stressful. The young woman had been an excellent worker until recently. Something had happened, and her captain wanted to provide her the help she needed. Thus, my reason for being there.

She was escorted in by her captain, who left. I invited her to sit and introduced myself. She appeared frightened. She was nice looking, about 20 years old. Her background had been described by her captain. She was a bright high school graduate, and her military tests showed high intelligence and education scores. I explained that her supervisors had noted her work performance was floundering, which was unlike her, so I was there to help. Instead of me asking what was wrong, we discussed her growing up. She was raised in a small, rural community back east by strict parents. They were very religious and kept a tight rein on her social life. Her dating had been limited and her social interaction with males almost nil. She had siblings, both older and younger. She joined the Air Force (against her parents' wishes) to find more out of life. While raised in an austere devout home, she, herself, was not as enchanted with her church as her parents or brother and sister.

I continued to seek information about her upbringing, what led her to join the Air Force, her military training, her job, what she enjoyed, what she didn't, her friends, and what her life goals were. Her previous life had mostly been dominated by older males, her father and church elders. Being twice her age, I fell into that category, but…. I was not controlling, I was not pressuring her in any way. I was quiet, calm, and obviously interested in her as a person, wanting to know her, learn what she wanted in life and how she planned to get there. I was not judging her, but intently listening to her describe her life and dreams. Eventually she came to accept me. She realized I was not going to criticize her, find fault with her, or make demands which could frighten or harm her. Ultimately, we closed in on what she feared.

As she described her job and how she was supervised, I noted her anxiety level was rising. Something was not right here. She discussed her role and how she perceived her captain (nice but neutral), then her NCO supervisors. Two were fine but one she dismissed without comment (an early 30s, male technical sergeant she avoided discussing, passing by any feelings or impressions). I inquired as to why she thought her work performance was becoming a problem. She said she didn't know but thought maybe she was not qualified to do her job; it was more than she could handle.

I asked her about her high school grades (mostly As), her military training (all above average), her feelings for her job when she first arrived. Together we arrived at the conclusion that she was qualified for the work she was doing. I moved to her after-work activities, what she liked to do. She had a roommate she adored, and together they went to movies, dining, and sight-seeing around San Antonio. No drinking, no barhopping, no night clubs or dances. No social interaction with males.

I moved our talk back to her work and questioned her about the tech sergeant supervisor, asking questions about their relationship. Finally, she admitted that was her problem, but she insisted it was her fault, not his. Clearly, she showed a little fear of him.

She described him as initially being very helpful, very supportive, praising her work. Soon, though, he became more intimate, touching her, brushing against her, leaning over her at her workstation, too close. She became confused. He was her supervisor, and she enjoyed their beginning relationship as he projected his admiration for her work. As time passed his praising became less, his physical behavior became more alarming, and his comments became more intimate. He was hitting on her, but her upbringing provided no defense or experience as to how this should be addressed. He asked for dates and she, not understanding how to say no, created excuses as to why she wasn't available each time. He pressed on and she became scared, depressed, and anxious, and her work suffered. He was her boss, her elder; he dominated what she did, so she found herself in a quandary she did not comprehend. Her background taught her to obey her elders, but her revulsion at the sergeant's behavior created a psychological conflict she was not prepared to handle.

We ended our session and I said I would be able to make things better for her in a way that would not get her in trouble. I received her permission to talk to her roommate and another good friend. We departed and I saw her captain and suggested that, for the next few days, she not be supervised by the tech sergeant. Then I left.

The next day I met with her roommate and her friend. They confirmed the sergeant was hitting on her and making it clear that if she would not date him, he would make her worklife miserable. I met with the young woman once more and confirmed everything I thought. Then a meeting with the captain, the major, and the colonel was requested.

I described to them what had been going on. I explained what was happening to her was wrong and should not have happened. The tech sergeant was a predator, taking advantage of a young Air Force woman. My recommendation was to remove him immediately, counsel him on his behavior, and place him in a position where he could not repeat this. Any legal action was up to them, but he should not be allowed in her work environment ever again, starting now. They agreed, and the colonel arranged for the sergeant's departure post haste.

I met with her one more time, explained what had happened and convinced her that what the sergeant did was in no way her fault. She was the victim, and he had to suffer the consequences of what he did, which happened. She thanked me profusely for what I did; she appeared happy, looking forward to a better future.

Becoming enmeshed in other matters, I moved on, testing and counseling at BAMC. A couple of weeks later, the Air Force colonel called, describing how well the young woman was now doing. He then asked if I would be willing to become the psychologist for his unit, helping as needed. My work regarding the young enlisted female and the sergeant was so well received, the captain asked the colonel to have me approved as the unit psychologist. Honored, I agreed.

A month or two later, another issue arose at the secret Air Force base to which I responded. It involved another airman who encountered personal problems affecting his work. His commander requested my help. After a few weeks of counseling, the problem was resolved. Even though available, I was never asked to help with any other problems.

Forensic Psychology

Occasionally, the Psychology Service would be asked to do a complete psychological work-up on a soldier regarding legal problems. The requests could come from the military for court-martial proceedings. Sometimes an Army prosecutor (a lawyer from the Judge Advocate General's Corps, JAG) would want a psych profile on someone being tried in a military court for a crime the soldier allegedly committed. At other times the defense counsel would want a report for the defendant's side. Infrequently, a soldier would be charged with a crime in a civil court, usually of a serious nature. In this case the soldier's defense attorney would ask us for a complete personality evaluation. The results would be used in the trial to verify or negate the defendant's behavior and to indicate if the accused would or would not be capable of doing what the charge was.

The evaluation could take a few hours or several days, depending on the information required and the seriousness of the crime. Because this type of evaluation could run several thousands of dollars in the civilian world, the civil prosecution rarely had more than a few minutes' cursory glance at the accused by a contract psychiatrist. On the defense side, though, the soldier was entitled (at no cost, of course) to whatever work-up the attorney and I agreed on. Most often a two-day psychological profile beat the impressions of a twenty-minute evaluation by a psychiatrist. Our service was a boon to attorneys defending soldiers.

My involvement with psychological evaluations for military courts martial was limited, although as a civilian police officer (when I was a college student), I had been to court several times, providing evidence and testimony regarding a crime. For me, there was never a court-martial of the Lieutenant Calley magnitude at BAMC; most trials were of much less serious offenses. But civilian charges being tried before a jury could be significant enough for the defense team to seek my assistance.

Civil trials consist of someone (the prosecutor) presenting evidence and telling a story of why and how a defendant committed the crime. On the other side, the defendant's attorneys want to present a different story of what happened. In either case, the accused's behavior plays a prominent role in trying to convince the jury one way or the other. Therefore, a behavioral scientist sometimes can become a major player for either the defense or the prosecution. More than once, I was asked by a civilian defense team to assist in creating a strategy explaining to the jury why the defendant's behavior was inconsistent with the prosecution's tale.

The prosecution, through evidence and testimony, offers the jury a scenario of how and why the accused behaved in a certain way to commit the crime. The defense presents another version of what occurred and an explanation of why the defendant either did the deed or why he/she could not have, based on their personality. This is where the psychologist comes in, to explore and define the defendant's behavior.

Initially my service would be approached by a member of the soldier's civilian defense team, explaining what they needed. Sometimes the information would be used to sway a jury. At other times the defense just wanted a more detailed, more scientific definition of the accused's behavior and personality. In either case a detailed psychological evaluation would be required. Here is what I did.

The first topic of the conversation with the defense team is the charges being faced. Then what evidence, testimony, witnesses, etc., would the prosecution have and what position would the defense want to project to the jury. My contribution would be to conduct a thorough psychological evaluation to determine the presence and level of current behavior (testing and personal interviews), collect data on past behavior (as a psychologist I believed that past behavior most often is the best predictor of future behavior), and create a psychological profile of the defendant which could assist in defining the defense strategy.

Sometimes I would serve as an expert witness and present my findings directly to the jury myself. Other times I would brief the lawyers on what instruments were used, what they did, how accurate and reliable they were, and what the results were. The final report, written by me, would be used in developing the defense used in the trial, presented as an exhibit to support the defendant's case. Much time would be spent educating the attorneys on how to use the testing administered and the results found.

An example of how this works happened to me a decade after I retired from the Army. I had become a professor and was on my motorcycle on campus, riding back to my office from a classroom during the day. A 19-year-old female freshman, driving a four-wheel drive pickup, looked to her right while turning left, plowing into my motorcycle. My left hip (knee to waist) was destroyed, and my left arm almost severed above the wrist. Over a year (and five operations) later, the driver's insurance company did not want to reach an amicable settlement. So, we went to trial.

My defense team consisted of four attorneys (the lead; a former emergency room physician, now an attorney; a legal strategist; and a new attorney, a former paralegal) and an experienced paralegal. Part of the problem was that I did not appear to be depressed or saddened from losing the use of my left leg. Why? I was a very stoic person with an attitude that if I want to change a situation and I am able, I will do it. If a situation is beyond my control, I will not waste time crying over what happened, but move on. Throughout my existence, this has been my philosophy, and it has served me well. Instead of moaning about what had happened to me, I procured a three-inch lift for my left shoe and learned how to maneuver using crutches, then a cane.

My attitude, though, presented a problem for my lawyers. Going before an insurance company-sponsored mediation judge, the company refused to accept the judge's decision for a settlement. We went to court, before a jury. The conundrum was my demeanor. I had accepted what happened to me and the limited mobility I now possessed. I was moving on with my life, despite the immense damage done.

Going in front of a jury, requesting it find the owner of the vehicle that hit me responsible for destroying part of my body and maiming me for life, could be extremely difficult because I was not sad, depressed, suffering from PTSD, or displaying any other visible attributes demonstrating how damaging the accident was to me and my family. The vehicle belonged to a car dealership the driver's father managed, who gave her the four-wheel drive pickup to use despite her having several citations for careless and reckless driving.

My behavior belied the actual damage done. The question was, how could my attitude be explained to the jury so it would still accept that I had suffered considerably and should be compensated for my physical loss and my reduced future earning power, as well as the diminished quality of my life? This is where a psychologist was needed, to scientifically explain my behavior and attitude. Ironically, the psychologist selected by the attorneys (the trial was in El Paso, Texas) happened to be a student I had supervised while in the Army, at BAMC.

A battery of various personality inventories and personal interviews documented my beliefs, attitudes, behavior, and philosophy as being a lifelong part of me, and while it appeared to the jury that I was not suffering, the physical fact of the damage could not be denied. Medical reports, x-rays, and testimony by orthopedic surgeons verified the immense permanent damage inflicted upon me. My limited range of motion was well-documented. The psychologist testified in front of the jury as to why I was not depressed or suffering mentally from the damage.

When my attorneys rested their case, the insurance company requested and presented an out of court settlement, which we accepted. In this case the work of the psychologist provided the jury with the reason why I was not depressed, allowing it to accept my behavior as normal for me. It would have found the driver and owner of the truck responsible and liable for considerable compensation if the insurance company did not agree to end the trial, thus financially settling with me.

This is one example of how a behavioral scientist can assist in a trial.

Soldier-killer?

The most notable trial I became a part of was when a soldier was accused of first-degree murder. First-degree murder is one of the most serious charges against a person. This charge implies that the accused willingly took the life of another person, by making plans before the killing (premeditation) to commit the crime. The soldier was charged with deliberately planning and then murdering the other boyfriend of his girlfriend. He claimed it was an accident. His defense wanted to know if the soldier had the personality commensurate to taking the life of another person.

Here is what was known (and undisputed) regarding the death. A man was shot outside an apartment in San Antonio. He was arguing with a woman who lived in the apartment complex. He was shot by a rifle belonging to a young soldier, who had exited his truck and held the rifle when it went off. The soldier rushed to the shot man, providing first aid, while someone called the police and ambulance. The police arrived quickly but the man was dead. The soldier was arrested.

Here is the district attorney's version. The woman, in her early thirties, was going out with both the soldier and the deceased. The 20-year-old soldier learned about the man, became jealous and made plans to kill him. He drove to the woman's apartment, took out his rifle and deliberately shot the man. Premeditated first-degree murder.

Here is the defense's version. The older woman was using the naïve young soldier to make her boyfriend (the shot man) jealous. She had a date with the soldier, who arrived at the same time the other man did. The man and the woman, standing outside her apartment, were embroiled in a heated argument, becoming physical. Just showing up, the soldier saw his perceived girlfriend being mauled by a man unknown to him, so he grabbed his .30–30 lever-action carbine from the window-rack above the seat, and as he pulled it out, it went off, hitting the man. The soldier saw his girl being attacked by an unknown person, so he grabbed his only weapon and it accidentally fired, killing the man.

The outcome of the jury trial would depend on which version the jury believed. I was asked to help the defense present to the jury why the defendant's account was what happened, not the DA's story. What we had to do was show the jury the soldier did not have the upbringing or personality to plan and commit a cold-blooded murder. The defense team began its own investigation while I began my psychological assessment of the soldier.

My mental health counselors and I did our interviewing and testing in the prison. I began by inquiring about the soldier's background. After high school he enlisted in the Army to serve as a chaplain's assistant, which he was doing at Fort Sam. His father was a minister in a small church in the Midwest, and the family also had a small farm. His mother, a homemaker, spent much time helping her husband. The soldier was a middle child with two siblings. His school grades were above average, mostly Bs with some As. His interaction with females was quite limited during his upbringing in a rural community, as he devoted considerable time to working on the family farm and his father's church. All members of his family enjoyed the outdoors, hunting and fishing.

The legal team investigators talked to his family, friends, schoolteachers, and others. All said the same thing: the soldier was kind, honest, never prone to violence, and always offering a helping hand when needed. He was polite, courteous, and respectful toward his elders. He completed basic and advanced training with no problems. As a chaplain's assistant, he received high praise from the chaplains he served. His first sergeant described him as a good soldier, always willing to do more than his share.

We administered several versions of personality inventories and IQ tests. Why? The results of a single test could be challenged by the DA. But if the conclusions of several, similar instruments all yield the same findings, that becomes very hard to successfully challenge. All tests used found comparable outcomes. The personality tests presented the soldier as kind; caring; considerate of others; and not prone to aggression, violence, hostility, or rage. All instruments clearly suggested the soldier was not capable of deliberately killing another person. His personality would seek other (peaceful, non-violent) means to settle personal differences.

Additionally, the assessments revealed evidence supporting his feelings of grief, guilt, and bereavement due to his hand in the man's death. During my interviews with him, he exhibited bouts of crying, feeling tired and drained, doubting his value as a person, and feeling alone and angry at God for allowing this to happen. Clearly, he was suffering over what happened, questioning why he found himself in this predicament.

Another aspect of my help was to research the education and background of the psychiatrist employed by the prosecution to conduct a psychiatric assessment. Two things were noted: first, the psychiatrist had almost no experience examining or treating killers. Also, his entire report was based on only 20 minutes spent with the soldier in his cell. My test administrators and I, collectively, had spent over 20 hours on this defense. We were ready for trial. The DA refused to consider any charge other than first-degree murder.

Nobody saw the actual shooting; witnesses arrived after hearing the single shot. Testimony by the woman and friends indicated the soldier had no knowledge of the deceased man. Upon cross-examination, the psychiatrist admitted he was not familiar with the soldier's background. He was told to visit him and describe his psychiatric finding. The defense quickly convinced the jury that a 20-minute talk could not compare to over twenty hours of interviews and testing.

Before the trial, the attorney and I walked through his questions and my responses. My testimony would be presented after all the other witnesses described their impression of the soldier and his behavior. We knew the prosecution would challenge the value and credibility of the interviews and tests, so we prepared for that. My education was extensive, and I had been practicing psychology for seven years. My experience as a police officer and a combat infantryman indicated death was not an unknown experience for me. Regarding the tests, I was prepared to cite research studies conducted verifying the validity (that the tests evaluated what they were supposed to) and reliability (the tests consistently yielded the same measurements).

On the stand for a couple of hours, the defense prevailed. The DA was unable to shatter the defense that the soldier was not capable of planning and killing another person as presented by the prosecution. The soldier was found not guilty and released from jail.

Other Programs and Research

BAMC was involved with numerous studies and research programs requested by other parts of the Army or the Department of Defense. One program psychology was involved in was Operation Homecoming (see Chapters 11 and 12), a DOD-mandated five-year physical and mental evaluation of those American military men held as prisoners of war in Southeast Asia during the Vietnam War. Our service did all the psychological evaluations of the Army's repatriated prisoners of war.

Another major research project was the psychological evaluation of champion Olympic athletes to determine if any human personality traits could be identified as predictors of world class performance in younger athletes (see Chapter 13). My involvement in both programs yielded numerous research papers being presented and published.

Because I had become a pilot (see Chapter 14) and studied human behavior, I combined these two interests into one of aviation psychology, examining pilot behavior in the cockpit. At American Psychological Association meetings, I encountered other psychologists who were also pilots. Together we formed a group of professionals interested in the employment of psychology to study flight training and learning, behavior in the cockpit, safety issues while flying, and mental aspects of flying.

This interest and research led to the creation of human behavior safety seminars for Army pilots, which I taught at Fort Sam to helicopter aviation units. After retirement from the Army, I became an FAA Safety Counselor and instructor presenting safety seminars for general aviation pilots.

BAMC had an Adolescent Medicine Clinic which had a child psychologist on staff. My creation of the special education program in DeRidder provided me with the training and experience to consult with the psychologist on developing evaluation and treatment programs for the patients.

The Psychology Service began a group therapy session specifically to help couples encountering marital discord in their lives. One treatment modality was to help a couple examine the differences between what they perceived as reality between them and what testing revealed to be fact. For example, one couple may spend Saturday evenings going out dancing. It may be an activity the wife thoroughly enjoyed, while the husband endured it only to keep the wife happy. Over time the husband (who would not acknowledge his dislike of dancing) became resentful of his wife, but they were unable to successfully communicate their feelings to each other.

Psychological testing, individual counseling sessions with each spouse, and then group meetings allowed the therapists to help the couples understand themselves better and improve how they communicate with each other. This program proved highly successful, and we helped quite a few couples.

Three local universities worked with us to create a 15-week internship program for psychology and counseling graduate students. This was a solution where everyone benefited. The schools were able to offer their students real-world experience practicing psychology. The students were able to enjoy working with patients in the clinical environment, and we got extra, free labor. The students were excellent and well-prepared for their practicums. Each student was paired with a staff psychologist and a mental health counselor. They would participate in counseling sessions, write reports, and observe testing procedures with our counselors. As the students gained experience and confidence, they were given greater

Susan receiving her U.S. Air Force scholarship with Julie in the middle and Anita and Bob in background, 1978.

responsibilities, such as conducting an intake interview or becoming the counselor doing the testing. As our program became better known on campus, we had to limit how many students we could supervise. Some students even helped me with various research projects.

Another program I instituted was a behavioral weight control clinic conducted by myself and members of the BAMC dietary staff. I would present seminars on how to use notes, journals, and other measurements for keeping track of eating, exercising, and other habits or behaviors related to adding or subtracting weight from our bodies. Examples included recognizing that watching TV at night would lead to a big helping of ice cream. Solutions may be to eat using much smaller cups or to substitute celery or carrot or fruit for the ice cream. Our clinic would teach how to monitor eating habits to reduce or eliminate bad ones and substitute better behaviors. The dieticians would teach how to eat healthy and stay full yet lose weight.

Another service we provided was pain management therapy, using hypnosis for dental, oncology, and burn unit patients. One of our psychologists would provide individual hypnotherapy sessions with patients to help mitigate their pain. Often, we would train them in self-hypnosis to manage pain levels on their own.

As more time was spent doing off-post, off-duty management

consulting (see Chapter 18), I realized how little I knew about managing a business or the financial components of running a company. In January 1978, I enrolled in an accelerated master's business degree program at the Fort Sam campus of Webster College. I graduated at the end of the year.

My military career was never a continuous upward slope. It also had its down times, because more than once, I was demoted. The following chapters describe my adventures, accomplishments, and rewards I enjoyed during my time running the Psychology Service.

11

Operation Homecoming

Returning Home

In February and March 1973, U.S. Air Force C-141A Starlifters (specifically configured as hospital aircraft) initiated the journey back home for the 591 Vietnam War military and civilian repatriated prisoners of war who had been detained in North Vietnam and various Southeast Asia countries who were allies of North Vietnam. The 27 January 1973 Paris Peace Accords terminated U.S. participation in the war and sanctioned the release of the repatriated POWs (RPOWs). They were freed in Hanoi, Saigon, and Hong Kong (three POWs were held in China).

In early 1973, when the Nixon administration announced the signing of the peace agreements signaling the end of the war for America, I was a PhD student at Utah. Newspapers, magazines, and books all heralded the coming home of the RPOWs and discussed at length what their physical conditions would be and what degree of psychological damage remained. I harbored a strong interest in what was happening. I was an Army officer, and these were my brothers-in-arms. I served two combat tours in Vietnam and was personally familiar with several of the locations in South Vietnam where the RPOWs were captured. And most important, with my research into the adjustment of Vietnam veterans, I needed to know how the RPOWs were psychologically and how well they would adjust after the war and years of being incarcerated. So I read and filed every newspaper or magazine article about them and began buying any books on the RPOWs.

In anticipation of the return of American RPOWs held in Southeast Asia, the Department of Defense created a plan for what needed to be done and how to do it. Noted was the fact that no long-term longitudinal data was available as no war America was involved in had any military POWs imprisoned as long as those in Vietnam. The U.S. Navy established the Center for POW Studies at the Navy Health Research Center in San Diego, California, in 1971. This organization was created to do research with the families of RPOWs.

DOD funded a five-year charter for all services to evaluate the effects of long-term captivity and the torture endured. As an aside, I had an uncle (a sergeant in the British Army) who was captured at Dunkirk and spent all of World War II as a POW held by Germany. As we discussed Vietnam and the American RPOWs, he postulated why the North Vietnamese treated the Americans so cruelly. Physically his appearance was no different from that of his German captors. Most of his time in captivity was not that bad (except when SS troops managed his prison). He believed that the physical difference between the larger and more affluent Americans incited the North Vietnamese to exert their dominance over the Americans through pain and beatings.

In 1972 all branches of the military met at the Center for POW Studies to develop a standard method for evaluating and treating the RPOWs and for collecting data. Air Force men went to Brooks AFB in San Antonio, Texas, and Army RPOWs went to Brooke Army Medical Center (BAMC), also in San Antonio. Navy and Marine RPOWs went to the Naval Aerospace Medical Institute in Pensacola, Florida.

In October 1972, when the Department of Defense thought the Peace Accords were imminent, plans were made to bring home about 400 POWs. This plan was named Operation Egress Recap (a title nobody really understood). In January, as the number of POWs increased to at least 587, the plan was renamed Operation Homecoming, a name everyone comprehended as it represented what was being done.

The Office for the Assistant Secretary of Defense for Health and Environment stated three general guidelines for the military medical facilities. The first guideline was complete individual medical care and support now and in the future for the returned POWs as well as support for their families and for the next of kin of those missing in action. The second was complete and careful recording of all medical care and support given as part of this program and retention of these medical data in each medical department. Finally, the third guildine was the analysis of such medical data to: (a) improve future medical care and assistance to those in the program; (b) assist in future planning relating to POW matters; and (c) allow the sharing of these with the general medical community. This five-year program would continue through January of 1979.

The Five-Year Plan

Once a year, for five years, the RPOWs would report to their respective military hospitals for physical and mental evaluations. After the first two years, several Army RPOWs did not report to BAMC but were evaluated at an Army hospital where they were stationed, while some sought private care. Not all Army RPOWs completed the five-year program, but voluntarily dropped out over time.

In the beginning the Psychology Service at BAMC initiated the evaluation of the RPOWs. The program began at BAMC shortly after the RPOWs arrived. For the first two years I was not part of this program as I was at William Beaumont, then Fort Polk. But when I was assigned to Fort Sam as the HSC Psychology consultant, I became involved. As the command staff representative for psychology, I became affiliated with the Center for POW Studies as the Army psychology liaison monitoring what was being done at Brooke regarding the psychological evaluations of the Army RPOWs.

I spent time with the BAMC chief of the Psychology Service, discussing what his service was doing. What I learned dismayed me. What was being done was properly executed: data was collected and analyzed, and evaluation reports were written and passed up through the chain of command. The Army psychologists doing the evaluations were clinicians in uniform, not career soldiers. Their interest in the RPOWs did not evolve beyond that of completing the psychological tests, analyzing the results collected, and writing a report. No one showed interest in the long-term psychological adjustment of this group of men beyond cataloging their status once a year.

Wanting to become more involved with the study of the RPOWs, I had joined the Center for POW Studies. I offered my services as a researcher to assist (I did not physically relocate, but added this to my duties as the HSC Psychology Consultant). Several times I would fly myself to San Diego, spend time getting to know the Center staff, and become an active participant. Several of my research papers were printed in various Center publications.

The Center had several projects being pursued simultaneously, from the five-year evaluation program to a variety of research studies examining the RPOWs and their adaptation into their renewed lives, and how the separation and reunion had impacted the families. The Center would host several different meetings annually to collect research findings, present them, and print classified copies of the papers presented.

Each year DOD funded the Annual Joint Meeting Concerning POW/MIA Matters. The location rotated among the various military medical institutes in the program. The purposes of these meetings were to share and exchange information between the military medical facilities regarding the health and adjustment of the RPOWs, their families, and the families of those service members listed as MIA during the Vietnam conflict and the discussions of policies to insure that similar clinical services were rendered by all the military departments to the RPOWs and families.

The first meeting was held at the National Naval Medical Center in

Bethesda, Maryland, in October 1973. The second was at Brooks Air Force Base in San Antonio, Texas, in November 1974, with the third at the Center for POW Studies in November 1975. The fourth was held at Health Services Command in November 1976, and the last at the USAF School of Aerospace Medicine in September 1978. I attended and was a participant in the last three meetings.

The primary concern of the five-year program was the physical health of the RPOWs. The first two meetings tended to present initial findings regarding the health and adjustment of the RPOWs. The third conference showed that the health of this group of men was much better than initially presumed. Much of the focus on this year's meeting concerned the welfare of the family and problems associated with an absent father returning home. The fourth year contributed to an overview of physical and psychological status since this project began. The last conference was mostly a summary (after five years) of the RPOWs and their families. The conclusions were that in almost all areas of concern, the RPOWs were adjusting better than predicted.

New Chief of Psych Evals

Assuming the role as Chief of the Psychology Service in the Fall of 1976 (and head of the evaluation program of the Army RPOWs), I had a personal interest in the program. I continued my research involving the adjustment of Vietnam veterans, and as a former combat advisor, I had fought in many locations where the RPOWs had been captured.

Most of the medical professionals who had contact with the RPOWs had no relationship with Vietnam or the war. To most, the RPOW was just another patient. Many, though, became involved in the program by collecting health and medical data on the RPOWs, analyzing the information, and writing their findings in research reports.

The psychological protocol summaries depended on our previous diagnosis of the RPOW. Upon arrival, the man would be evaluated with the instruments selected for previous tests and current condition. When the test results were finalized and reviewed by me, we would engage in a lengthy interview. During the interview his current psychological status and the test results were presented to him. The interview would be conducted in my office, in a relaxed manner. Often medical personnel would wear a white lab coat (denoting a medical professional), which I had no interest in. I would wear my short-sleeve khaki uniform with my Combat Infantryman badge and all my decorations. Immediately, the RPOW could see that at one time, I had been the same as them (but not captured). They would not have to explain terms or conditions surrounding their time in Vietnam or combat. This made the interviews more comfortable for both me and them.

How Operation Homecoming Worked

The initial phase of Operation Homecoming began with the transport of the RPOWs to Clark AFB in the Philippines. Onboard the aircraft were a couple of flight surgeons (the planners thought that since most RPOWs were pilots, they would prefer a flight surgeon to a regular physician), nurses and aeromedical technicians. Over the next few weeks, 54 flights transported 325 Air Force, 138 Navy, 77 Army, 26 Marine, and 25 civilians to Clark, as well as two German nurses, Bernhard Diehl and Monika Schwinn, health aid workers who were captured outside of Da Nang. Schwinn was the only woman POW.

At Clark, the RPOWs were evaluated for their medical and psychological conditions and debriefed. Some family and health professionals questioned the priority of the debriefing being as essential as concern for the health of the RPOWs, but it was important to learn, immediately, as much as possible about POWs who might still be alive or who had died, and any other information about American MIAs.

At Clark the American RPOWs were joined by previously trained two-man teams. One member was part of the debriefing team and the other was an escort, matched as closely as possible to the individual RPOW. The escort was trained to serve as a shock absorber to assist the RPOW in dealing with his change from being a tortured captive with no freedom, rights, or future to a free person. The escort was a buffer to help the man adapt to his sudden and drastic re-entry into a new and vastly different world.

James Daly, a black enlisted Army RPOW, describes the escorts as: "The white prisoners had white escorts, black prisoners, a black escort, Puerto Rican prisoners, a Puerto Rican escort." Daly guessed that was the Army's way to make the former prisoners more comfortable.

In addition to the debriefing and medical/psychological evaluations and treatment, the men also visited the base exchange for personal supplies and were able to call home. Next, the men were flown to California via a stop in Hawaii, and then transferred to a military hospital near their homes or wherever they wanted to go.

Coming Home

While overall the people of the U.S. greeted the returning men openly and warmly, some conflict and hostility were present. Some saw the Paris

Peace Accords as a political expedient to selling the South Vietnamese out, deserting an ally in the time of most need. Others viewed the RPOWs not as heroes, but as war criminals. This hostility was mostly directed toward those crew members who flew bombers.

In addition to the physical damage done to the men's bodies (torture, improperly healed combat wounds and injuries, malnourishment due to substandard diets, and the disastrous effects of various diseases), three more major difficulties existed. First was the introduction into a society that did not exist prior to the captivity of many RPOWs; second was the reunion with a family that had changed significantly during the absence of the husband/father; and third was the considerable vocational gap and career experience void the RPOWs had to endure.

Many career military men were married, and most had families. This group consisted mainly of Navy and Air Force pilots. Family separations due to unaccompanied tours or combat were accepted as part of the job. The prolonged separation due to captivity, though, added another unknown dimension to the family dynamics. In addition, during the 1960s and 1970s, the role of women in society was also undergoing considerable change, such as the women's liberation movement.

The military man, head of his household, turned this role over to the wife and mother of their children. But the extended separation made the woman totally in charge of the family, minus her mate. Some wives performed admirably while others faltered. The women had to cope, and what they did varied greatly. Some were able to successfully keep the family together, and some sought relief by bonding with other males. One result of prolonged absence of the father is that the mother thus became the central focus of the family structure. Many of the wives also saw themselves as captives, because they did not know if they were wives or widows. Upon reunion, the actual roles of husband-wife/father-mother and their perceived functions become divergent, causing role and marital conflicts. Some wives and mothers sought emotional relief in the arms of other men.

Regarding vocational experience, many RPOWs spent what would be their initial career-building assignments just trying to survive as a POW. Leadership roles, career education, and participation in the military technology and regulation changes escaped the POWs. In short, they were not vocationally competitive with their non–POW peers. They were left behind.

For example, one Army officer, Special Forces Captain Floyd "Jim" Thompson, was captured on 26 March 1964 and repatriated on 16 March 1973 as a major. He spent 10 days short of nine years as a POW. During that same time, I as an Infantry officer went from a first lieutenant to a senior major; served as a platoon leader and a company commander;

held two different staff positions in an infantry battalion spent a year as a full-time Army competitive pistol shooter and the executive officer of an Army Marksmanship Detachment; graduated from the Army JFK Special Warfare School, the Defense Language Institute, and the Armor Officer's Career Course; served two combat tours in Vietnam; and earned a master's degree and was five months away from being awarded a PhD. Quite a difference.

Additionally, history had passed them by, and many RPOWs could not believe what had happened during their captivity. Many left behind toddlers and came home to pre-teens. In the late 1960s the hippie movement began (anti-war, free-love, open use of drugs, communal living), and by the time the repatriated POWs returned, the hippie lifestyle had moved into mainstream American society.

This was the much different world the RPOWs entered. DOD had major concerns regarding how to best assist the RPOWs' integration into this strange new world as well as to accept vocational challenges they may not be prepared to master, re-establish family relationships, and adapt and function successfully in an environment so foreign to them.

As a participant in this program, I can say that as time passed, collection, analysis, and documentation of the evaluations gave way to the needs of expediency and efficiency.

Once a year, for five years, the RPOWs would report to their respective military hospitals for physical and mental evaluations. After the first two years, several Army RPOWs did not report to BAMC but were evaluated at an Army hospital where they were stationed, while some sought private care. Not all Army RPOWs completed the five-year program, but voluntarily dropped out over time.

The Psychological Evaluation Process for the Army RPOWs[1]

The Army group of RPOWs was different from the other branches because most of the other POWs were pilots, therefore commissioned officers. Most Army RPOWs were enlisted and NCOs. Not all Army RPOWs were a part of Operation Homecoming. Those who had been previously repatriated or escaped (such as Special Forces Major James Rowe who was captured in 1963 and escaped in 1968 ... see *Five Years to Freedom*, 1971) were on their own evaluation schedule after returning to Army control.

During the Vietnam War period in all combat areas in Southeast Asia, there were 179 Army men captured and imprisoned from 1 January 1961 through 31 December 1976, according to data in the DOD document

Number of Casualties Incurred by US Military Personnel in Connection with the Conflict in Vietnam (20 January 1977). Of these men, 11 were still classified as POWs at the end of 1976. Thirty-four died in captivity; 57 either returned to the U.S. military or escaped prior to 27 January 1973; and 77 returned via Operation Homecoming.

The 77 Army RPOWs were captured in South Vietnam and suffered greatly due to the horrendous captivity circumstances (poor diets, very little shelter from extreme climatic conditions, a lack of proper medical care, and often chained or imprisoned in small cages).

This group of 77 men, when released in 1973, consisted of 28 officers and 49 enlisted. The average age when captured was almost 28 years for officers and 23 for enlisted. Twenty-five men were aviators or aircraft crewmembers, 16 infantry, 18 Special Forces or combat advisors, 7 transportation and 11 in other Army occupations. All but 18 were eventually moved into prisons in North Vietnam, with the 18 remaining in South Vietnam. The medical condition of the Army RPOWs reflected their subhuman treatment, as most bore the effects of infections and diseases; dietary symptoms; untreated wounds and injuries; damage from beatings; and, for some of the younger RPOWs, maturation deficiencies due to malnutrition, disease, and infections.

Each military branch had its own system for how its RPOWs would be evaluated. The questions to be answered involved the overall health of the men, the presence of permanent damage and the help each man needed to improve their mental and physical well-being. Because the health care providers met every year, we shared what we found and what we were doing. While the process at each medical facility might have differed slightly, we were all seeking common responses to how the RPOWs were doing. And I believe we succeeded at this.

As each RPOW arrived at our offices, I made sure that I would be there to greet each one. I welcomed him there and introduced myself. I explained what we would be doing over the next few days (even though they had done this more than once on previous visits). First, the enlisted mental health counselors would conduct all the tests to be given to the RPOW. The evaluations included IQ tests, a battery of personality tests, and neurological tests for some (to assess any brain damage or neurological dysfunction). These tests were quickly scored, and the results given to me.

The purpose of the lengthy interview (after reviewing all the test results) was to determine if my interpersonal interaction with the RPOW confirmed the analysis of the psychological evaluations. I began the sessions (for my initial visit) with the introduction, leading into gathering background information about them. Then we would cover their military experience, Vietnam and then their captivity. Lastly, we would discuss their current life, their vocation, their family (if they had one), adjustment problems, and their expected future. If I had seen them previously, we would begin with what had happened since we last met and how life was in general.

Because of my military background and combat experiences, I found that we could readily discuss their Army background, Vietnam, and captivity. Several RPOWs I saw had been captured in locations where I had fought. I am convinced that my combat background allowed our interviews to explore more about their past and their current lives.

I was interested in two findings. First, I wanted to evaluate the current psychological status of the RPOW and, based on the overall test outcomes, assign the man to one of three groups: successful adjustment group, borderline adjustment group or unsuccessful adjustment group. The second was to compare this year's findings to those of previous years to see if the man, psychologically, was the same, regressing, or improving.

The successful adjustment group consisted of those men seen as successfully coping with the demands of life. This was determined by a lack of any psychiatric diagnosis and evidence of their social, vocational, and family lives being satisfactory and productive.

A second group, the borderline adjustment group, consisted of those men experiencing minor difficulty in their post-captivity adjustment process. Psychiatrically this group was viewed as having mild personality disorders or neuroses, or experiencing transient situational disturbances.

The third group, the unsuccessful adjustment group, comprised those men who were clinically evaluated as encountering severe adjustment difficulties. They were diagnosed as having a psychotic disorder or a severe non-psychotic mental disorder. All diagnoses were based on the Diagnostic and Statistical Manual of Mental Disorders II (1968–1980).

After the psychological testing of the RPOW, I conducted my interview. I created a two-page questionnaire which I used during our discussion. It consisted of military information, including data on when, where, and how he had been captured; captivity status; post-captivity disposition; military problems; prior service background; jobs held; education; family or marital life; and a list of all psychiatric findings during previous visits. Some of this information was already in his files, but much was not. Family background details were not available; neither was military history, captivity particulars, and post-military history. The previous file (before me) on each RPOW had little data except for the psychological and psychiatric testing and the results. From my point of view, a gold mine of information was sorely lacking for rendering any useful conclusions regarding "why" the RPOWs belonged in one of the three groups. I now had the opportunity to remedy this vital component of the evaluations of these men.

Establishing rapport was not difficult. I had been a Marine private, a Marine NCO and an Army officer. I could relate to each rank. Regarding situations that might lead to capture, I had found myself in similar circumstances but had not been captured. We spoke the same language (military), we had been in the same places (in Vietnam), and we had experienced related situations such as being wounded. I found it easy to talk to most of the RPOWs. Some were reticent, others did not want to discuss any of their captivity, while still others found life after being released exceedingly difficult. But all were able to talk enough for me to complete both pages of my forms.

My interactions with several of the RPOWs will remain with me forever. The group contained exceptional leaders; beaten men who lost their family during captivity; some who found life after being released too difficult; and others who were able to recover and enjoy life to the fullest.

Adjustment back into a "normal" lifestyle varied according to the age, education, family background, and position in the Army of the individual. The older officers and NCOs were mostly married with families. Being career soldiers (and volunteers), they understood the danger of being captured (as an accepted risk of their chosen occupation) and placed value in the Code of Conduct. Their military experience, their value of the "Code," their strong family ties, and their staunch belief in the military system and survival guided their ability to resist and endure. The younger RPOWs, though, possessed a different mind-set. They were not career-oriented, were less educated and experienced, did not have wives or children to return to, and were less able to deter the will of their captors and sustain a resistant posture. They did what they could to survive, which was different from their older "brothers."

From the moment a soldier was captured, their known universe ceased to exist. They were no longer a part of the evolving world, and as events in the U.S. happened, they were not participants. As new captives explained what was happening back in the "world," many POWs were unable to accept emotionally, psychologically, or intellectually what they were told. This phenomenon is seen today in which people who hated former President Trump or President Biden were unable to accept anything but negative aspects of the men, regardless of what they did. Conversely, those who admired either man ignored any information reflecting their flaws. So the POW was ensconced in a world that had changed so it was unrecognizable to the POW.

The POWs were not alone in their time warp. Their spouses and children were also trapped in their own changing world. Often the military husband and father made major financial decisions, maintained where they lived, disciplined the children, and set the family tone for how they lived. When the man deployed, all of this fell onto the wife, until the husband/father returned 12 or 13 months later. But when he was captured, future plans for the family went into a tailspin. Not knowing what was happening to the husband/father, or if he would ever return, placed the wife/mother into her own prison of loneliness, fear, anxiety, apprehension, and dread, facing a future with too many unknowns. A two-parent family became a single-parent household where the wife/mother now became solely responsible, maybe forever, for the future of her family.

When the POWs were repatriated, medical, psychological, and social experts recognized that the lives of the men and their families went in very diverse directions and for many, that separation would be so great that they could never rejoin again as a cohesive family unit. Consider that the men were psychologically returning to a world that no longer existed, while the family survived and functioned for much of their lives without their father. Consider that when they were rejoined, with diverse backgrounds and experiences and totally different perspectives on what the future should be like, violent clashes must occur. And this certainly did happen.

The Operation Homecoming experts were aware that lifestyle challenges were imminent, and the families would need help, especially because the RPOWs would have to become aware of and accept what changes have occurred in both the world and their families. The RPOWs could not successfully re-enter a realm that no longer existed, but must accept the changes and learn how to function in the new and different reality.

Fortunately, most Army RPOWs were able to successfully move forward and function "normally" after captivity. It should be noted that the Army RPOWs were unlike the RPOWs of the other services. Most were enlisted infantry soldiers, and some were drafted. Most of the captives from the other services were officers and flight crews. This meant double volunteers, first as officers and second as pilots or flight crew members. They were older, better educated, and more with families than the Army prisoners. These differences made a considerable impact on the return adjustment of the various incarcerated service members.

The initial psychological evaluation of the RPOWs consisted of different psychological personality inventories and tests designed by the Center for POW Studies, as well as individual interviews. Additional psychological testing was completed as decided by the psychologist (where the RPOW was evaluated) if such testing was needed to obtain more information. The data collected indicated that the RPOWs could be placed into one of three groups according to the clinical evaluation of their post-captivity lives and careers, be it military or civilian.

In 1973 all 77 Army RPOWs were psychologically evaluated during their first three to six months after release and of these men, 51 (66 percent) were seen as successfully adjusting, 15 (20 percent) were evaluated as experiencing some difficulty adjusting, with 11 (14 percent) encountering severe adjustment problems. The successful group consisted of 22 officers and 29 enlisted (based on their rank upon repatriation). The borderline group contained five officers and 10 enlisted. The unsuccessful group comprised one officer and 10 enlisted. (See chart 1)

Chart 1. 1973 Evaluation Results
77 RPOWs evaluated (100%)

Ranks listed are at time of evaluation
Successful Adjustment Group 51 men (66 percent)

Enlisted	Warrant Officers	Commissioned Officers
E8 = 3	CWO 3 = 1	COL = 1
E7 = 3	CWO 2 = 7	LTC = 1
E6 = 17		MAJ = 4
E5 = 5		CPT = 8
E4 = 1		
29	8	14

Borderline Adjustment Group 15 men (20 percent)

Enlisted	Warrant Officers	Commissioned Officers
E6 = 4	CWO 2 = 2	MAJ = 1
E5 = 5		CPT = 2
E4 = 1		
10	2	3

Unsuccessful Adjustment Group 11 men (14 percent)

Enlisted	Warrant Officers	Commissioned Officers
E6 = 2	none	MAJ = 1
E5 = 7		
E3 = 1		
10	0	1

As time passed, fewer men were evaluated at BAMC. The second evaluation consisted of 74 men while in the last (1978) evaluation 30 men (70 percent) were classified as successful, 9 (21 percent) as borderline, and four

(9 percent) were experiencing severe adjustment problems. This evaluation included active-duty Army, some civilians, some medically retired individuals, and regular military retirees. (See chart 2)

Chart 2. 1978 Evaluation Results
43 RPOWs Evaluated (100%)

Ranks/status listed are at time of evaluation
Successful Adjustment Group 30 men (70 percent)
Rank/status at time of evaluation

Enlisted	Warrant Officers	Commissioned Officers	CIV	MED RET	RET
E8 = 1	CWO 4 = 1	COL = 1	5	3	3
E7 = 2	CWO 3 = 3	MAJ = 3			
E6 = 2		CPT = 4			
E5 = 1		1LT = 1			
6	4	9	5	3	3

Borderline Adjustment Group 9 men (21 percent)

Enlisted	Commissioned Officers	CIV	MED RET
E8 = 1	MAJ = 1	1	2
E7 = 2			
E6 = 2			
5	1	1	2

Unsuccessful Adjustment Group 4 men (9 percent)

Enlisted	Commissioned Officers	CIV	MED RET
E6 = 1	LTC = 1	1	1
1	1	1	1

One unusual occurrence was noted during the final evaluation. Six RPOWs were stationed in Germany (one a retired NCO turned Department of Army Civilian; one warrant officer aviator; and four NCOs). All four NCOs were experiencing mild to severe adjustment difficulty, with three reporting feeling states like those in the latter stages of the captivity and initial post-captivity periods. All four explained the hardships of serving in Germany, which affected them in separate ways. Essentially, they were experiencing, again, a re-entry into a foreign and perceived hostile environment with much of their support systems absent (wives, families, unrestricted freedom of movement, and familiar language).

During the Operation Homecoming period 25 RPOWS elected to not continue the full five years of evaluations. Of this group, most were civilians (released from active duty) or medically retired. The active duty RPOWS were two majors, two warrant officers, and two NOCs. Fifty-six percent of the RPOWS who did not complete the five years of evaluation were civilians. At their last evaluation 56 percent were in the successful adjustment group, 20 percent were facing some adjustment problems, and 24 percent had received a psychiatric diagnosis at their last evaluation. (See chart 3)

Chart 3. 25 RPOWs did not complete all five evaluations (100 percent)

Ranks/status are at time of their last evaluation

Successful Adjustment Group 14 men (56 percent)

Warrant Officers	*Commissioned Officers*	*CIV*	*MED RET*
CWO 2 = 1	MAJ = 1	9	2
WO 1 = 1			
2	1	9	2

Borderline Adjustment Group 5 men (20 percent)

Enlisted	*CIV*	*MED RET*
E7 = 1	2	2
1	2	2

Unsuccessful Adjustment Group 6 men (24 percent)

Enlisted	*Commissioned Officers*	*CIV*	*MED RET*
E5 = 1	MAJ = 1	3	1
1	1	3	1

During the five-year evaluations it appeared that the first two years after repatriation were the hardest in terms of the RPOWs' re-adjustment to their careers and normal behavioral patterns. There also appeared to be a relationship between age at time of captivity and length of captivity and their post-captivity adjustment. The most successful RPOWS were older at the time of their capture and spent less time as POWs than either the borderline or unsuccessful RPOWs.

In addition to being older, the successful RPOWs had more time in the Army and were better educated. More of them had families, suggesting they had more reasons or better survival skills to enable them to return to a more normal life. The soldiers who experienced greater difficulty adjusting upon return were younger; possessed fewer survival skills; were not career military; and were less equipped to cope with incarceration, deprivation, and torture.

The final psychological evaluation reveals that only nine percent of the RPOWs were experiencing severe adjustment problems in their post-captivity lives. At the same time, 70 percent of the Vietnam War RPOWs were successfully coping with the demands of life, raising families, pursuing life, and enjoying their post-captivity lives.

It is generally accepted that being in combat in Vietnam and becoming a POW was one of the most traumatic experiences a soldier could ever be subjected to. Yet most of our POWs were able to re-enter life and adjust normally.

In December 1978, the Center for POW Studies closed. Some of the behavioral scientists working there believed it was a mistake, and premature, as the collected data warranted much more analysis, with conclusions and recommendations for the future.

At BAMC the working files on all the RPOWs were to be relegated into storage files and then, after a few years, destroyed. Our working files were not extinguished, as I continued to use the data for research purposes. I even received approval from the Pentagon to present my RPOW research at a professional national psychology conference and published in an official DOD proceedings and **VIETNAM** magazine. After the closure of the Center for POW Studies, not much research on the adjustment of the POWs was conducted or published. Today, most people 40 or younger know nothing about the plight of the American Vietnam prisoners of war and I am guessing (in 2023) most RPOWs have already died from POW injuries or diseases and Agent Orange.

What I found interesting is the fact that the percentage of the Army RPOWs experiencing severe difficulty adapting to their post-captivity lives was even less than my findings of Vietnam vets. This was amazing, since few Vietnam vets suffered more than our RPOWs.

12

Some Repatriated
POWs I Met

Each Army RPOW I met was a unique individual. Their backgrounds, their military service, their captivity, and their post-captivity lives share the spectrum of human emotions. Some adjusted extremely well, living full, happy, and productive lives. Others overcame horrific beginnings upon repatriation and were able to seek normalcy. Some never overcame their captivity and faced depression or worse throughout their lives. All suffered some effects due to being wounded or tortured as a POW. A few unfortunate ones, returning home to a family that no longer existed, were unable to adjust to the differences nor to their own changes.

Most returned to a world that only existed in their minds. The longer the incarceration, the greater the differences between reality and the RPOWs' perception of what should be. Here are the stories of four Army RPOWs I spent time with ... and will never forget.

The College Athlete

The most remarkable RPOW I met was former Captain Luis Chirichigno. He was one of the finest soldiers I have ever known.

The first time I saw Chirichigno, he was dressed casually in civilian clothes. Of average height, tanned, with medium length dark hair, he looked like a movie star. He was cheerful, had a broad smile, and was easy to talk to. His mannerisms were relaxed and stress-free.

Born in Peru in 1937 (he was my age), he worked for an Air Cargo company and was able to immigrate to Miami in 1959, where he was awarded a swimming scholarship at the University of Miami. Since he had trouble with English, school was not going very well, so he enlisted in the Army in mid–1960. Upon graduation from Airborne School, he was assigned to the 82nd Airborne Division and completed Jumpmaster and Pathfinder schools. In August 1963, as a sergeant, he left active duty. Three months later, as a reservist, he joined the 20th Special Forces Group (Reserve). Attending the University of Alabama on a football scholarship, he was a kicker for Coach Bear Bryant. Joe Namath was the quarterback when Luis' team won two national championships. He did not graduate from Alabama, but left after his third year. In 1964 he was granted his U.S. citizenship.

In January 1965 he went through the Army Reserve Officer Candidate School, then re-entered active duty with the 101st Airborne Division. After graduating from Ranger School, in mid–1967, he deployed to Vietnam as a platoon leader with the 25th Infantry Division, until he was wounded and hospitalized in Japan. A few months later he returned to Vietnam, joining the 5th Special Forces Group, where he stayed until May 1968. Upon returning stateside, he entered helicopter flight training, earning his wings in February 1969. Four months later he returned to Vietnam as an AH-1G Cobra gunship pilot and aero-weapons Platoon Commander.

On 2 November 1969, Luis was on a helicopter rescue mission, defending a sister helicopter and its downed crew when he was shot down. The pilot with him was killed (the crew of the helicopter he was protecting did get away). Luis, shot up in both hands and left arm, evaded capture for two days. He was imprisoned in a bamboo cage in Cambodia, then was forced to walk to North Vietnam in May 1970, where he was moved three times, spending his final days in captivity in the Hanoi Hilton. He was repatriated on 27 March 1973.

His wounds were severe enough that he was hospitalized for reconstructive surgery at Brooke Army Medical Center until spring 1975. During this time, he attended his final year in college at St. Mary's University in San Antonio, receiving his BA in Math and Spanish.

When he first returned to the states after repatriation, Luis was mildly depressed. He struggled with his hospitalization, health situation, marital issues, and concerns about his future, since he wanted to remain an Army aviator.

In April he was medically retired from the Army with a 100 percent disability, and then joined the U.S. State Department, where he was initially assigned to the embassy in Bogota, Columbia. He was no longer depressed, as his health had improved a little and he had a future planned. Returning to Washington, D.C., for a year, in May 1977, he became the Cultural Vice-Consul with the U.S. Embassy in India. When I last saw Luis (August 1978), he was incredibly happy, as he was engaged to a woman, a native of India. He served 30 years in the State Department.

During his 10 years of active duty, Luis was awarded the Distinguished

Service Cross; four Bronze Stars; three Purple Hearts; three Air Medals; two Army Commendation Medals; six Vietnamese Crosses of Gallantry; and the Combat Infantryman Badge, Aviator Wings, and Master Parachutist Badge. I admired him for his devotion to duty and his success as an officer and a leader. This was the most amazing RPOW I met.

Luis died on 3 February 2021 of leukemia, age 83.

The Special Forces Veterinarian

One day I was completing an interview with a former Special Forces NCO, now a survival expert with the USN SEAL School. As we shook hands, I mentioned that tomorrow I would be seeing one of his colleagues, another former SF NCO and RPOW who I named. The man swung his fist into the side of my government steel file cabinet, resulting in a small dent. Cursing, he spit out words of disgust and anger regarding the RPOW he considered a coward for not having been killed. He said that sergeant had been in an SF camp that was attacked, and was the only one to survive; he claimed that the man was found hidden in a bunker, where he stayed during the fighting. This was surprising to me because the RPOW I was to see the next day was a Medal of Honor recipient. I never understood this man's dislike of Sergeant Cavaiani.

The man I saw the next day was Sergeant First Class Jon Cavaiani, another foreign-born soldier, naturalized in 1968. He was born in 1943 in England, and his parents were killed during World War II. He was adopted by a U.S. Air Force man and his wife. He moved to California with his family in 1947. His adopted mother remarried, and Cavaiani took his stepfather's name. In the early 1960s he worked on a ranch and went to California State Polytechnic College. From the mid- to late 1960s he worked as a district sales manager for a chemical corporation. In 1968 he tried to enlist in the Army but was found 4-F (medically unfit for military service due to allergic reaction to bee stings). He located another physician who stated he was medically qualified for the Army, so he enlisted in 1969, completing basic and advanced infantry training at Fort Ord, California, and the airborne School at Fort Benning. He took Special Forces training in 1970 as a medic and heavy weapons specialist.

Reporting to Vietnam in July 1970, Staff Sergeant Cavaiani was assigned for a brief time as a SF veterinarian and agriculture advisor because of his farming/ranching background. Subsequently he was stationed at an isolated radio relay site in I Corps, near the DMZ, where he commanded a security force of 70 Vietnamese soldiers and 13 Americans. The camp was attacked the morning of 4 June 1971 where SSG Cavaiani repeatedly fought off the enemy, allowing three helicopters to evacuate some of the defenders. Remaining in the camp overnight, he continued to battle the aggressors.

The next morning, dense fog prevented any helicopter rescue, so Cavaiani ordered the remaining security troops to escape while he covered their departure. He was wounded over twenty times but still escaped, evading the enemy for five days; then, the severely wounded and burned NCO was captured by an 80-year-old man with a weapon. For two months he was held captive in South Vietnam, then moved north where he was imprisoned in prisons such as the "Plantation," ending up in the Hanoi Hilton.

The PC Group

In the late 1960s the POW Camp "Plantation Gardens" (in northeast Hanoi) was seen as a showcase prison, where films of the POWs were made, and where famous visitors to North Vietnam could see staged prisoner activities. It closed in mid–1970 but opened again in November due to the raid on Son Tay prison (Camp Hope). The senior ranking officer (SRO), Air Force POW Colonel Ted Guy, a shot-down fighter pilot, became the commander of the American POWs in the Plantation. Just before repatriation, all the POWs were moved to the Hanoi Hilton (Hoa Lo Camp in downtown Hanoi).

During this time five young, enlisted POW men became known as anti-war activists, referred to as "Ducks" because they followed their guards like ducks behind their mother. These men were noticeably young (late teens, early twenties), not career warriors, and caught up in a war not of their making. They were little understood, endured excruciating torture, and subsisted on a diet unable to sustain healthy American males (many POWs lost over half their pre-captive weight). In short, they were in a very painful situation they did not comprehend and wanted out, at any cost. They were not just against the war in Vietnam, but any and all wars. Additionally, their captors were foreign to them. Physically smaller, with different colored skin, and shabby hair and clothes, the Vietnamese soldiers delighted in abusing, beating, and forcing the much larger (and hated) American aggressors to submit to constant punishment and humiliation. Some young POWs just wanted out. There were some American POW officers who also voiced anti-war sentiments but were not overtly active in their beliefs. At the end of 1971, three more young POWs joined the Ducks, now called the Peace Committee (PC). One of them was a black man from Brooklyn, New York, named James Daly.

A self-proclaimed conscientious objector before the Army, he had no evidence to support his position. An assertive Army recruiter conned Daly into enlisting, promising him a non-combat assignment. Nine months after enlisting, he was in an infantry unit, fighting in Vietnam. Three months later he was captured.

Colonel Guy became alarmed with the PCs, as they were accepting favors from their guards, getting better food, and receiving special treatment. Some PCs were openly defying the POW officers, cursing them, and insisting the officers had no right to command them. Now the PCs had eight members (five Army and three Marines).

When the bombing of North Vietnam began again in April 1972, the PCs became devastated. All signed a memo to their captors denouncing the attacks (although after being repatriated, two PC members denied signing).

Over time several POWs capitulated and signed propaganda missives for several reasons: to avoid torture, to get their names (as live POWs) out to the public, and to express their anti-war feelings (some 30 percent to 50 percent of the POWs were disillusioned about the war).

My Escape and Evasion training, my combat experiences, and then my time as a psychologist has taught me that every person can be broken (or they will die in the process). And many POWs were broken, and many died because they refused to quit their fight against their captors. TV shows, movies and books depicted the hero undergoing extreme torture (captors pulling out his fingernails, waterboarding him, cutting off his digits, and destroying his kneecaps) while remaining resistant to the pain. In real life, most humans would give up to escape the maiming of their bodies. Then there is the psychological abuse that can also destroy a person's will to fight. Sleep deprivation, physical exhaustion, and warping of the mind are other ways to break a person. All were employed on the American POWs.

Colonel Guy issued a combat order to the senior NCO POWs to form a squad to infiltrate the PCs and learn what they were doing. In 1972, four more POWs joined the PCs, one being SSG Jon Cavaiani. Upon returning to the States after being released, Colonel Guy brought court-martial charges against the original eight members of the PC. The charges were: aiding the enemy, disrespect to superior officers, conspiracy, and carrying out a conspiracy. SSG Cavaiani was not one of the eight charged.

One Marine sergeant (one of the eight accused) committed suicide. At this point the Secretaries of the Army and Navy stepped in. Officially investigations determined insufficient evidence was present, so all charges were dropped (this included those against the two Marines and five Army soldiers). Unofficially the two Secretaries pointed out that the men had exhibited good behavior during captivity in South Vietnam and endured a very hard time in North Vietnam, so for political reasons, all charges were dismissed. The branches of the military did create committees to evaluate the records and behavior of the RPOWs, and several were discharged from the military.

Returning to Sergeant Cavaiani

The day I saw Cavaiani, he was in uniform, immaculate, brown hair short to medium in length, and at the top of his ribbons was the Medal of Honor, the decoration awarded for his defense of the radio station before he was captured. Looking healthy and young despite losing around 100 pounds and suffering dozens of wounds, he had worked long and hard to retain his pre-captivity size and strength. After captivity he graduated from Jumpmaster School and Pathfinder School, became HALO qualified (a parachute term for jumping at a high altitude but opening the parachute at low altitude), and completed a course in heavy and light weapons, as well as an advanced Intelligence program. Though friendly, he was initially guarded and reluctant to talk about himself very much; but as the interview continued, he was more open.

When Cavaiani was first seen in his psych eval upon his return, he, like most RPOWs, had encountered some difficulty in his life. He was hurting from all his combat injuries, had trouble walking (fractured spine), was hard of hearing, and was still recovering from malaria and migraine headaches. Additionally, he was going through a second divorce and was seen as experiencing adjustment reaction. When I last saw SFC Cavaiani, he was functioning fine, but some residual behavioral traits remained. For example, when he would read articles about his Medal of Honor it would remind him of Vietnam, and that was not a good part of his life.

He was assigned (in 1978) as the Operations NCO in the 6th Infantry Brigade in Berlin, Germany. Describing this assignment as good for his career (he expected to make E-8, master sergeant, in this job), he found it personally distasteful. He attended the Defense Language Institute to study German and had been in Germany almost a year. His complaints about soldiers in Germany echoed my thoughts when I received orders for Europe while at Fort Bliss in 1974. He also was not happy with the recent riffing of many good officers (reduction in force due to downsizing the Army). Additionally, he was in a foreign country, with the Germans not that enthusiastic about American troops, evoking feelings of being in Vietnam as a POW.

We discussed the PCs and how he was involved. He explained that what happened was not realized by many people. Because of his sense of patriotism and his Special Forces training, he was disgusted with the PCs. After Colonel Guy ordered the senior POW NCOs to do something, Cavaiani decided to do something on his own. Thus, he joined the PCs, hoping somehow to disrupt what they were doing and cause the group to break up. He made it clear that he was not personally ordered by Guy to join the PCs, but clearly understood that his colonel wanted the POW NCOs to do something, so Cavaiani did.

Cavaiani retired from the Army as a sergeant major (the highest enlisted rank) in 1990, after spending most of his Army career in the Special Forces. His decorations included the Medal of Honor, the Legion of Merit, two Bronze Stars, two Purple Hearts, the Meritorious Service Medal, four Army Commendation Medals, and the Combat Infantryman Badge, Master Parachute badge, Pathfinder Badge, and the Ranger Tab.

He died on 29 July 2014 of a bone marrow disorder, age 70.

The Conscientious Objector

James Alexander Daly had just turned 19 when he enlisted in the Army in January 1967. A good-looking, short-haired, big man with a bright smile, Daly enlisted because his recruiter guaranteed him that he would be trained as a cook or clerk and never see combat. That was important to Daly because he was a conscientious objector. He wanted to serve in the Jehovah's Witness ministry but was unable to qualify for a draft deferment. In Advanced Individual Training he applied for CO status because of a conflict between his pacifism and being taught to kill, but his paperwork was rejected.

Nine months after enlisting he found himself as a rifleman in A Company, 3rd Battalion, 196th Light Infantry Brigade. He refused to shoot; while he carried his rifle, he did not load it. In Que Son valley (in northern South Vietnam), on 9 January 1968, during a fierce battle, Daly was slightly shot in the shoulder and captured with two other soldiers. One died that night and the other was released in 1969. Daly was retained for three years in various POW camps in South Vietnam. His living conditions were extremely harsh. Disease, dysentery, beatings, and a lack of food and hygiene brought death to many POWs in the south. A two-month trek at the end of 1970 and early 1971 brought him to North Vietnam and the Plantation POW Camp (and later the Hanoi Hilton). Daly possessed good self-preservation skills, but as a black enlisted man with a high school education, he found his anti-war beliefs not tolerated by the many Air Force pilots incarcerated with him.

Growing up in Brooklyn, New York, his life was normal with no legal difficulties. Raised by his mother (his father was deceased), he had several brothers and sisters. After graduating from high school, he was classified as 1-A, eligible for the draft. He wanted to enroll in a local community college in the fall but needed a job first. He found getting a job difficult as no one wanted to hire an 18-year-old 1-A male. That is when he unsuccessfully sought CO exemption and then decided to enlist.

In the Plantation Gardens, he became acquainted with the five "Ducks" who shared his anti-war beliefs. He wrote anti-war letters and partook of the benefits the Peace Committee enjoyed. His life in this POW Camp was quite different from what he endured in the south. He ate better food and was allowed more time outside.

Upon being repatriated, he remained friends with his fellow PCs. When the Marine sergeant committed suicide, Daly went to Denver to be a pallbearer. Initially Daly experienced feelings of anxiety, depression, and adjustment reactions. After the Secretary of the Army dismissed Colonel Guy's court-martial charges, several of the PCs, still on active duty, were charged again by an Air Force major. In September 1973, these charges were dropped, and Staff Sergeant Daly was informed he would not be able to re-enlist. He did not receive a Purple Heart medal for being wounded. After discharge he found employment as a gift buyer at the B. Altman and Company department store in New York City.

When I first met Daly, he looked confident but still had worries and problems. In April 1974, he married, and he and his wife had one daughter. In August 1974, he was the first Vietnam RPOW to receive a Small Business Administration guaranteed business loan to buy a small automatic laundry in New Jersey. Unfortunately, the business did not do well; it closed in July 1977, but he said he owed $62,000 in debt (which he hoped the government would write off). He then became employed with the U.S. Post Office where he worked almost two decades.

In 1975 he co-authored a book, *A Hero's Welcome*, about his seven years in the Army (with five being a POW). It did not do well, but was released again in 2000 under the title *Black Prisoner of War*, more as a sociological treatise on his POW experiences as a black man.

We did discuss his involvement as a PC member. They continued to correspond and visit around the country for a weekend of friendship. Daly exhibited mixed feelings. At Clark AFB he was identified several times as a special POW (as a member of the PC). This classification bothered him, as did being charged twice as a traitor and then waiting a long time until the Army decided what to do with him (keep in or force out).

We did talk about the PCs and Jon Cavaiani and his joining the PCs. Daly said that Cavaiani was always telling war stories (with himself as the good guy). Daly believed that Cavaiani spent a lot of time trying to influence the members to fight among themselves by spreading rumors. From what Daly told me, it appeared that Cavaiani, was in fact, trying to disrupt the PCs by introducing discord.

James Daly died in 1998, in his early 50s.

The POW Held the Longest

I doubt if any RPOW has suffered more than Jim Thompson. He was a captive the longest, 10 days shy of 9 years. One man has never given so much to survive, refusing to quit or give in, existing on the hope that he would live and be able to return to his wife and children. Upon returning home, however, he learned he had no family; they now belonged to another man. His story is the most tragic one I encountered regarding the post-captivity lives of the repatriated American POWs.

Born in 1933, Floyd James (Jim) Thompson graduated from high school, then worked in an A & P grocery store until being drafted in 1956. He was married in 1953, but his first child was not born until 1958. At first Jim did not like the Army and was rebellious, but came to like it and went to OCS, then Airborne and Ranger schools.

As a junior officer, he was praised for his quick mind but faulted for making rash decisions. He served in different infantry units both stateside and in Korea. In the early 1960s, Jim was recruited into the Special Forces and received a six-month assignment to Vietnam, arriving in December 1963 as a captain. By then he had two more daughters and his wife was pregnant with their fourth child. After he had been in Vietnam three months, his L-19 was shot down during an aerial recon flight. Jim suffered burns, a broken back, and a gunshot wound, and was captured. The pilot's remains were located and identified in 2013–2014.

For his first five years, Jim never spoke to another American. He was imprisoned in small bamboo cages, deprived of food, beaten, tortured, diseased and still recovering from his injuries. One fellow prisoner described him as a corpse, with his skin almost falling off. Another told the story of Jim suffering a heart attack and being dragged away so the POWs thought he had died. Five times Jim escaped (once for two days), but was recaptured five times. In 1967 Jim was moved north into different POW camps, eventually ending at the Hanoi Hilton. At the time of his release, Thompson was emaciated, with sparse white hair, looking closer to 70 than his almost 40 years.

After being processed at Clark AFB, Thompson was flown to Valley Forge General Hospital (Army) in Pennsylvania, where he spent some time being treated for his fractured back, gunshot wound and burns, heart seizure, malaria, dysentery, weight loss, internal health issues, dental problems, and the list goes on.

Thompson's life before captivity has two sides. His wife claimed he paid more attention to the Army than his family. She said he was absent for the birth of all his children, and his macho military bearing became abusive. In short, she said their marriage before he went to Vietnam was rocky. Jim's version is much gentler.

When I saw Lieutenant Colonel Thompson (upon repatriation he was made a major and less than a month later he was promoted again), he had been seen by others over the past few years. He appeared to be a gaunt, fragile man with thinning hair, stooped over and not very healthy-looking. Our conversation was not upbeat; his words were more like that of a person who finds life difficult and depressing. He did not have much to say, and was reticent about his life.

He acknowledged that when he arrived home, his wife and kids had been living with a retired Army NCO; the kids viewed this man as their father, which bothered Thompson very much. His wife agreed to return to him, but that did not work out, so in October 1974, they divorced. He just could not accept his wife living with another man while he was a POW.

In addition to his health issues and his marital discord, he faced other serious problems. He had difficulty being in the "new" volunteer Army. It was different. He lacked the military background of most lieutenant colonels in that he had never commanded a company or battalion, and he had no formal education beyond high school (most of his peers had at least a college degree, many with master's and some with doctoral degrees). Add to this the fact that America had changed significantly in the decade he was absent.

This was not the world he dreamed of returning to. His perception of his life after captivity was totally different from reality. The world he envisioned kept him alive as a prisoner. Sadly, though, that world no longer existed.

Thompson realized he no longer fit in. His family was gone, and while the Army created jobs for him to keep him occupied, he defined them as not much of anything. On a speaking tour he met a female Air Force lieutenant colonel. They married in early 1975 but divorced almost three years later; he said it was because they had different values.

He was an alcoholic, tried drugs, and wandered through life, with his hope vanished, almost like a broken man. A year before I saw Jim, he had attempted suicide by abusing drugs and alcohol. This occurred two days after President Carter signed Executive Order 12017 on 3 November 1977 changing the Military Code of Conduct (essentially making it not as restrictive regarding the conduct of Americans who become POWs).

Thompson was devastated because of the changes and became deeply depressed, saying it was the final straw.

He said he expected to make full colonel, which he did. His military decorations included the Distinguished Service Medal, Silver Star, Legion of Merit, Bronze Star, two Purple Hearts, Air Medal, parachutist Badge, Ranger Tab, and Combat Infantryman Badge. Because of all he had lost due to his captivity, the Army refused to deny him anything else; thus, he was promoted accordingly.

In 1981 he suffered a heart attack and a stroke, rendering him partially paralyzed. He was medically retired in 1982.

In 2002, at age 69, he died.

Other RPOWs I Met

No two Army RPOWs possessed an identical full story of their lives. For some, the differences began before they entered the Army. Others evolved while in the military or because of captivity. A few survived being a prisoner of war for years: the deadly tortures, the subhuman food, lack of human interaction, solitary confinement, isolation, and family deprivation—only to be crushed beyond repair upon returning home. In fact, the greatest difficulty experienced by several RPOWS after coming home was divorce.

Most RPOWs overcame their captivity and were able to get on with their lives, while others never could.

One man I saw lived out west. He was never able to discard the trauma of fear and being attacked and captured again. His house was on the side of a mountain with a long dirt road (i.e., several miles) clearly visible from the house. If he heard a car that was not known to him, he would shoulder his rifle and shoot at the approaching car.

One RPOW became the ward of his sister who owned a bar and grill on a beach. The man would wake up each morning, go to a hammock and lie down, spending the day there, eating and drinking, until bedtime. Day in and day out, this was his life after being a POW.

Another would get up each day and bid his wife goodbye as she went to work. Moving to his basement (with blacked-out windows), he would get comfortable in his eggshell chair (a large, plastic, eggshell-shaped chair with a hole large enough for a person to easily sit inside the shell, with legs outside). The seat was cushioned, and the inside insulated with speakers around the inside of the shell. Turning on the music, settling inside the chair, the man would spend his day in his chair, smoking marijuana.

Several RPOWs who were imprisoned in the south told me about a white man who was a VC. They described him as being healthy, nice looking, but armed and guarding the Americans. Some thought he was a Frenchman, left over from the 1950s (which did not make sense, since they described him as being in his mid-twenties to early thirties). Some said he only spoke Vietnamese, and others said he was able to converse in English. Some thought he was a converted American POW, but none of the RPOWs I talked to knew much about him. I knew all the RPOWs had been debriefed by military intelligence, and they admitted they had told their interrogators what they had seen, so I listened to them, very curious about the identity of the white man. It was not until 1979 that I discovered the "white VC" was actually U.S. Marine PFC Bobby Garwood. Garwood had been captured, or deserted, or disappeared at age 19 in 1965 outside Da Nang. In 1979, he returned to the States with quite a story of his life with the Viet Cong and the North Vietnamese.

Several were still working through marital issues but committed to making their family whole again. Many sought counseling where they lived or where they were stationed. No Army RPOWs lived in or near San Antonio, so I never saw any as a therapist. I was not a counselor to any of them or their family members. I was there to psychologically evaluate them, record their current diagnosis, recommend treatment as necessary, and repeat the process with the next RPOW. I collected data, analyzed findings, arrived at conclusions, and wrote professional papers and magazine articles on what I found in hopes of offering some advice to other therapists or researchers with their patients or clients after another war.

One book on post-service adjustment of Vietnam vets I had a chapter in (*Stress Disorders among Vietnam Veterans*, 1978) was recently noted by a VA therapist as a bible still used for counseling Vietnam vets. A decade ago, a fellow psychologist sent me a clipping of a research study completed in Israel which cited some of my research on the adjustment of post-war veterans.

My studies of the RPOWs and my final findings regarding the degree of adjustment difficulties experienced by this group of men echoed my research on the adjustment of Vietnam veterans. In the final (1978) psychological evaluation, nine percent of the RPOWs seen were found as unable to adjust to life after being incarcerated. My Vietnam vets research (done in Utah) showed that few showed severe problems adapting after military service. Again, my research was finding less post-service adjustment problems than that of many other behavioral scientists. And throughout my military career as a psychologist, I continued to validate my initial conclusions that service in Vietnam did not adversely affect every soldier, only a few.

Seeing this group of men intensified my understanding of the horrors of war and reaffirmed my iron-clad belief that no Vietnam veterans suffered more than our POWs. These men are the real heroes of the war; they gave and gave for several years. Each year my tour ended; I was able to return home to my family. They could not, never knowing if they would ever return home; for many of our POWs, they did not.

13

U.S. Olympics and Sports Psychology

The Modern Pentathlon

In January 1977, a friend, a local psychologist and a member of the Sports Medicine Committee of the U.S. Modern Pentathlon and Biathlon Association, spoke to me about a major project the U.S. Olympics wished to be conducted at Fort Sam Houston in San Antonio, Texas. The U.S. Modern Pentathlon Team resided at Fort Sam, where the Army provided training facilities, coaches, and other resources for the team. Additionally, several team members were in the Army, now stationed at Fort Sam.

The Modern Pentathlon is a unique sport. It was created in 1912, just for the Olympics. It is not found in high school or college athletics or even professional sports such as football, soccer, basketball, or baseball. The Modern Pentathlon is a team sport, but performed as individuals; the Pentathlon team members come from other sports such as swimming and running.

The sport was designed to emulate the tasks a 19th century cavalry soldier (courier) must endure in combat situations. The soldier must be able to cover territory by foot and on horseback; swim rivers; and fend off the enemy using a sword or pistol. These military skills became the capstone of the sport. The actual requirements of the sport have changed considerably over the past 100 years, but it still retains the five sports originally developed: running, swimming, shooting, fencing, and horseback riding (although now the running and shooting are combined into a single event).

In the mid- to late 1970s, the sport consisted of certain specific events. Participants ran a winding and twisting 4000-meter course of hilly terrain, woods, and rocky trails. It was not an easy run, requiring endurance and the ability to readily transverse uneven, obstacle-strewn paths quickly. The swimming event was a 300-meter freestyle timed distance, calling for endurance and speed. Shooting called for firing, off-hand, .22 caliber semi-automatic handguns, rapid-fire, at paper targets about 30 feet away. Fencing involved two athletes competing using fencing swords (foils … long, slim, flexible, metal blades). This was a one-touch event where the first to hit his opponent wins. The hit was determined by an electrical contact between the competitors' foils and chest protection. The horseback riding event took place over a 1000-meter course requiring the rider and horse to cover the distance and jump over 15 obstacles. The horse was provided to the competitor just before the event, so rider and horse must immediately form an aggressive and spirited relationship. The competition was spaced over five days, with one event held each day.

Pentathletes typically come from high school or college track and swimming teams. There are not enough sports events in shooting, fencing or horseback riding to locate world-class pentathlon athletes. It is easiest to take runners and swimmers and teach them the other events.

As mentioned, these events have changed considerably since 1912. Originally any caliber handgun could be used (as a young officer, General George Patton, shooting a .38 caliber revolver, represented the U.S. in the first Olympic Pentathlon competition, finishing fifth overall). Eventually only a .22 could be used. In 1994 the pistols were changed to .177 caliber air pistols (some said because the lead bullets were too poisonous). In 2009 the handguns were changed to laser pistols for safety reasons. Also, at that time (to increase spectator participation), the five-day competition was converted to a single-day event where the shooting and running events were combined (even though there are now only four events, it is still called the Modern Pentathlon). This was the sport I became involved in and my introduction to sport psychology.

What Is Sport Psychology?

Sport psychology is the use of behavioral science techniques to enable athletes to reduce competition anxiety and to improve performance. In the 1970s it is a little-known sidebar to clinical and counseling psychology and practiced by even fewer professionals. It was first employed in the late 1800s, then reappeared in the 1920s and 30s, only to fade away again. By the late 1970s, more psychologists were finding collegiate and professional athletes who were benefiting from what we had to offer. It was not until the mid–1980s that sports psychology was accepted as a legitimate practice of psychology. In 1985 the Association for the Advancement of Applied Sport Psychology was founded, and the next year the American Psychological Association created Division 47, Exercise and Sport Psychology.

Sport psychology can involve both individual and group sessions with athletes, coaches, and parents to improve the performance of athletes. Techniques include setting goals, concentration, relaxation exercises, and mental imagery or hypnosis to increase consistent performance. Sport psychologists are found in high school sports, college and professional teams, and individual athletes.

I became a sport psychologist by default. A research project conducted with the Modern Pentathlon Team led to me realize that I had experience related to two of the events, and in one, I was better than the pentathletes. Therefore, I believed that I could help some team members.

Medical and Psychological Evaluation of Pentathletes

My psychologist friend was providing a heads-up about a massive project for the U.S. Olympics that would be conducted by Brooke Medical Center. One day my boss, Colonel Otto Schreiber (Chief of the Department of Psychiatry), and I were summoned to the office of the medical center Chief of Staff. Other hospital department chiefs were in attendance, as well as some officials from the U.S. Modern Pentathlon and Biathlon Association. They were seeking support to perform a study to determine if there were any medical (physical) or psychological means to predict the world-class potential of young athletes. The physical study would be conducted by various medical services, while the psychological study would be headed by me and my psychologist friend. I assumed the reason for the study being done at Brooke was because the Modern Pentathlon Team was located at Fort Sam, and if the Army did the study, there would be no cost to the Olympics.

The plan for the psych study would be to first evaluate some world-class pentathletes to establish some kind of psychological profile of the top athletes. Then we would evaluate the younger and less talented pentathletes and create a psychological profile for them. We would compare profiles and work with the coaches to see if we could use psychological means to predict world-class potential. Additionally, the request was for the psychologists to aid the coaches regarding the management of the athletes.

The Modern Pentathlon was an event for males only, but in 1977 women were allowed in some of the competitions. There were 40 male pentathletes and eight females, but not all at Fort Sam. Several athletes lived, worked, and trained elsewhere in the country. Probably around 30 lived in the vicinity of the Army post.

First, we had to design the tests to be used, then devise a testing schedule, followed by the test analysis. I thought that, before devising a test battery for a group of athletes, it would benefit me to understand exactly what the Modern Pentathlon was. I set aside a week to find out.

Training of Pentathlon Athletes

I discussed what I wanted to do with the officer in charge of the pentathlon training. He explained every event of the competition and then covered what the training consisted of. Each event had a different coach and assistants. Most of the coaches were civilians, but the shooting coach was a retired Army NCO and a former Army competitive pistol shooter. Appointments were set up for me to visit every coach. We worked out a schedule where I would spend time training with them in every event.

When this project began, I was a couple of months shy of 40 years. But I had three things in my favor. Some time ago (like 14 years), I had been, like them, a professional athlete who spent his weekdays training and one weekend a month in competition. I was a pistol shooter for an Army Marksmanship Detachment, representing the Army in pistol matches around the country. In addition to shooting handguns, I, then a lieutenant, was also the unit executive officer. During the year I shot competitively, I won the Third Army indoor .22 pistol championship and was awarded the highest competitive pistol rating, that of Master. In short, I was not a bad shot with a pistol. Essentially, I had spent a year dedicating my life to increasing my performance and achieving the best I was capable of. Thus, I was aware of the life of a full-time competitive athlete.

I was a long-distance runner and competed at Fort Sam and San Antonio in monthly races such as the 5K (3.1 miles), the 10K (6.2 miles), and the mini marathon (also called the half marathon, 13.1 miles). Most races collected entry fees to cover the costs of hosting the races and to provide some financial benefits to local non-profit organizations. One competed in age brackets, so at age 40 I was not competing with 20-year-olds. Long distance running is not as much about speed as endurance. To win, one must set a steady pace and hold that throughout the race. I was not fast, but I did have endurance (during the week, mornings before work, I would run five miles each day and 10 to 15 miles on weekends). In most races I would finish somewhere in the top 10 for my age.

Therefore, I entered the pentathlon training with athletic experiences similar to what they were doing. There were two major differences, however: I was nowhere near a world-class competitor, and I was a decade or two older than the pentathletes.

We started with swimming. At the indoor pool I just watched their practice. Back and forth, as fast as possible. Since most pentathletes are selected based on their running or swimming competition times, many were (to my mind) super-fast. Smooth, coordinated, they could glide through the water like fish. If I were to join them in the water, I would only block their path, causing an aquatic traffic jam. Where I grew up, we had lakes, ponds, and rivers, and I learned to swim at an early age. But compared to them I was an ungodly thrasher, flailing about. Yes, I was a good swimmer but could not in any sense be a challenge to them. I spent an afternoon as a watcher, not a participant.

The next day was fencing. They wore white, tight clothes, and their safety gear included gloves, a chest protector, and a face mask (like a baseball catcher's or umpire's mask, but instead of the front having metal strips, the entire face was obscured by a fine steel mesh). The fight took place in a narrow lane with the fencers attacking or defending, their long, thin, flexible blade circling in front of them, awaiting an opening to push forward, hitting their opponent. I was dressed up in the protective equipment (minus the pants and shirt), and then a fencer began to show me some basic steps. For an hour or so, I began to learn the rudiments of fencing, and quickly realized that this was not a sport for me. I honestly knew that my adversary would end the bout in less than two seconds. While I became familiar with the sport, I recognized that this was not anything I could accomplish.

I arrived for my experience in the horse-jumping event, wearing old jeans; a pair of well-worn, low-heel, soft leather pull-on Red Wing boots; and a denim shirt. I was not a horseman, although I once had a large pony. Right after World War II ended, when I was age 8, my parents moved from our rented home in a small town into the country. They had a one-year lease, and as part of the deal, we had to care for the owners' pets, Ginger and Sugar. Ginger was a friendly collie and Sugar was a monstrous big pony (at least to an 8-year-old). Sugar's care became my responsibility. Unlike Ginger, Sugar did not cater to me, and our relationship quickly became strained and wary. Next to her barn was a long pasture where I would ride her quite often. Sometimes I would even ride her to school and leave her in a field behind the school. But during our treacherous year together, she had kicked me, thrown me, bitten me, stomped on my feet, and pinned me between her body and the walls of her stall—her favorite activity. Pushing me hard, she would try to shove me through the sides. She only succeeded in hurting me; I never fell. My experiences with equines were not enjoyable.

The coach walked me over the training course, explaining what the horse and rider had to do. The horses were trained jumpers and did not belong to the Army; they were leased. On different days, some horses were not the same ones as previously used. And the pentathletes would ride unknown horses during competition. Because pentathletes were not equestrians, they had to be taught how to ride and jump, from the beginning. The horses were bred for endurance, strength, and agility. They were trained to quickly run between obstacles, and readily and gracefully leap over the wooden hurdles.

My introduction to this event began with my presentation to my horse. I knew how to mount and dismount a horse and how to make it move or turn. This introduction did not go well. Although I was much bigger and stronger than my 8-year-old self, the beast in front of me appeared even larger than Sugar. The competitor must control the horse, yet it was noticeably clear to both of us that this horse was never going to be controlled by me. The coach had the horse and me walking the course but sauntering around the jumps instead of over them. Unfortunately the horse had its own idea of what to do and no matter what I did, it went its own way. After 15 to 20 minutes, it was obvious to the coach that I was not an effective rider, so that part of my training terminated. For the rest of my time, I only observed as a spectator.

Early the next morning, clad in running shoes, shorts, and a tee-shirt, I met the athletes and running coaches at the beginning of the three-to-five mile cross-country running path. I was the oldest runner by 15 to 20 years. The racers lined up, single file, with me at the end. At the start, we all took off. They kept ahead of me, and as each of us reached the end, our time was recorded by one of the coaches. As I started, I was the last to cross the finish line. The coaches looked at several measurements to note improvement. Much of this event depended on endurance. One measure employed was to note the pulse rate at the end of the run, and then to check recovery, by taking the pulse again, one minute later. The stronger the runner, the quicker the pulse would return to normal. Since I was used to running five miles every weekday morning, my pulse rate returned to normal as quickly as the other runners, which impressed them and their coaches.

The last event was the shooting. I arranged with the shooting coach to arrive early. I wanted to go over the firing course and do some practice before the team showed up. As mentioned, most pentathletes are swimmers or runners; none are competitive pistol shooters. Therefore, it is the coach's job to teach them .22-caliber, rapid-fire target shooting with a semi-automatic pistol. The targets are paper and the shooter fires one-handed. In 1912 when George Patton represented the U.S., target shooting was his strongest event. Unfortunately for him, all his shots went into a single ragged hole, so the judges, instead of allowing him all bull's-eyes, said some of his shots missed the target. After that, the back of the target moved to record every shot individually.

I found the course easy and comfortable, and practiced while adjusting the rear sight so my bullets would hit the target at my point of aim. Shortly the athletes arrived and began practicing while I watched. warm-up and sight adjusting were completed, the coach said all would run through the regular course for the event. The shooters lined up (to include me) and I am sure they thought, after watching me try the other events, that my performance would be similar. I blistered the course, getting a near perfect score, better than any of the pentathletes. Some even approached me after practice, asking how I could do that and seeking advice for improving their own performance.

Now I was ready to create a battery of psychological tests to begin the study.

The Modern Pentathlon Study

To begin, we looked at the research already done. An appreciable amount of research data was available examining psychological variables and athlete success or power. The research suggested that there was no correlation between IQ and sports achievement, but champion athletes did differ from the normal population on several traits. Also, no relationships existed between physical abilities and personality traits. We would conduct our research to determine if there were psychological factors related to success in pentathlon events. Success was defined as winning world-class competition events.

The tests selected include the Sixteen Personality Factor, the Personality Research Form and the Shipley Institute of Living Scale. The tests were administered between April and July 1977. We tested two small groups of pentathletes.[1] One group consisted of those athletes selected for the upcoming World Championships, and the second contained three world-class U.S. Pentathletes.

Due to the small size of our athlete sample, our results must be viewed with caution. But some differences from the normal population were noted in our tests of all athletes. They had higher IQs and their endurance traits were higher than normal.

There were differences between the three U.S. champions and the other pentathletes. The champions were brighter, and scored higher on indicators of endurance and the qualities of being seen in a favorable light, being success oriented, being perceptive, and being aloof and impersonable. Thus, the champions did differ in certain personality traits from the other pentathletes.

This study did have its problems. And these problems also rendered our findings even more dubious. The tests were administered in group sessions, and the behavior of some of the athletes was juvenile, antagonistic, and counter-productive. Twenty-nine (17 males and 12 females) were scheduled to be evaluated, but only 19 were completed and considered valid. The coaches and trainers for the team did not consider our project to be worthwhile and did not share the same degree of seriousness we did.

Because the results of the testing were not conclusive (due to the problems noted), the local psychologist and I decided to change the testing for 1978.[2] We would test the pentathletes individually and would add more test instruments.

For the second year of testing, we added the MMPI (Minnesota Multiphasic Personality Inventory), the WAIS (Wechsler Adult Intelligence Scale), and two parts from the Halstead-Reitan Neuropsychological battery (this test is lengthy but evaluates specific aspects of the condition and functioning of the brain by completing a variety of manual eye-hand coordination tasks). While endurance, speed, and agility are the hallmarks of successful pentathletes, concentration, focus, and brain-eye-hand functioning are essential in events such as shooting and fencing. For these reasons we added the Halstead-Reitan evaluations.

For the second round of testing, we had three females, seven junior males (under 21) and 14 senior males. The mean age of the women was 22, the junior men 19½, and the seniors 25. Seven were just out of high school, six had some college, and 11 had college degrees. Of the 24 tested, 21 were on active duty in the Army, and only three were civilians. The males were divided into two groups (there were not enough females to separate), superior performers (over 5000 Pentathlon scoring points) and average performers. These two groups were further divided into seniors and juniors. The testing was done between March and July 1978.

While all four male groups scored above normal on their IQ tests, there was no difference between groups. The females also scored above normal, but their scores were slightly lower than the males. Most personality tests were unproductive in distinguishing differences between male groups, yet some differences were noted. The younger athletes, being at the inception of their Olympic careers, scored above normal in areas of aspiring to accomplish difficult tasks, striving, being productive and driven, and being ambitious. The average juniors scored higher in traits of attempting to control their environment, and to influence or direct others. All four groups scored higher than normal in areas of achievement and endurance. The neuropsychological tests showed no discrimination between groups.

Historically it has been difficult to either find consistent personality correlates for athletic success or to predict athletic achievement using personality measures. This present study was no exception. Our findings indicate that while world-class athletes do have personality traits consistent with athletic prowess and achievement, many of the younger athletes also possess the same characteristics. Our conclusions were that there are certain personality characteristics in which all pentathletes do differ from normal people. But these traits do not identify future world-class athletes. The differences between champion pentathletes and average pentathletes lie in innate, unmeasurable traits such as drive, motivation, and a powerful desire to be the best. Along the way, many exceptionally good pentathletes drop out because of the rigid and demanding personal way of life that champions must endure for many years. These traits cannot be measured or assessed, but develop and become stronger over time. Not all superior athletes will devote this much time and effort to their sport, so they move on to something else.

Basically, those pentathletes with the potential for world-class performance could be identified by their coaches. But not all would stick with the regimented and brutal training regime to attain what they were actually capable of. Because of this factor, predicting who would remain with the program to become champions was not possible using the medical and psychological measurements.

This was a most frustrating project because it was unappreciated by those we were doing it for. Quite often athletes never showed for test appointments and had to be rescheduled, which was not easy when the tests took 5 to 6 hours for each session. Both the athletes and their training staff showed no enthusiasm for the project; their priority for ensuring schedules and appointments were kept was exceptionally low. The attitude shown by the training staff was manifested by the athletes reflecting ambivalence and even hostility toward the research. In fact, this time none of the coaches or trainers even asked for feedback or assistance concerning their athletes' test results. In summary, our labors were not seen as worthwhile contributions to the training effort. Additionally, on the medical side of the study, it was also found that there were no medical or physical means to predict which athlete would achieve success at the championship level.

The Life of a Pentathlete

Most of the pentathletes were young, single, and in the Army. Additionally, most were lower rank enlisted, recruited into the Army as a pentathlete. Some were officers, which was typically a career-ending decision. Competing as an Army athlete was disdained for officers and viewed as a dereliction of the oath of office. In early 1964, I won the Fort Benning

Post pistol championship and was selected to join an Army Marksmanship Detachment as a full-time pistol competitor. My battalion commander had a long talk with me about how becoming a shooter would kill my career and was vehemently against it. But I was a lieutenant, proud of my accomplishments as a pistol shooter and eager to enjoy the chance to become even better. I chose to become a full-time shooter. The year spent competing, in the long run, did not hurt me. That was probably because we became involved in a war and my combat record outweighed my year as an Army athlete.

Most athletes had little money, lived in inexpensive apartments close to the base, and had almost no life beyond training and competing. As I began working with some of the athletes as a sport psychologist, we became friends. I would visit them where they lived. Usually, two or more shared an apartment. These people were young, in superior physical condition, nice-looking, but totally devoted to their sport. Their living arrangements were spartan and simplistic, almost monk-like. Clothes were mostly sports gear. Because of their lifestyle, dressy outfits were not needed or desired. The apartments I visited were bare of furniture except for essentials (like a table and chair for dining purposes and a mattress on the floor for sleeping). Clothes were strewn in a corner or hanging in closets or stuffed in back packs.

One pentathlete I befriended was a regular Army captain, a West Point graduate. After the Infantry Officer Basic Course, he completed Airborne (parachute school) and Ranger training. Assigned to the 82nd Airborne Division, he was a platoon leader in a rifle company. Along the way he became a pentathlete. For a West Pointer, becoming an Army athlete was a kiss of death; he was passed over for captain (but was selected for promotion the second time around). He realized his career as an Infantry officer was dead, so he came up with another plan. His degree was in engineering. San Antonio College (a local community college) had a remarkably successful program to provide college graduates lacking a pre-med background with the courses needed to gain entrance into medical schools. As a pentathlete, he joined that program. He enjoyed the Army and did not want to leave.

Retaining career physicians in the Army was a challenging task. If one was a competent doctor, promotions to full colonel were fast and virtually guaranteed. This young man applied to the Uniformed Services University of the Health Sciences Medical School and was accepted. Med school regulations required him to resign his regular Army commission and accept a reserve commission as a second lieutenant. But time in med school would count toward promotion, so he calculated he would graduate as an MD and be promoted to major. If he was good as a physician, he would rapidly be promoted to lieutenant colonel and then colonel. He figured he would make colonel as a doctor at the same time his classmates would in their branch of service. He would remain a pentathlete until entering med school in the fall.

To me, the life of a pentathlete was an existence I would not tolerate.

Sport Psychologist for an Olympic Team

While the pentathlon study revealed that personality traits were not meaningful predictors of athletic success, the research did lead into other areas of psychological consultation, primarily that of teaching pentathletes how psychological theory and principles might augment their sports' preparation.[3]

My concept of sports training can be divided into three primary areas: endurance, skill, and mental. Endurance training encompasses physical development such as strength, stamina, and conditioning. Skill training relates to development of precise brain-motor-muscle coordination. Mental training is used to prepare the athlete (1) to cope with pressures and stress of competition more effectively; (2) to employ self-hypnosis as a means of relaxing during periods of intense physical and mental strain; and (3) to utilize mental imagery as an adjunct to their skill training.

Stress management is controlling stress. The less control one has over situations, the greater the chance for negative effects of stress to manifest. The more options the athlete has to manage stress, the more effective he or she becomes in handling stressful conditions. Stress management training consists of the athlete developing realistic plans for competing and training. Goals, objectives, measurement criteria and time schedules are clearly defined and prepared. Counseling sessions are held periodically to evaluate progress and emotional state. Harmful stress and relaxation are incompatible states, so knowing how to relax is vital.

My primary use of hypnosis was to train the pentathletes in self-hypnosis as a means of relaxation. Increasing self-confidence, minimizing feelings of pain, and reinforcing specific components of skill training are additional goals of hypnosis. Initial sessions accent the importance of a hypnotic trance to achieve mental and physical release from stress, tension, and fatigue. As the hypnotic sessions progress, the athletes learn how to achieve this on their own.

Simulation saves time, money, and effort. Many professions utilize simulators for training, such as aircraft pilots, golfers, and others. Using simulation reduces training time and enhances safety. These same principles apply to my use of mental imagery. This technique requires the athlete's application of self-hypnosis skills to achieve a level of maximum concentration. The concentration then focuses on specific aspects of training in the mind instead of on the broader field. The athlete is taught how to control concentration to produce the desired images. Skill coordination procedures, rehearsing competition strategies, or cognitively preparing for an athletic event are some applications of mental imagery. This process invites relaxation and increases confidence.

Psychological training for athletes combines the psychologist's knowledge of the sport with clinical skills and rapport with the athlete. Sport psychology can become a valuable adjunct to the endurance and skill training of the athlete.

Despite the sorry conditions of the research study, the impact of sport psychology consultation did contribute to athletic success, especially in areas of anxiety reduction, and increased awareness and concentration. By the end of summer 1977, we were completing our analysis of the research data collected. In October 1977, the Modern Pentathlon World Championships would be held at Fort Sam Houston. Six pentathletes requested assistance from me in muscle relaxation, mental imagery, and hypnosis. Individually we discussed what each wanted to achieve using my skills. Unfortunately, their requests did not come until shortly before the World Games; therefore, our time together was limited.

Behaviors to improve included proper trigger squeeze and sight alignment during pistol competition (requiring total concentration and mental focus), reduction of weariness or pain during swimming and running, and maintaining appropriate distancing during the cross-country run. These behaviors as described by the athletes were confirmed by their coaches. The correct techniques were reinforced with mental imagery while in a light to moderate trance. Specific goals heightened awareness while focusing on areas of stress; anxiety was reduced.

Four of the six continued with my assistance throughout the competition. One was the highest scorer on the U.S. team and came in sixth overall. Three of the four achieved significant success during competition and reached their stated goals.

I continued to work with a few pentathletes until the summer of 1981, before I retired. For the 1978 World Championships in Sweden, the U.S. finished fourth, with an American winning the bronze medal. In the 1979 World Championships in Budapest, the U.S. won the gold medal. I never attended any foreign competitions, but for the pentathletes I worked with, we made a series of audio tapes to assist in self-hypnosis, mental imagery, and relaxation.

The big competition during my time with the Modern Pentathlon

Team was the upcoming 1980 Summer Olympics to be held in Moscow. In March 1980, though, President Jimmy Carter declared that the U.S. would not participate because of the Russian involvement in Afghanistan.

As an aside, my involvement with sport psychology and my research papers led me to join a group of like-minded clinical psychologists who shared what we were doing, praising our successes and dissecting our failures. When I retired from the Army, I left psychology, yet our small group increased and, by the mid–1980s, became a recognized and legitimate part of psychology.

Even though I no longer practiced as a psychologist, I did continue to offer my services as a sport psychologist. I worked for several years with a university women's winning basketball team, continuing doing the same as I did for the pentathletes.

Not everything I did was totally Army-related. Professionally there were other non-military activities I engaged in to add more variety to my life. These were fun, stimulating, and sometimes financially productive.

14

Continued Adventures in Flying

My last flight at Fort Polk was on 26 August 1975. Due to my transfer to San Antonio, I had to quit flight training. Shortly after arriving at Fort Sam Houston, I joined the post's flying club. It was located at Martindale Army Air Field (10 miles east of downtown San Antonio but only four miles southeast of Fort Sam Houston). Martindale (MDA) was a little-used former auxiliary field, built during World War II for Randolph AAF, 10 miles further east. Now it only was home to the flying club. It had a clubhouse building, hangars, some other unused buildings, and a single, well-worn 3000-foot runway. In the 1970s it was listed as an active airfield but became abandoned in 1983, only to be reclaimed in 1992 by the Texas Army National Guard as a helicopter training base, which it is today.

The club had four Cessna 150s, a Cessna 172, and a couple of surplus Army T-41s (a military souped-up C-172). The cost for a C-150, wet, plus flight instructor was $12 an hour. My first flight at Martindale (with an instructor) was 24 September. This aeronautical nightmare almost caused me to give up flying.

Martindale has no control tower, so pilots land and depart under their own supervision. My initial flight with Daniel J. Mitchell, the club's civilian flight instructor, was primarily an introduction to flying around San Antonio. Soon after getting airborne, it seemed all he did was switch radio frequencies, without referring to any list of aviation radio stations. I said to myself, "I can never do this; it is too confusing, more than I can handle."

You see, because Martindale has no radio station, you don't need to talk to anyone until you are in the air. San Antonio International Airport (SAT) is north of Martindale, Randolph Air Force Base is just east, and to the southwest are two more Air Force bases as well as a municipal airport. Each controls its own airspace, so no matter where you fly, you must talk to someone. And typically, one will fly through airspace controlled by more than one facility.

To me, it was so confusing that I told Daniel I could never learn to do that, but he convinced me that I could, and soon would be doing what he did, just as easily. You know what? He was right. In the next month I flew 10 times, preparing again for my Private Pilot check ride.

We flew all around the area, in and out of SAT, cross-country and night flights. Mitchell was an excellent instructor. Younger than me, he was a former Army recruiter as well as a flight instructor.

Sometimes, I would over-control the 150 and Mitchell would tell me to relax. I would counter that the plane was hard to fly and I was just applying pressure on the yoke to keep it straight. He advised me that the plane could fly itself, so I should relax. I expressed my disbelief that the plane could fly itself, as I knew it was hard for me to remain in steady flight because the plane wanted to do something else. Then he told me this story.

The Plane That Flew Itself

A few years ago, Mitchell, as an Army recruiter, was stationed at Yuma, Arizona. He would often fly himself to small towns in western Arizona and southeastern California, trying to encourage young men and women to enlist. At the time he was also a flight instructor at Yuma International Airport.

Yuma Airport is an unusual airport as it is both a military facility and a civilian field. The U.S. Marine Corps Air Station Yuma operates from the airport, as well as all civilian traffic. One hot summer day, one of Mitchell's civilian students was preparing for a solo flight in a C-150.

He had taxied to the departure end of the runway with his door open, due to the suffocating heat. While holding on the runway, ready for departure, his map flew out of the open door. It landed on the ground just below. He slid out the door, bending over to grab the map when it blew a few feet further away. Crouching under the wing strut, he moved again and stretched out to reach the map when the plane moved forward. Turning and twisting, he attempted to grasp the strut, but the plane motored down the runway, without a pilot, and slowly became airborne. It gently banked to the north and eventually settled at a cruise altitude, floating over the ranges of the U.S. Army Yuma Proving Grounds. There it circled until it ran out of fuel and crashed.

Mitchell told that story (which I did not believe) to get me to realize that the plane could fly itself, so I should stop trying to control every little bump or twist. Several years later I landed at Yuma for fuel. As I waited in the FBO (Fixed Base Operator, the on-airport service station for planes) for my plane to be fueled, I noticed a photo of a crashed plane in the desert.

Walking over to the bulletin board I noticed an old newspaper clipping, dated in the early 1970s. The article described how a Cessna 150 took off without its pilot and flew over the military artillery ranges until running out of fuel. The photo was of the crashed 150.

Mitchell arranged for my Private Pilot FAA check ride for the afternoon of 19 October 1975.

Getting Lost, Twice!

I was to meet the FAA examiner at the municipal airport in Castroville, about 25 miles west of San Antonio. I departed Martindale and tried to follow IH 10, westbound, as I crossed the city. Flying from the left seat, I was on the north side of several major highways which bisected San Antonio. Keeping watch out the window to my left, I kept the freeway under my left wing. Unbeknownst to me, instead of following IH 10 west, I was following IH 35, southwest. Watching the compass, I noted I was no longer flying west but more to the south. I did not realize IH 10 went north and I needed to follow highway 90, westbound. I became worried that I was lost.

Studying my map, I believed I had followed the wrong highway out of the city. I had not noticed when the two highways split. I calculated that if I turned right, and flew due north, I should quickly cross highway 90 and a left turn, west, should take me to Castroville. Which it did.

At the airport, the examiner, Mr. Valentine, went through the oral exam with proper responses from me. Then came the air work where I had to demonstrate I was capable of flying a plane. I did different landings at Castroville, and then we flew north for aerial maneuvers. I did banks, stalls, and turns around a point, and somewhere north of Castroville I was told to fly to another airport.

I did not know where that airport was; in fact I had no clue as to where we were now. I was lost again. Valentine opened my map and pointed to the airport I was to fly to. I was dumbfounded. I had no idea of what direction to fly in, because I was lost and did not know where we were. Stalling for time, I asked him to point out again where he wanted me to go, and he did. As his finger pointed to the airport, I noted a small lake north of the airport; I also noted that it was the only lake anywhere near us on the map. Glancing out the window, I saw the lake. Shifting my eyes between the map in my lap, the lake, and the compass, I then knew where we were. I quickly calculated how I needed to cross the lake to fly to the airport. I explained to the examiner that, when we reached the lake, I would turn south, and we would soon be at the airport. As we started to cross the lake he said to return to Castroville. I knew Castroville was on IH 10, so I quickly located it on my map. I flew southwest, saw 10 and followed it back to Castroville. On the way, Valentine complimented me on my excellent navigation skills. If he only knew the truth. On landing he signed off on passing my FAA check ride. I was now a legal pilot.

Flying Anita

I had heard several horror stories where a new (and young) pilot wanted to take a friend, spouse, or special other for a flight. Unfortunately, the new pilot wants to show off his aerial skills, so he takes the passenger through stalls, steep turns, and other stomach-turning maneuvers, scaring the person in the right seat to death where they vow never to ride in

Anita and Bob in their plane, preparing for a flight, 1979.

a small plane again. I learned to fly so I could fly myself on trips for the Army. I also wanted my wife to accompany me on these trips.

I had to introduce her to flying as a safe, comfortable, hassle-free mode of transportation to fun places to visit. I selected a very calm, clear Saturday for her first flight. I explained the pre-flight examination, going over details so she would feel this procedure would ensure the plane was safe, then helped her into the plane and buckled her in. Moving around the plane, I entered, closed my door, and buckled myself up.

My describing the starting process, the checking of the control surfaces, and the run-up to check all the instruments and the health of the engine relaxed her. After slowly moving down the runway, I rose very gently, the transition from wheels on the ground to flight being so smooth, it was not noticeable. We cruised around San Antonio and by now my ability to switch frequencies made my performance appear like that of a professional pilot. Anita had a headset so she could hear everyone I spoke to. We did not go very high; the turns were gentle and fully coordinated, and our flight brought us back to the airport in under 30 minutes. My pattern was high and wide, so the turns were slow and easy. The landing was almost perfect. I parked the plane and tied it down. Anita thought the short flight was fun and safe.

After that time, she accumulated several thousand hours in the right seat, flying in every state except Hawaii as well as Canada and the Bahamas, and surviving two crashes. In fact, for a while she authored a column titled *The Right Seat* for an aviation magazine. She named her column for the seat in a small plane where the passenger sits.

Weather Delays and Flights Canceled

My certificate to fly would only allow me to fly in clear weather when I could see. If the weather was bad (thunderstorms, clouds, obscured visibility), I stayed on the ground. One day I had a business trip planned but the weather was not cooperating. It was cloudy, with low ceilings, drizzle, and poor visibility. I hoped the weather would improve, allowing me to launch safely and legally. I kept calling the local FAA weather briefer and finally the man (who by regulation could not tell me it was either safe or unsafe to fly) said to me, "son, if you do not fly today, you will be around to fly tomorrow."

I seriously reflected on his sage advice. I was fully aware of the risks in flying (mostly related to bad weather). I had survived three combat tours in my military career; I had been shot at multiple times, and hit once. A combat infantryman could not tell a superior, when being given a combat mission, "that's not looking so good, I will stay here today and go out tomorrow." It does not work like that; if told to go, you go.

But flying is different. I have total control over my flights, If the weather or the plane or the pilot (me) is in any way iffy, I can say, "not today." In over 7100 hours of flying, I have canceled flights several times, left airplanes to fly home commercially, or stopped en route because I felt something was unsafe (me, the plane, or the weather). I have never regretted any trip not taken, flight canceled, or plane left behind. I have always felt comfortable saying "not today."

Purchasing My First Airplane

I was accumulating quite a few hours, as I would fly on either trips for the Army or back to DeRidder for the Special Education project. Continued flying with my flight instructor, Daniel Mitchell, increased my skill, making me a better and safer pilot. Early on, shortly after I obtained my Private Pilot certificate, he explained how to get the Army to pay for my flights for them.

He explained that as a recruiter he flew to small towns, trying to find enlistees. He said that for Army-authorized travel, typically the orders allowed travel by commercial means (bus, train, airlines) or privately-owned vehicle (POV). He further stated that there were no specifics on what a POV is. Other regulations covered travel by private plane. Mitchell cited the regulations that governed this travel and advised me to contact the travel section of our Health Services Command finance office. I did and Mitchell was correct. There was one caveat, though: I would be compensated for using my own airplane, but reimbursements would not exceed the cost of a regular airplane ticket. For my flights, most of my costs were covered, but not 100 percent. At any rate, the Army did pay me to fly; and what was not paid by Uncle Sam became an employee tax deduction.

Being a member of a flying club allowed one to lease aircraft from the club for flying local or cross-country trips. I belonged to both the Fort Sam Houston club and another club at San Antonio International (SAT), so I had more planes available to fly for business, fun, or more training. Being a club member, though, I encountered problems which thwarted some of my trips, so alternate means of travel had to be found (drive myself or commercial air). Why?

Aircraft, like cars, have regularly scheduled maintenance. The owner of a car may choose to neglect the required maintenance (and of course risk vehicle damage), because there are no laws requiring the work be done. But, unlike cars, aircraft maintenance is required by law (the Federal

Aviation Administration), and if it is not done as required, the aircraft cannot be flown. The scheduled time for mandatory upkeep is usually measured by hours flown.

Often the obligatory work is to inspect a part of the aircraft and repair or replace if needed. Club planes may be reserved for a trip. Because the planes are booked in advance, if the hours flown between being booked and the actual trip reach an inspection time, the plane is grounded until the examination is completed and appropriately certified in the aircraft logbook. The club maintenance officer keeps track of the times for necessary work and many times, I would not know the plane had been grounded until the day before.

Sometimes the last pilot to fly the plane forgot to turn off the master switch (after shutting the plane down), and I showed up for my trip and

Bob cleaning the rear windows on his plane, 1978. Photo taken before the plane was painted.

found out the battery was dead, and the plane would not be flyable until the next day.

Therefore, at times, I would have a trip planned but no plane to fly. The club I belonged to at SAT was part of a large corporation at the San Antonio airport. It had the flight school (with several planes), a flying club (using the same planes), an aircraft maintenance facility, an FBO, and an aircraft sales department. After I related my woes to the owner of the entire corporation, he suggested buying my own plane. I said I could not afford to own and fly an airplane. He said I could. He then explained how.

He said he had a 10-year-old Cessna 172 for sale. Originally the owners asked him to sell it, but it was in such attractive shape, and the price was so right, that he bought it to sell.

His maintenance shop had thoroughly inspected the plane before purchase, and it had no problems. He planned on doing some cosmetic work, painting the exterior and making it pretty for sale. He said if I would buy it now, as is, he could offer me a very good price: $10,000.

He suggested I make an appointment with the maintenance section of the local FAA Flight Standards District Office, take the Cessna's logbooks

Bob standing next to his plane after it was painted, 1980.

and his inspection, and ask the person there to review it all and tell me what he thought. And I did.

The FAA Maintenance Section Chief went through the logbooks and explained the accidents and repairs to the plane. He knew all the repair shops that worked on the plane, and pronounced them very competent. Next, he reviewed the inspection report. He commented that the business that had the plane for sale enjoyed an excellent reputation and did honest work. In his opinion the plane looked okay on paper, the logbooks were complete and detailed, and he thought the deal was good.

I bought the plane.

Instrument Training ... How I Failed the Tests, Twice

Now that I owned my plane, I was responsible for all maintenance, and it was up to me to ensure that the plane was available for every planned trip. One other problem hindered my trips: the weather. I was trained such that I could only fly in clear weather, where I could see the ground and around me in the air. If the weather was cloudy, rainy, or foggy, or otherwise had obscured visibility, I could not legally fly.

One day I had a trip to DeRidder but the clouds were too low for safe flying, so I drove. About 20 miles out of San Antonio, the low ceilings dissipated, and the skies were clear and sunny all the way to DeRidder. I decided that I needed to get my instrument rating, allowing me to fly in poor visibility, in the clouds, when I could not see, navigating solely via the flight instruments in the plane.

I enrolled in the instrument training program at the flight school where I bought the plane. I learned what additional navigation equipment I needed to fly by instruments. Contacting a local avionics shop, I agreed to purchase the new (and used) navigation devices for an affordable price. As the shop was examining my plane to determine what was needed, I was told that there was another problem. The airplane was configured for VFR (visual flight rules) flying only; it did not have the electrical capacity to power the new equipment. Now what? Did I have a white elephant? Did I waste ten grand?

In short, no, I did not. Between 1967 (when my plane was made) and the time of my instrument training, many owners wanted to upgrade similar planes to be capable of instrument flying. Therefore, Cessna produced a fix. The generator system could be converted to an alternator and my plane would have ample electricity to allow the new instruments to function.

Another weekend course (this time for the instrument test) resulted in a high score. The training went well, and I was signed off for the instrument check ride. I scheduled an examiner for the flight test. He started with an oral exam, on which I did fine, and then we climbed into my plane. I started up and someone came running out of his office, banging on the door. The examiner motioned for me to not move as he opened the door. He was told that his wife had been in an accident and that he was needed at the hospital. He told me to shut down, and he left.

Several days later we rescheduled for a time at the end of the day. I had a remarkably busy and difficult day at work, so my mind was split between work issues and passing the instrument flight test. Because of approaching darkness, we were rushed, and I did not do well. The examiner called a halt and we returned to land and park. He believed being rushed was not fair to me, so instead of failing me, he said I never took the test so I could reschedule for another, more convenient time.

My attempt to pass the instrument flight test was a disaster. I felt I was not destined to become an IFR (instrument flight rules) pilot. A good friend of mine was a Certified Flight Instructor—Instrument. He took me under his wing. In a couple of weeks, he announced I was ready for the test again.

I set up an appointment with a different examiner, this time at Stinson Municipal Airport, six miles south of the city. Built in 1915 by the Stinson aviation family, the field had a long and interesting history. I had set aside another afternoon for the test.

When I landed at Stinson, I taxied to the examiner's office and went in. His secretary said he was on a flight test and would return soon. I waited over two hours until he finally arrived; it was almost early evening. He was astounded to learn that he had missed my appointment. Apparently, another pilot needing his instrument examination showed up before me; the examiner thought he was me, and proceeded with the test. He said to me, "let us go," and off we went. It did not go well. He was trying to administer a 90-to-120-minute test in half an hour. Seeing my discomfort at trying to play catch-up, he said to return home, so we did.

He apologized profusely, saying it was all his fault. If I could fly Saturday afternoon, he would keep the entire afternoon open for me. I pointed out that my test scores would expire in a day, so my written test would be invalid come Saturday. I would have to take the instrument written test over again before I could take the flight exam. He thought for a minute and, rummaging through his desk, extracted some papers.

He said he was going to "pink slip" me for having the flight test terminated due to an instrument failure. When the instrument is repaired, the testing can resume. If I successfully pass, the date of passing (and receiving my Instrument Rating) would be the date of the original test, before the expiration of my written exam. I agreed to Saturday.

I was crestfallen. Twice I had failed the instrument test. My friend said we could go through the flight test protocol on Saturday morning, which we did. I was nervous and feared I would mess up the test again. For some reason, my family was elsewhere that day. I got home in the late morning, ate a light lunch by myself, and laid down on our bed.

I used self-hypnosis to relax me and allow my mind to focus on the flight I had just completed earlier that morning. Out of my trance, I was calm and rested. I flew to Stinson and picked up the examiner. He was relaxed and we took the test slowly, without haste. I did well. I nailed it. Upon landing he apologized again and said that I did great, and he was happy to approve my flight test. I was now an instrument-rated pilot.

Flying with My Family

Flying with family members can be great. In some families, the love of aviation passes from one generation to the next. In other families, the pilot has no one who shares his or her passion. My family sort of falls between the two extremes. While my wife, Anita, has several thousand hours in the right seat, our kids saw our plane as only a means of getting somewhere quickly. Their combined attitude, in flight, became, "Are we there yet?" In fact, our youngest daughter thought for some time that every family had a small plane stashed somewhere as an airborne family station wagon.

When I became a pilot, I was 38. Our three daughters were Suzi (14), Julie (10), and Karen (7). Because our 172 only allowed three passengers, someone had to stay home. So often, our teenager, with school obligations and newly-found social activities, remained home for our single-day trips. Yet sometimes, Anita would remain on the ground so Daddy could enjoy flight time with his three girls. Here are some flights I will never forget.

The $100 Hamburger

One younger daughter had a friend who wanted to fly with her. After I convinced the friend's mother that I was a safe pilot, a Saturday morning was scheduled for a flight to another airport for the proverbial "expensive" hamburger (because the cost of flying the plane to another airport for a $10 hamburger is $90). The little girl's mom was a nurse, and told me that her daughter never suffered from motion sickness (yet she gave the girl some Dramamine before our trip).

I planned a short flight (30 minutes) for lunch and both small girls responded with glee, looking forward to the trip. The girls occupied the

Karen riding in the back seat of the family's airplane, 1978.

back seats. My daughter, being the "expert" on flying, showed her little friend where the sick sacks were in the rear pockets of the seats in front of them.

Unfortunately, before arriving at our cruise altitude, the friend got sick. It seemed like buckets of vomit exploded from her tiny body, not into a sick sack, but all over the entire back of the plane. My daughter comforted her sick companion, while I immediately turned around, returned to our airport, and landed as quickly as I could. We had no $100 hamburger; instead, we spent several hours cleaning up the plane. As I was a quick learner, that was my only flight with a daughter's friend.

Flights to Padre Island, Texas

The white beaches of the barrier islands off the Texas coast became an attractive destination. Sometimes we went for an overnight camping trip, but often flew over for a day on Padre Island. Being less than 100 miles away, it was an easy flight, under an hour. We could land on the beach (very tricky as too far inland, the wheels would dig into the soft sand and flip over; the same could happen if landing too near the water). Northeast of the island was a deactivated U.S. Air Force bomber base (now privately

Bob and Julie loading his plane to visit Northern Arizona University, 1980.

owned) where we could land, taxi to the beach, park and walk a few yards to the water.

As much fun as this was, there was a slight catch: balls of tar. Apparently, the tar came from offshore oil wells, floated ashore, and coated the bare feet of anyone swimming or strolling. So flying to the island required carrying a few plastic jugs of water, WD-40, a roll of paper towels, and plenty of soap. Upon landing, the jugs would be set on the ground to be heated by the sun.

Before departing, I sprayed each small foot and leg with WD-40 to remove the tar. The warm soapy water would cleanse the lower extremities and the girls could board the aircraft. Climbing to cruise altitude, I would tune the ADF (Automatic Direction Finder, a navigation radio) to the frequency of 1200, the AM radio station of WOAI, in San Antonio, near the airport. Being a clear channel station (a powerful radio broadcast frequency), we could easily pick up the radio station and just follow the needle back home.

Going Away to College

For those pilots with kids, nothing beats general aviation for checking out colleges. Suzi knew she wanted to go to a women's college in New

Orleans. Being about 550 miles away we would stop in Lake Charles, Louisiana, for fuel and food, then continue. The trip by car would have taken 12–14 hours but by plane it was under seven hours. Now the four of us left behind could fly to visit Suzi.

When it was Julie's turn to select a college, I suggested Northern Arizona University in Flagstaff (where I received a master's degree). The two of us planned a visit, along with a dad-daughter fun camping trip. We would fly from San Antonio to Lake Powell, camp there a couple of days, fly next to Flagstaff to visit NAU, then land on a dirt strip on a mountain in southwestern New Mexico to camp, then finally head home.

Lake Powell is a national recreation area managed by the National Park Service. We planned to camp at the Park Service campground, Wahweap, on the southern end of the lake, just across from Page, Arizona. On the mesa just above the campground was a collection of trailers, and right down the middle was a short dirt strip. One could fly in, park, and hike the short distance to the campground.

We did just that, and set up our tent next to an older couple (early 60s) staying in their pick-up camper. Seventeen-year-old Julie could have easily passed for being in her twenties. So, this scruffy-looking guy in his late

Julie backpacking during visit to Northern Arizona University, 1980.

30s or early 40s and a young attractive female came trudging down with packs, appearing to the couple to be hitch hikers.

Our neighbors were very curious as to who or what we were but dared not seek answers. The day before we left, they asked Julie where she was going next. She replied, "Flagstaff." Believing we were hitchhiking since we walked into the campground, they asked her how long she thought it would take to hitch a ride for the 120 miles to Flag. She replied about an hour. Their incredulous faces reflected disbelief. Julie then pointed to the mesa (where only trailers could be seen from the campground), explaining that we had a plane parked between the trailers. For the rest of our stay the couple avoided any contact with us.

Weight and Balance and Daughters

Aircraft weight and balance (meaning the weight of people and baggage must be distributed in the plane to ensure it was balanced so the plane would fly straight and level, not nose up or nose down) had little meaning to my daughters. Small aircraft have very rigid weight limitations; if exceeded, the plane becomes too heavy and unsafe. We planned a spring break in Santa Barbara, California.

Anita and the two girls (Julie and Karen) packed what they each thought they needed. So three sets of everything, from hair dryers to combs and brushes, went into their duffels. Once the duffels were packed, I weighed the bags; each was considerably overweight. I explained the weight limits of the plane, including the number of pounds that needed to be removed from each bag. Back to their rooms Julie and Karen went, returning with much lighter bags, certainly within weight limits.

Glancing back at the girls, I almost cried. The clothing removed from the bags never went back into drawers or closets, but on their bodies. Two shirts, multiple sweaters, long pants, shorts, and a skirt, scarfs, coats and who knows what else removed from the bags did not reduce our weight, but only transferred it from suitcases to daughters. My wife had a talk with our girls, and finally bodies and bags remained within limits.

Flying for Business and Pleasure

Anita and I loved our little plane and our flying adventures. Often, I could combine both on the Army's dime. Once I had orders to attend a psychology conference in San Francisco. The meeting did not end until Friday and I did not have to be at work until Monday morning. A local newspaper article stated Frank Sinatra would be spending the weekend in Las Vegas, singing at the Caesars Palace Hotel and Casino.

We reserved a room at Caesars for Saturday night and thus were able to procure tickets for Sinatra's Saturday evening show. Saturday morning, we flew to Las Vegas, a 4.4-hour flight. Early Sunday morning we departed for San Antonio, with a fuel stop in El Paso, Texas, a total of 10 and a half hours in the air. This could only be done by our small plane.

Six years after I became a pilot, I retired from the Army. In that time, I had spent 903 hours in the air with 600 hours flying my Cessna (and the Army paid for the flying).

When I became a civilian, though, the Army no longer financed my flying, so I needed to find another source of money. I joined the Civil Air Patrol (a non-military auxiliary of the U.S. Air Force, created to execute search missions for downed civilian aircraft for the Air Force) as a search and rescue pilot. I could use my own aircraft for these missions and the USAF would reimburse me for gas and oil. Additionally, I convinced the editor of an aviation weekly newspaper (*General Aviation News*) to hire me as a writer. I believed that my flying would now become a business expense, and therefore tax deductible. I was hired and four decades later, I am still an aviation writer.

15

Being Demoted, Three Times

In the Marines I was promoted to corporal in the fall of 1958. A Marine corporal was a leader at the lowest rank, a junior non-commissioned officer. At this time, the military had seven enlisted pay grades (E-1 through E-7) and the corresponding ranks, with private as the lowest and either master sergeant or sergeant major as the highest.

Effective 1 January 1959, the military added two more enlisted grades, E-8 and E-9. So now a corporal had the pay grade of E-4. Even though I remained in the E-3 pay grade, I was allowed to retain the rank of corporal. But six weeks later, when I was released from active duty, I lost one stripe. Administratively reduced to the new rank of lance corporal, still in pay grade E-3. I was no longer an NCO. This was my first demotion.

Returning to Dartmouth College, I entered Army ROTC, which would not allow me to remain in the Marine Reserve, so I received a branch transfer into the Army Reserve. I enlisted as an E-3, except an E-3 in the Army is a private first class. Going from a lance corporal to being a PFC again is another demotion. As both these demotions were administrative, I never lost my E-3 pay grade, only the rank.

As a commissioned officer in the Army, promotions are more complicated. Throughout this book I refer to the U.S. Army and my serving in both the Reserve and on active duty. The U.S. Army comprised four separate components: the Regular Army (some view this as the corps of career, active-duty soldiers), the Army Reserve (part-time soldiers serving one weekend a month plus two weeks of active duty, annually), the Army National Guard (with dual responsibilities…. Army and state), and the Army of the United States (AUS), which includes everyone who serves full time on active duty in the Army.

All commissioned officers (Regular, Reserve, or National Guard) could serve on full-time active duty for specific periods of time, or continuously in what was called Voluntary Indefinite status (Vol Indef). I held an Army Reserve commission (via college Reserve Officer Training Corps) and was on active duty as a career officer on Vol Indef status.

Commissioned Army officers (lieutenants, captains, majors, colonels, etc.) become an officer via several ways. West Point graduates become commissioned in the Regular Army and most ROTC graduates (and OCS grads) receive reserve commissions (USAR or sometimes National Guard commissions). All regular officers serve on active duty, all the time. Reserve and National Guard officers can serve on active duty or part-time in a reserve or National Guard unit.

To add to this confusion, all officers serving on active duty would hold two ranks, a temporary rank and a permanent one. The permanent rank would be determined by which commission (Regular, Reserve, or National Guard) they held, their time as a commissioned officer and their time in grade. My permanent commission was in the Army Reserve (USAR). The temporary grade is determined by what the Army of the U.S. needs, cited as an AUS promotion. In war time, promotions can be fast (like my promotion from second lieutenant to major) or slow in peace time (like my promotion from major to lieutenant colonel). An officer could have a permanent grade of captain but serve on active duty with a temporary grade of major. Think of George A. Custer, a West Point graduate with a permanent grade of first lieutenant, then captain, who still served during the Civil War in various temporary flag (general officer) positions.

Add to this perplexity of promotions various rules and regulations that implement more changes in the promotion system. Here is an example.

In August 1968 (when on active duty) I was promoted to major, AUS with a permanent rank of Army Reserve captain. A year later I was released from active duty, but remained in the reserve. At the time of my switch from full-time service (Vol Indef) to join the Army Reserve, the Army had issued a new regulation which declared that any person with a temporary grade of major and one year of active-duty service in that rank would receive a permanent promotion to major upon moving from the active Army to reserve status. This meant that my permanent USAR grade (of major) awarded on 21 August 1969 was several years before the normal promotion procedure.

After I returned to active duty as a psychologist, I received a letter from the Department of the Army Personnel Center announcing my promotion to permanent lieutenant colonel (USAR) as of 20 August 1976, seven years after promotion to major (permanent grade). Thus my permanent grade was lieutenant colonel, while my temporary grade remained major. This was quite a switch as normally the temporary grade was the highest.

Almost one year later, on 13 May 1977, I was promoted to the temporary grade of lieutenant colonel, AUS. For a lieutenant colonel to be promoted to full colonel, he or she would need 21 years of commissioned

Bob being promoted to lieutenant colonel with Anita on the right and deputy commander of the Brooke Army Medical Center on the left (U.S. Army photo, 1977).

service. Because I was appointed a second lieutenant on 25 August 1961, I would not be eligible for promotion to colonel until 24 August 1982.

In 1979 I received a notification that I was in the zone to be considered for permanent full colonel. I wrote the board a letter explaining that I did not believe I would be eligible because I would not have 21 years of commissioned service until August 1982. I had a quick response stating I was correct in that I was not eligible to be considered for colonel.

The letter also said, after a thorough review of my records, I had been erroneously promoted to lieutenant colonel too early, so my date of rank would be administratively overturned and I was given a new date for permanent lieutenant colonel, 20 August 1978.

The reason was that, although I certainly had the proper amount of time as a major (which is what the promotion was based on), I also needed 17 years since being commissioned. In August 1976 (the first time I was considered for promotion to lieutenant colonel) I only had 15 years of commissioned service. Therefore, I could not be promoted to lieutenant colonel until August 1978, 17 years after commissioning. The letter noted that I had served ad hoc in that position, so nothing else would be done. Additionally, the letter did affirm that I would become eligible for consideration for promotion to colonel as of 20 August 1981.

This was the third time in my military profession that I was demoted. Each time was an administrative action that had no effect on my career, but I doubt if many lieutenant colonels can boast of being demoted in rank three times.

Moving On

As the pages of the calendar turned to my second summer at BAMC, Colonel Schreiber, Chief of the Department of Psychiatry, began learning about problems associated with the Community Mental Health Service, run by a lieutenant colonel psychiatrist. A year before, his psychologist committed suicide. Now all the enlisted mental health counselors officially requested a transfer out of CMHS, as did the civilian secretary.

The local military community was also voicing concerns about a perceived absence of interest by the CMHS chief. The assigned CMHS officers complained of the lack of any in-service meetings or training. The staff was pretty much operating on their own and very unhappy about that. They wanted new leadership.

By mid-summer Colonel Schreiber asked if I would be willing to become chief of the CMHS and turn it around. It meant going back to the troops again. I couldn't say yes fast enough.

On 31 July 1978, I was re-assigned as chief of the Fort Sam Houston CMHS.

PART V

Doing What I Love Most: Community Psychology
July 1978 to September 1981

16

Community
Mental Health Service
The Previous Chief and His Problem

The psychiatrist chief I replaced was responsible for everything the clinic did or failed to do. He reported directly to the Chief of Psychiatry. He was responsible for the Community Mental Health Service (CMHS) providing all the necessary psychological, psychiatric, and social work services to all the active-duty troops at Fort Sam as well as assisting their commanders to manage any aberrant behavior problems within a unit. Additionally, he was accountable for the behavior, training, and clinical expertise of every person, military or civilian, assigned to CMHS. Also, the clinic's community outreach programs, records management, and overall credibility within the military community it served was his obligation. The previous chief's being fired was due to his failure to accomplish most of these requirements. My job was to reinstate all of this again.

The Community Mental Health Service at Fort Sam Houston

The Community Mental Health Service provides psychological and psychiatric support to the over 6000-person military population at Fort Sam Houston (referred to as our catchment area). The main post has 3200 acres while the maneuvering areas and ranges of nearby Camp Bullis add another 27,000 acres. CMHS is normally staffed with a chief, two or three more professional officers, 4–6 enlisted mental health counselors, a civilian secretary, and several other medical and mental health students doing internships or clinical experiences. The CMHS comes under the Department of Psychiatry at Brooke Army Medical Center, with the chief working for the department chief. Normally the CMHS chief is a lieutenant colonel psychiatrist. Because the psychiatrist chief had been relieved, I now became its chief.

The building itself was a temporary World War II single-story wooden office building. Built off the ground on pilings, it was entered by a short flight of stairs on both ends of the structure. Inside to the right was a large, comfortable waiting area, with padded armchairs located around the room. To the left was the secretary's desk; behind her stood several file cabinets, with my office door to the side of her desk. Through the rest of the building was a long hallway, with various offices facing the hall. The hall itself terminated into a large conference room, spanning the width of the building at its end. Restrooms also faced into the hall. Our home had been maintained fairly well during its 35 years of life; though rather spartan in décor, it was located in the troop area, and it served its purpose.

Community Mental Health Center Staff

The CMHS was staffed with three officers (mental health professionals), six mental health counselors (enlisted men and women trained in both counseling and administering psychological tests), one secretary, and several graduate students, Army Reserve PhD psychologists, and students in the Army's Physician Assistant program. I inherited the following staff.

Officers

Major Pete Boston was a Psychiatric Nurse Practitioner (PNP). Pete was a large man with very short hair, a pleasant smile, and always calm, patient, and very smart. He held a master's degree in nursing which allowed him to assess patients, diagnose and interpret lab reports, treat patients, and prescribe psychotropic medication (antidepressants, antipsychotics, anti-anxiety meds, mood stabilizers, and stimulants). He was also the deputy chief of CMHS in my absence. Pete was a highly valuable asset to me and the clinic, because of his education, clinical experience, and relaxed demeanor. He had a relaxed supervisory relationship with a psychiatrist in the Department of Psychiatry overseeing Pete's authority to prescribe medication.

Captain Walt Wilson, who held a master's degree in social work, was the staff social worker. Walt was, like Pete, extremely qualified in his field. Slim, of average height, with short light brown hair, he never appeared assertive or antagonistic and was quiet and thoughtful. His role was to help individuals, families, groups, and the military community to enhance both individual and collective well-being, and to assist in the improvement of the outcomes in their lives. He conducted individual and group counseling, and created and initiated different programs to identify and thwart difficulties found within various military organizations (such as a sexual assault prevention program, anti-anxiety reduction seminars for Academy of Health Sciences students, or other intervention agendas for the troops).

Because of HSC's mission of working with Army Reserve medical units for training, it was not difficult to bring reserve psychologists on active duty for their two weeks of training, serving as staff for CMHS. Some spent their time seeing patients, teaching, or supervising our enlisted staff, while a few joined me full time doing research. We also had a local psychologist (whom I recruited and was commissioned in the Army Reserve) who met his reserve obligation by spending half a day each week with us. He supervised enlisted counselors, taught them psychological testing, and reviewed their written reports with them.

Enlisted Mental Health Counselors

Staff Sergeant Ralph Prince, NCOIC, held three jobs in CMHS. First, as the NCOIC of our clinic, he was responsible for all administration and management of CMHS. His duties ran from ensuring all patient records were complete and that we complied with all hospital medical and military requirements, to maintaining toilet paper and paper towels in our restrooms. Second, he was the senior enlisted man in charge of all enlisted and civilian counselors—their training, duty schedules, leave time, supervision—and also prepared their efficiency reports. I wrote the academic reports for our civilian interns (with input from Prince). Of average size, athletic with a proud military bearing, he was a perfect example for the other counselors to follow. A graduate of Reed College (a private liberal arts school in Portland, Oregon), he was intelligent, educated, and a master of Army regulations.

Under Sergeant Prince were five enlisted counselors. Sergeant Oliver Grey, a quiet man in his late 20s, married with children, was an exceptional worker and a student of improving his skills as a therapist. Sergeant Chuck Murray, a very large (and slightly overweight) man with thinning hair, married, was dedicated to his job and willing to learn more. Sergeant Roberto Perez, the only bachelor, drove a muscle car, and worked hard at his job. There were two female counselors, both Specialist Four, single and early twenties. Ann Ferguson was quiet, shy, reserved, and consumed with her counseling responsibilities. Joan Owens was outgoing and extroverted, the opposite of Ann. But she was a conscientious counselor, always seeking ways to improve herself.

Last was the clinic secretary, records keeper, and regulation monitor, Rose Ramirez. In her mid-thirties, she was quietly efficient, exceptionally knowledgeable in medical record keeping, friendly and a very hard worker.

Students

We had a wide variety of graduate students serving in internships, doing clinical on-the-job training, and fulfilling licensing or certification requirements, as well as PhD candidates, and students completing the clinical phase of the Army's two-year Physician Assistant program.

What Happened Before My Arrival

The mental health center, under the lieutenant colonel psychiatrist, was organized primarily as an outpatient clinic. In addition to normal clinical duties, it was responsible for creating and managing mental health outreach programs in its catchment area.

Very little community consultation, though, was accomplished, except for liaison work or visits to follow up in the community on patients being seen in the clinic. There was almost no psychological testing done and no in-service training. The entire staff was treated more as servants or drones rather than team members assisting in the planning of training, duties, and other aspects of managing a mental health clinic. No one felt like a part of the clinic; they felt they were just being used. The morale of the workforce was so low that everyone had requested to be transferred elsewhere.

What the CMHS Should Be Doing

The Community Mental Health Service is a semiautonomous outpatient clinic in that its chief is dependent on the Department of Psychiatry for both administrative support and medical supervision. The chief is additionally responsible to the BAMC chief of Professional Services for the overall management of the mental health center. The mission of the Community Mental Health Service is to provide psychiatric, psychological, social work, and consultation services as appropriate to maintain the mental health of those eligible military personnel assigned to Fort Sam or Camp Bullis. The functions of the clinic include (1) operating an outpatient mental health facility to provide the diagnosis, treatment, and proper medical disposition of patients; (2) providing mental health consultation services to the community; (3) conducting in-service training programs as necessary; (4) evaluating medical care as prescribed by the medical center chief of Professional Services or the chief of the Department of Psychiatry; (5) conducting research relevant to the field of mental health; (6) initiating, maintaining, completing, and storing patient medical (mental health portion only) records; (7) maintaining an appropriate liaison with other military and local civilian mental health facilities; and (8) establishing and conducting community mental health education programs and preventive mental health programs as necessary.

Taking Over, Instituting Change[1]

My first task was to hold a meeting with all nine staff members attending. This was held at the end of my first day at CMHS (I had spent the day being shown around and moving into my office). It was short and to the point. I explained that I was aware that the staff was not happy with the way the clinic had been run and that was about to change. I made it clear I could not do that alone, and I needed everyone's help. To do this, in the coming days, I would talk to everyone individually about how the clinic was managed and what should be done. I requested that everyone make a brief list of what they believed was wrong or not working in our clinic and what could be done to make it better. I asked two major questions: "If you were in charge of CMHS, what changes would you make to improve the clinic?" and, "What would you like to do or have happen to you in the next year at CMHS?" Their comments should be written, and we would discuss their observations when I met with them individually. In less than fifteen minutes the meeting was concluded, and all departed.

One day after my short clinic meeting, and after everyone else had gone home, I asked Pete to stay while we discussed what to do. Pete said that there was a lot of work for both of us. He felt Rose knew a great deal more than the previous chief gave her credit for. When it came to hospital rules and regulations, she was an expert. She was also a very friendly person, eager to help wherever she could and willing to assume a more responsible role than previously allowed. The counselors were not happy with their jobs. They were bright and motivated but had received almost no training since they arrived. They had not been allowed to do much more than see patients initially when they first entered the clinic, collecting background information and finding out why they were seeking help. Pete acknowledged that the future didn't look too bright either. He was leaving and the hospital said it would be unable to get a replacement until next spring. This would leave Walt as the number two professional in the clinic, and he had limited clinical experience. I would then become the only officer with clinical experience. Propping my feet on my desk, leaning back in my swivel chair, and glancing at my nurse practitioner, I asked, "Well, Pete, what do we do now?"

Later, I hunched over my desk, scrutinizing my notes, thinking of what must be done. I recalled what one of my graduate school professors had preached over and over: "A good community mental health program has two primary objectives: The first is to recognize the needs of the people and the second is to design a system to go into the community and meet these needs."

During the first week on the job, I set an individual appointment with every member of CMHS. I began with Rose Ramirez, then Pete Boston, followed by Walt Wilson and next Sergeant Prince, and finally the counselors. During each session I asked for their list, read it, and began talking with them about how to make the clinic better and a place each enjoyed working in.

Rose spoke of her inability to do her job. She was a qualified medical secretary but relegated to receptionist duties. She took me to a back room that had a year of old, unfiled patient records which had been dumped there. She hoped to be able to regain the ability to do what she had been trained for (record keeping and office management) and not just someone who greeted patients.

Pete reminded me he had no future at CMHS since he believed his request for transfer would be approved. He did offer his observations. When new counselors came to CMHS, they were eager to work and highly motivated. There had been no formal training for them, and they were limited to only conducting intake interviews; they had not been able to do any counseling with patients by themselves (even though some had counseling experience from their previous assignment). Pete felt they were mature, intelligent people who could do an excellent counseling job if only given the chance and the proper training.

Walt related that his major talents lay in family and community work, but he had done very little of that since he was assigned to CMHS. When asked why, he remarked that no one knew what we had to offer. People in the community who have family problems knew what we had see us as a provider of those kinds of services; they would go to their church or a private counselor; they saw us as only helping "crazy people." Part of the problem was our image; the center was seen as a clinic where mentally ill people came to us. We did not go out in the community; we waited for sick people to come to us.

Sergeant Prince expressed disappointment with his job. He had come to CMHS to help normal people who were experiencing some problems coping with life. Instead, all he was doing was interviewing people who had problems even he had difficulty understanding. During his service as the clinic NCOIC, many of his responsibilities to the other enlisted counselors had been negated by the previous chief.

Oliver Grey said he felt inadequate. He had learned just enough in school to know what should be done, but he lacked the advanced clinical skills to know how to help more severe mental problems.

Roberto expressed confusion. He was not sure where he fit in. Major Boston had been very helpful in teaching the counselors, but his time was limited because of his own patient load. Roberto also mentioned in passing something he had heard. He was dating a young woman who was a technician in the emergency room. One night she was feeling down when they had a date. When Roberto asked why, she explained what had happened to her on the shift she'd just finished. An 18-year-old female soldier was brought to the emergency room, the victim of a sexual assault. The ER was trained and equipped to provide excellent treatment, but the staff members felt stymied because the hospital had no official follow-up procedures. All they could do was recommend that the woman seek counseling and give her the phone number of CMHS. Roberto knew that no sexual victims had contacted CMHS since he had been there. His date said the ER had seen three military women in the past few months.

Chuck Murray was an older hand, counseling soldiers. His complaints echoed those of the other counselors: not enough responsibility, no outreach programs, and little training or supervision. He explained he'd indicated on his transfer request that he would go anywhere to get out of this CMHS.

The female counselors, Ann and Joan, said the same things. They were new as mental health workers and felt they needed more supervision and should also be allowed to do counseling, as their work had been severely restricted with no supervision.

Taking all the lists and my notes from meeting with each person, I began to formulate changes necessary for our clinic.

Creating Change, Together

A week after my short staff meeting, having met with each staff member, I asked all to collectively set aside half a day for another group meeting. I asked Rose to schedule this with the counselors and the two officers and also requested her attendance. This was arranged.

Our conference room was furnished with an easel and a large pad of paper, with magic markers for writing. I explained that while I would moderate this meeting, no single person's comments or beliefs should be considered of less value due to rank or assigned position. I pointed out that while I was now the chief of CMHS, I was the least informed about managing this clinic. The staff were the experts, not me. Therefore, we would have to work together, compromise if necessary, but collectively decide on what needed to be changed, and how to do it. We would also assign staff members to become responsible for ensuring our changes become implemented and effective.

For change to be productive, everyone had to own part of the change. After all, someone who championed for a specific change, and then became responsible for making it work, would do their best to see it through to success. Part of my own personal goal was to form the staff into a cohesive unit, all wanting the same thing, and all willing to give 100 percent to make it work. Each staff member should realize the recommended changes were their ideas and it was their duty to create the change. Changes in the clinic were not to be forced upon them by me; the changes were what they wanted themselves, and they should become proud to initiate and manage their recommendations themselves.

Before the meeting I had studied each member's list, and taking the most shared eight or ten ideas, considered how they could most easily be employed in our clinic. Additionally, I contemplated who might be best in overseeing each change. On the pad of paper on the easel, before the meeting, I had written several changes requested by several staff (and which I believed would not be difficult to implement and would become successful). I did not want us to pursue changes that would be hard to implement or lacked the ability to be productive. We needed adjustments on how the clinic was to be managed but would also be easy to execute and destined to prove effective.

As the moderator, I took charge of the meeting. I described how I read every list and discussed it with its author. I then took all the lists and combined the most frequently voiced complaints. These were written on the large pad. I said we would discuss each item on the pad and try to reach a conclusion on what to do, how to do it, and who would be responsible. When one item was completed, we would move on to the next. And this is how we spent one Wednesday afternoon, in our clinic. Here are the results of that meeting.

We discussed changing the intake interview process and assignment of patients. Under the old chief, all counselors did intake interviews, but the chief decided which counselor would see what patient. Typically, the younger counselors did not see any patients on their own. Essentially the counselors had no input on who they would see initially or if they would even counsel anyone. This was not an effective way to treat patients and definitely not a way to enhance job satisfaction.

This is how we decided to change that problem. Each counselor would create a list of the kind of patients they would be most comfortable seeing. Pete and I, being the most educated and experienced counselors, would take the more complex cases or those patients the counselors did not believe they could help. Rose and Sergeant Prince would be responsible for assigning patients (and making this work). Our innovative approach was readily accepted by the staff and successfully implemented.

Another issue raised was that patient counseling supervision was never done properly. Although both Pete and Walt would work with some counselors and their patients, the former chief would not allow the younger counselors to treat any patients; they could only do intakes.

First, Pete, Walt, and Ralph Prince each would be assigned as mentors to two other counselors. The counselors would conduct the intake interviews (sometimes with their mentor present) and develop a treatment plan with the mentor's concurrence (and sometimes their mentor would also assist the counselor during patient visits). This would increase the use of staff (enable them to help more patients) and improve training for the less experienced counselors. My role would be to oversee this plan and to assist in any way needed. Greater job satisfaction and increased training of staff was attained, both for the mentors and the younger staff.

One item everyone agreed was a major fault was the lack of training. We decided to attack this deficit three ways. Pete, Walt, and I would provide specific training in our areas of expertise. I would present seminars on psychological testing, why it is done and how the results are used. Pete would cover psychotropic medications: their uses, expected results, and potential negative side-effects. Walt would discuss the resources available within our military community, what they do, and how to access them. Resources available on-post include drug and alcohol advisors available at the clinics; family services, which provided a variety of clothes, food, or furniture ready to take or borrow; religious leaders; school counselors; JAG attorneys; and the list continues.

Our counselors were intelligent, educated (all had at least some college), and well trained. They totally appreciated this furtherance of their professional education, now expecting to benefit by being in CMHS rather than be totally used as before. In addition to what we would provide within our clinic, we three officers would call on other experts in our fields of expertise to also present seminars to our staff. This was one more educational perk greatly appreciated by our staff.

Another suggestion by the staff was in-service time where counselors could present a case study of one of their patients they were struggling with, asking for suggestions from all the staff or to just brainstorm optional treatment plans. Sometimes if one of us had a very unusual patient we treated successfully, we would present what we did, why, and the outcome.

Proper record keeping and compliance with all Army, medical, and hospital regulations would be taught by Rose and Prince.

To accomplish this, we needed to block out a specific time every week. Friday morning was selected, with two hours for in-service training and the next two hours for didactic sessions. This morning exercise kept everyone on their toes and sharp. One summer, with several counselors on leave and some being transferred, we had to cancel our Friday morning training and use the time to see patients due to reduced staff. After a few weeks of missed in-service training, we found numerous errors in the maintenance of our records and some counselors became stressed due to our lack of supervision and education. I quickly reinstated our Friday morning in-service sessions, and our record errors and stress pretty much went away. I never canceled any more valuable staff training as long as I was chief.

Other duties were accepted eagerly by staff members. Prince and Rose became responsible for managing the administrative aspect of our clinic. Walt assumed responsibility for reaching out to our military community and commanders (as well as hospital departments), informing them that CMHS was now back in the business of coming directly to units to help solve behavioral problems. This involved him creating a positive public relations image for our clinic within the military community we served. Additionally, he was to consider various programs we could develop for commanders, such as a sexual assault prevention program or a behavioral weight control program.

All counselors were now assigned a mentor (I worked with Walt and Pete worked with Ralph Prince). My supervision came from Colonel Schreiber, who received written reports from the ever-present variety of inspections by different post or hospital teams, examining how well we were doing our business, as well as commanders' assessments on our ability to address their behavioral issues. Also, we utilized a management by objectives (MBO) program in which Colonel Schreiber and I would create objectives (goals) for the clinic to achieve, along with a method to measure results. For example, one goal was to improve the efficiency of the clinic by increasing our patient load (seeing patients, intakes, and treatment) by 25 percent without a concomitant expansion of staff. This we achieved in a few months. Colonel Schreiber and I met every four to six weeks to examine our MBO goals and how well they were met.

The afternoon meeting to begin the process of change was seen by all as very productive. The team left with smiles and renewed energy, involving a clinic they now began to see as theirs.

Change Results

Within a few weeks the staff began to appear eager to come to work. Every person was friendlier and all requests to be transferred were withdrawn, even Sergeant Murray's. Rose blossomed in her management of our clinic and total responsibility for maintaining our records. Military discipline and courtesy, uniform conformation, and overall military bearing were never issues. This was without a doubt the best assignment I ever had in the military. I reported to a great boss, had a tremendous staff, and never encountered any conflicts or personnel problems. In fact, Pete even requested he be allowed to remain, which was granted.

Career Supervision and Promotion Issues

One of my duties as chief was the career supervision of my two officers. Pete as a senior major and a nurse needed no career assistance as he knew what was essential (and one of his supervisors was the senior nurse at BAMC, who provided career advice as desired). Walt, though, had a problem. Shortly after I took over CMHS, Walt learned he had been passed over for promotion to major. After I gained access to his personnel files, it quickly became apparent why he was passed over. During my military career, I had served as a member of an Army field grade selection board. I was aware of why some officers went to the top of a promotion selection board without question and why other officers were not seen as competitive. Walt fell into the latter category.

As a social worker, he was professionally competent and skilled. As an Army officer, he was unnoticeable, invisible. He had nothing in his records to indicate he was outstanding, superior, or the best social worker ever. His records suggested he was someone just skating by, someone just filling a slot, and almost accused of just taking up space. While his personnel records did not contain any negative or derogatory comments, it did lack high praise for any exemplary work accomplished and notes indicating superior work as a social worker. As a person, Walt was reticent, almost shy, never one to assert himself or engage in any type of self-promotion. Throughout his career, he remained in the background, allowing others, even those less competent than him, to shine while he appeared to sit back and observe. If he was to be promoted, something had to change. Accordingly, I became his change agent.

Walt had to move out from under his basket and parade to the front of the room. In short, Walt had to show the next promotion board he was an officer the Army could not afford to lose. Here is how Army promotion boards work.

If an officer has less than 19 years of active-duty service and is passed over (not selected for promotion) twice, he or she is released from active duty (no longer serving in the Army). The promotion boards meet almost annually (a single board for each rank; some officers are competing for selection only among their branch), taking a few months to select those found eligible for promotion and then another year to promote those officers selected.

How many officers are promoted depends on the needs of the Army. During times of war when the military expands, many officers are needed at every rank, so promotions come quickly (and a greater percentage of considered officers are selected). In peacetime, though, the size of the Army shrinks; therefore, fewer officers are necessary, so promotions take longer (and the percentage of passed-over officers increases). Therefore, we had a year, maybe 14 months at most, to make Walt selectable for promotion. During that time, we had to do everything possible to prepare our social worker to be capable of serving as a major.

I could write two officer efficiency reports (the normal annual one and a special one for the selection board). He had to enroll in some military correspondence courses, and have completed several notable accomplishments, above and beyond his normal work routine. One crucial area examined by selection boards is the officer's ability to assume positions of increased responsibility and authority. Therefore, we had to provide Walt with the ability to create and manage programs beyond that assumed appropriate for captains. Our work was cut out for us.

The military has a plethora of correspondence courses available in almost every discipline possible, as do many civilian educational institutions. For example, I completed two military-sponsored correspondence courses from the University of Maryland while in the Marine Corps. Walt enrolled in a correspondence one-year course in advanced administration management for Army Medical Department officers. If he pushed it, he could finish before a year was up. He also created and ran several community mental health programs designed to meet the needs of unit commanders at Fort Sam. Additionally, he was placed in charge of a program for two local universities where graduate social work students served a one-semester internship at CMHS. The dean of each school wrote letters testifying to the success of the program, due primarily to Walt's efforts. All of this was completed in a year.

I wrote two perfect officer efficiency reports citing Walt's brilliant work and dedication to his profession as well as lauding all his extra efforts, benefiting the Army. On the second go-round, he was selected for major.

Our Work Activities

During my first year as the chief of the CMHS we won recognition for our patient care, records management, and several graduate student internship programs (to include our psychiatric training for the Army Physician Assistant program). The annual Health Services Command IG inspection gave us a "noteworthy" commendation for our effective and efficient clinical service. Our clinic increased the number of patients we helped; created and implemented four new community mental health outreach programs; and completed five research projects. My time at CMHS was rewarding, fascinating, educational, and the best job I ever had in the Army.

17

What Community Mental Health Services Are Provided

What I Do at CMHS

As chief of the mental health clinic I had the most capable staff ever. Implementing the changes suggested by the staff quickly turned CMHS around to where it became a very enjoyable place to work. My work duties were nothing compared to my year as a company commander (which I hated), where my battalion commander (a lieutenant colonel) demanded I work 10- to 14-hour days, six and a half days a week, and he always demanded more, never satisfied with honors won or outstanding accomplishments. My belief was that he wanted a perfect score commanding a battalion in the States so he would not have to command one in combat (this was in 1968, during the height of the Vietnam War). Because of him and his relentless nagging, I left the Army, only to return as a clinical psychologist. Within the Army medical field, I found that one's value and credibility is more related to his or her professional practice, not rank. In the infantry a colonel always knew more than a major. In Army medicine, many majors were experts in their field, so colonels listened to them. This assignment was the best and I was happy.

The CMHS staff was eclectic. We had seven males and three females. Plus, our graduate students, interns, Physician Assistant students, and Army Reserve professionals added more very capable and motivated men and women. Of the assigned full-time staff, we had five Caucasians, three African Americans, and two Hispanics. Age-wise we ranged from the early twenties (our two female counselors) to early forties (me). Together we worked as a well-oiled team, always professional and always respecting each other. As I said, this was a great place to work.

I was still the HSC Psychology Consultant so occasionally took military trips for HSC. As a researcher, I had several military research studies accepted for presentation, so BAMC allowed me time off to present my findings (and paid for the trip). Essentially, I traveled quite a bit, almost always flying my own plane (on the Army's dime). Life could not get better.

My CMHS activities were divided among the following undertakings: seeing patients, psychological testing (administering instruments, analyzing test results, or teaching the counselors testing procedures), participating in legal actions as a forensic psychologist, community consulting with unit commanders, conducting research, supervising the PAs and graduate student programs we supported, and creating and managing various other mental health programs for the community we served.

Our primary patients were mostly young, enlisted students from the Academy of Health Sciences, then enlisted soldiers from various units assigned to Fort Sam. But we could (and did) see members of other branches of the military, mostly Air Force as San Antonio was surrounded by several AF bases. Any active-duty military member could request our services but as mentioned, most were young Army soldiers.

Some of My Patients

Not Everyone Can Be Helped

One day a young Air Force psychologist called me. We had met professionally previously so he knew who I was. He had a patient, an Air Force staff sergeant, command referred, and was at a loss to help. Because we could help any military person, providing our services to Air Force personnel was not uncommon. The psychologist explained the NCO was narcissistic, overbearing, egotistical, self-centered, and verbally abusive, all at the same time. While the sergeant willingly came to the counseling sessions, it was all a game to him. Instead of trying to change his adverse behavior, he was constantly conning his therapist. The psychologist was unable to accomplish anything and asked if I could see his patient. I agreed to see him.

The sergeant arrived at the time scheduled for his first appointment. In his early thirties, he was married with no children. Average sized, with light-colored hair, he was neat in his uniform. It was immediately apparent his behavior was exactly as described by his previous therapist. I had an advantage over the Air Force psychologist. I was older (in my early 40s), had over 20 years in the military, and had been an NCO myself (a corporal in the Marines). Unlike his Air Force counselor, I was not the same age as the NCO nor brand new to the military.

I told the sergeant our working together depended on his commitment to changing his behavior. If he would not actively participate in our sessions, I would discharge him. While he tried to dominate our first meeting, I would not allow that. Knowing his past, I took control by managing our interaction, cutting off his attempts to take charge. When I inquired why he had been referred to counseling by his commander, he countered that he was not at fault; his commander just wanted to hurt him. He explained he was better at being an NCO than his commander was at being an officer. Thus began his litany of his life; everything that happened to him was never his fault. He was perfect and others were always the cause of his problems.

He saw himself as smarter and better than everyone he encountered, including me. Nothing was ever his fault; he just had to deal with people who were always beneath him. As hard as I tried, I could not connect with him. He was a con artist, always trying to control our sessions, always believing others had personality problems, never him. Despite all my effort pointing out how his behavior was detrimental to how he interacted with others, he refused to recognize that. He maintained his superiority was not readily accepted by lesser people who then created the problems.

Two things were quickly becoming apparent. First, the sergeant's feelings of superiority were clearly interfering with productive interacting and socializing with others; and second, he was not inclined to change anything. In short, I was unable to help.

I contacted the Air Force psychologist, describing my inability to do anything with the sergeant. I said I was going to quit wasting my time with him. I suggested he refer the sergeant to an Air Force psychiatrist I knew, a full colonel. I said I would send the sergeant back to him so he could arrange for the colonel to see what he could do.

On our fourth session (a month into our visits) I told the sergeant I was terminating our sessions. Looking shocked, he stammered, "Why?" I described my impressions of him, his behaviors, his feelings of superiority, and his game-playing as well as his inability to understand how his aberrant behaviors were the cause of his poor interactions with others. I continued by explaining that he had no desire to change and no inclination to participate meaningfully in our counseling sessions. Consequently, I could not be of any help to him. For an instant I glimpsed a look of astonishment, like he had been caught with his hand in the cookie jar. But, quickly recovering, he began his defense of his behaviors and how I was just another officer, who was intellectually and otherwise inferior to him, blaming him for my professional incompetence. Cutting short our session, I told him to return to the Air Force psychologist who would arrange for another therapist to see him.

A few weeks later, early in the morning, I received a call from the Air Force psychologist. He took some time to tell me what had happened to our sergeant. The psychiatrist saw him a couple of times and promptly ended his counseling, as the sergeant had no interest in changing his behavior. During the sessions the sergeant constantly tried to take control of the counseling, so the psychiatrist just terminated the therapy.

Then the sergeant and his wife hosted a dinner for another NCO and his wife. Throughout the evening, the sergeant controlled everything that occurred. He dominated the conversation; he manipulated his guests, limiting their active participation during dinner. Inviting them (demanding, really) to sit in the living room for after-dinner drinks, he arranged where everyone should be seated (almost like setting a stage). After everyone was in place, he said he wanted to show them something. All eyes were on him as he reached between the cushions he and his wife were sitting on, retrieving a small semi-automatic pistol. Mesmerized, his wife and guests were speechless, frozen in awe or fear as he grasped the trigger, placing the muzzle against his temple … and squeezed. This was his last act of dominating and controlling the situation and everyone in it.

The sergeant always had to be in control. But honestly, I never suspected him to be suicidal. I had no inkling he would be prone to killing himself. Twice I had failed. First, I was not able to help him perceive his behavior and how it was impacting his life in such negative ways. And second, I never realized his potential for suicide. Obviously, not everyone can be helped.

Another Positive Aspect of Psychological Testing

Because of my participation as a forensic psychologist aiding trial attorneys, my use of in-depth psychological evaluations was well-received among local defense lawyers. I received a call once from a civilian attorney defending an Air Force sergeant being tried on family abuse charges. The attorney believed his client to be innocent and sought help convincing a judge of that. Now, I like to think that my expertise as a forensic psychologist was so well-known that every trial attorney needed me, when the actual truth was considerably different. My work was free.

My psychological evaluations could require as much testing and personal interviews as necessary to prepare the report. Typically, this could take several hours and, if done by a civilian psychologist, cost several thousand dollars. Few defendants could afford this, but if the defendant was in the military, this could be accomplished at no cost to the defense team. Like I said, I worked for free.

In this case, it involved an Air Force NCO and his divorced wife over the custody of their children. The sergeant wanted equally shared custody and the wife, wanting the sergeant out of the picture, accused him of family abuse and unfitness as a father. The settlement of custody was solely at the discretion of a judge. The sergeant's attorney found no evidence of any abuse in the sergeant's past, neither within his family or on his job. My task was to provide corroboration that abuse was never in the sergeant's repertoire of behavior.

Initially, an interview was scheduled with the NCO. I explained my duty was to establish, via psychological evaluations, that the sergeant was not abusive nor had any abusive tendencies. I talked to the sergeant about his upbringing, his family, his job, his leisure-time activities, his friends, and how he envisioned his future. I was also convinced he was not an abuser. Copies of his military efficiency reports showed him to be a caring, personable supervisor. His superiors praised him as did friends and acquaintances. There were zero indications of any abuse, anywhere.

The psychological protocols included personality inventories such as the Minnesota Multiphasic Personality Inventory and others, intelligence testing and various aptitude and interest assessment instruments, all designed to provide an overall appraisal of the sergeant's total behavioral patterns, past, present, and propensity for the future.

All told, our evaluation of the sergeant required around 20-odd hours (and all of it free). The data on his work-related behaviors as well as his off-duty behaviors yielded no patterns of any abuse (or tendencies for abuse). The psychological inventories were all in agreement that this person harbored no predispositions for manipulation, cruelty, or violence. The testing revealed a person who cared for others and enjoyed helping, not abusing. My final report was several pages long.

The sergeant's attorney said he did not need me in court as the report sufficed. In court the lawyer, using the NCO's official efficiency and other reports as well as the psychological evaluations, provided overwhelming evidence the NCO was not, nor had ever been an abusive person. The ex-wife's attorney had no evidence the sergeant had ever been abusive toward anyone. He only had the ex-wife's testimony, which, in the end, was not accepted by the judge.

There was another instance where past behavior predicts future behavior, where psychological testing can be used to foresee behaviors to calculate what a person may have the potential for undertaking down the road.

Community and Command Consultation

Considerable time was spent consulting with unit commanders, the medical center, and the Academy of Health Sciences. Additionally, as the

Health Services Command Psychology Consultant, I still traveled around the U.S. providing seminars and consulting with hospital and medical center staff regarding mental health issues and conducting command consultation.

One unusual assignment as the HSC Psych Consultant was my involvement working with the U.S. Embassy in Mexico City on a classified project. It was not exactly related to my typical HSC or CMHS duties, but interesting. I did receive accolades for the work achieved.

The VA Seeks Help

Another consultation request, in early 1980, was from a psychologist in the Veterans Administration regarding a major research project being considered by the VA.

During the Vietnam War (the dates are ambiguous as different agencies cite different dates) from 5 August 1964 to 7 May 1975, 2,709,918 Americans served in the war. Some 1 to 1.6 million of these military personnel saw combat, provided close combat support, or regularly were exposed to attack by the enemy. Most of the 7484 women who served in Vietnam were nurses (83.5 percent of the women, with one being killed in action). Of the total number who served in Vietnam, 58,202 died, with 47,378 being killed in combat. There were 303,704 wounded (and I am on that list), 2338 missing in action, and 766 POWs. And the numbers of tragedy and sorrow continue.

The big question that remained unsolved, with no consensus on a definitive answer, is: how many service men and women encounter post-service adjustment difficulties after returning home? Those researchers defined as hawks (behavioral scientists who support the U.S. assistance to the government of South Vietnam) believe that the number of Vietnam vets who experience adjustment problems is between 10 to 20 percent of all who served in-country. The researchers seen as doves (those who opposed the war, and especially America's involvement) quote much higher figures, stating that most vets who served in Vietnam faced problems due to the war. Some postulated that every person who served in Vietnam was mentally hurt by the war.

I would be classified as a hawk; my research showed 15 percent of Vietnam veterans encountered serious difficulty returning to a civilian society. I personally never had any problems; my transition from combat to a return home as husband and father was smooth, without any trauma. Was this typical or atypical? The VA wanted to learn the truth regarding the severity of PTSD (post-traumatic stress disorder) among Vietnam vets.

As a Vietnam Vet, I Had to Have PTSD

Ironically, 45 years after I departed Vietnam, after my second tour, I had requested a physical evaluation by the Veterans Administration of disabilities caused by injuries sustained during combat. My request went unanswered, but a neighbor knew a VA mental health counselor at our local VA Vet Center, and an appointment for me was made.

I was told to bring my DD214 form with me. This document is a snapshot of a person's military career (be it six months or 20 years), which shows the person's rank, time served on active duty, military education, job title, overseas service and war time, and decorations earned. This document is received by everyone who is released from active duty or retired. I have three: one from the Marines, one from when I left active duty as a major in 1969, and the third from when I retired in 1981.

My three DD214s confirm three combat tours, seven medals for valor, the Purple Heart, and other combat decorations. Entering the counselor's office, I met two counselors sitting behind a desk. After reading my DD214, they questioned me about loud noises bothering me, sleep disturbances, anxiety, depression, and other queries related to PTSD, because my extensive time in combat should have had a negative impact on me. As I answered no to all their questions, I noticed a familiar, red-covered book[1] on the shelf behind them. Pointing to the book, I asked if they had read it.

Reaching behind him, one counselor retrieved the book, telling me it was their bible in treating Vietnam vets with behavioral issues. I explained I knew about PTSD, I did not suffer from it, and my time in combat did not create any ill effects for me. I opened the book, turned to Chapter 8 (on page 173), and showed them I was one of the authors of the book, confirming I understood PTSD.

Even 45 years after the war ended, some people expect all veterans to have some adjustment issues, which I did not have. The questions terminated, a call was made to the state VA office, and a few days later, I received a date for my physical exam.

Back to the VA in the Early 1980s

But in the early 1980s, there was no conclusive evidence to clearly document how many Vietnam vets experienced adjustment problems after service. The VA was working on a proposal to implement a national study on Vietnam veterans.

Because different researchers (doves versus hawks) found differing rates of psychological disorder among Vietnam vets, the research was suspect regarding their outcomes. Additionally, the sample of Vietnam vets examined by the different researchers was minuscule compared to the 2.7 million Americans who served in Vietnam. The total number of soldiers I examined did not exceed several hundred men.

My research found about 15 percent of Vietnam vets suffered post-service adjustment problems, and many of these had pre-service maladaptive issues in their lives. My conclusions: serving in Vietnam, for most veterans, did not result in PTSD. My research also discovered that for many veterans, regardless of where they served, pre-service maladaptive behaviors (due to dysfunctional families, dropping out of high school, drug and alcohol addiction, job instability, marital difficulties, etc.) continued during the military, and did not abate after service. Other behavioral scientists found comparable results. The U.S. government felt obligated to provide mental health services for its vets but had no idea how extensive the problem was. Mass media, books, newspaper articles, and anecdotal reports by mental health therapists presented a grim view of a veteran's life post–Vietnam service. Thus, more information was needed.

Congress Becomes Involved

Realizing this was a problem needing answers, the Senate Committee on Veterans' Affairs, in 1974, published a 935-page volume consisting of articles, reports, and other materials on Vietnam veterans to disseminate information on what little was known about the plight of these vets. It recognized the controversy over the number of vets unable to return home and successfully continue with their lives and thus compiled this tome. Even so, as Chairman Vance Hartke stated in his preface: "This volume is intended to present a representative spectrum of views ... no reader will or could be expected to agree with all the views in these articles." Throughout the 1970s different researchers and scholars offered different theories and opinions regarding the mental health of our Vietnam vets.

The VA, though, decided to pursue ways to better define the problem by creating a national survey. I was one of many researchers contacted by the VA Readjustment Counseling Planning Task Force to lend assistance. Questions were posed regarding how I located my samples, how I contacted them, psychological instruments used, survey questions asked, what I was looking for, and what follow-up research projects were conducted. My relationship with the VA psychologist continued, off and on, for almost two years and terminated after I retired in late 1981.

In 1981, Congress mandated the VA evaluate its readjustment programs and the effectiveness of its Vet Centers. On 12 September 1984 the VA awarded to the Research Triangle Institute a contract, titled The National Vietnam Veterans Readjustment Study (NVVRS), to determine the extent of PTSD among Vietnam veterans. This study took four years to and evaluated a sample size of 2348 veterans (1632 served in Vietnam and 716 veterans served elsewhere). The study cost $9,350,000.

When I received the results of the study in November 1988, I was ecstatic. While the study findings were released in 1988, the book[2] on the project was not published until 1990. This study found that only 15.2 percent of Vietnam vets experienced post-traumatic stress disorder (PTSD). Follow-up studies indicated that pre-service personal difficulty and trauma increased the risk of experiencing post-service adaptation problems. This news was important to me because it vindicated the results of my research. I also learned that my research on the adjustment of Vietnam-era veterans was cited as a reference for the NVVRS project. I was pleased that the results of my early research examining the adjustment of Vietnam vets were validated by a much more extensive and complex national study.

Running with the Sergeants

I kept fit at the University of Utah by running, as well as training and competing in karate and judo. At William Beaumont during my post-doc fellowship, though, I was too busy to spend time working out. That continued at Fort Polk. By the time I arrived at Fort Sam Houston in 1975, I had packed on over 20 pounds (none of it muscle) and my clothes did not fit. I decided I had to do something and do it now. I bought a set of weights and dug out my running duds.

I began long distance running in the winter of 1955–56 as a member of the Dartmouth freshman rowing team. This continued in the Marines and the Army infantry. I resumed running and by early 1976 I had lost the flab and was running five miles early each morning during the week and 10 to 15 miles on the weekends. I enjoyed running so much I began to enter competitive races.

San Antonio held long distance races about once every month. Most were to raise money for local charities. I competed in the 5 K (5 kilometers or 3.1 miles), 10 K (6.2 miles), and the mini marathon (13.1 miles or half a marathon). Long distance racing is not about speed but rather pacing and endurance. I was not a fast runner, but I did have endurance. Racers would be placed in age and gender classes, so most often I would place in the top 10 for my age.

In the combat arms, physical training (PT) is a part of a soldier's daily

Bob in the white headband checking in for a long-distance competitive race in San Antonio, 1980.

life. That's not so in the Army Medical Department. Hospitals do not shut down so all the Army personnel can do PT. To offset this issue, Army medical facilities allow its personnel an afternoon off to do PT individually. I would guess that few soldiers use this time for PT.

Often the male head of a military unit is called "the old man" because he is usually older than the rest of the unit and always senior in rank. One day the four sergeants and I were discussing the afternoon off for PT and what we actually did. Soldiers are required to pass an Army PT test annually, but during my decade as an Army medical officer, I never took any PT tests. Keep in mind that I was 15 to 20 years older than my sergeants and I chided them for their physical condition (or lack thereof) and the poor shape of the youth of today. This led to other comments on exercise and fitness, and a challenge for their "old man." The sergeants wanted to race me. They were unaware that I was a competitive long-distance runner. They were sure they could run faster than me (which over a short distance I know most of them could). I agreed to race them on one condition: I would set the pace and all they had to do was keep up with me. After some discussion among themselves, they agreed.

The next day, the challenge began. For a couple of miles, everyone stayed with me (but I had set a slow pace for me). First, Chuck Murray dropped out; he was out of shape and overweight. After five miles I ramped up the pace and soon each sergeant dropped out. After everyone else had stopped, I quit and began running back. I returned to our clinic first; later the others struggled in. In their minds, their opinion of me as a leader increased, because no one could keep up with their "old man."

Sergeant Murray took umbrage with the running outcome and vowed to beat me. He began running on his own and started to lose weight. Before he could beat me, though, he received a one-year hardship assignment (no family) to Alaska. Upon completion of his tour, he returned to Fort Sam and our clinic. He had exercised in Alaska, and the next time my four sergeants and I ran together, he did beat me.

Running Can Be Dangerous (at Least for Me)

One weekend morning in the fall, I had nearly completed my 10-mile run, and was only a couple of blocks from my home. A single-story house was about 75 feet back from the street, with two cars parked in front, next to the curb. Alongside the first car, I heard a loud crash. Now, next to the space between the two cars, a massive black dog flew through the opening, snarling, grabbing my left thigh with its jaws. It hit me with such force I was spun around and violently knocked on my back, skidding across the pavement.

Someone started yelling and I saw a young man lock his fist around the dog's collar, pull the dog back inside the house, and shut the door. I could see a huge hole in the bottom section of the screen door. Apparently, the front door was open, with only a screen door guarding the entrance. The dog, hearing me, went through the mesh like it was wet toilet paper. The man returned, asking if I was okay.

Slowly rising, I hurt. My back and butt suffered from sliding across the rough street, and where the dog bit me, blood flowed. Tying a large handkerchief around the wound on my thigh, I replied I was not sure and said I would go home. The man replied okay, saying he had to make sure the dog stayed inside. Turning around, I limped home.

My wife, inspecting and cleaning the puncture holes left by the dog's teeth, said I had to go to the BAMC emergency room, now. I complied. The ER treated the wound and educated me on dog bites where we lived. Apparently, some agency has responsibility for rabies control from animal bites. For some municipalities, it is animal control; for others, it is the police. In Terrill Hills, it is the police.

I was warned that the animal must be identified and either verified as being vaccinated against rabies, or I must undergo four (very painful) rabies shots, spread over two weeks. Asking what I needed to do, I was told to report the dog bite to the police, and they had to investigate. A vaccination tag would not suffice; the dog owner must have the vaccination certificate, which can then be verified by the veterinarian who issued the certificate. Otherwise, the dog had to be brought to a veterinarian for 10 days of quarantine. If proof of vaccination is not provided within 24 hours after being bitten, my rabies shots must begin.

Returning home, I contacted the police department. Terrill Hills has a small law enforcement force and on weekends, only one police officer is on duty at a time. The officer on duty listened to my description of the incident and how it was his duty to either locate the vaccination certificate and get it verified by the vet or take the dog to a vet for 10 days of quarantine and observation for rabies. The police officer did not appreciate me telling him what to do. He said he was too busy, and someone would tend to that the next day. I countered with the 24-hour requirement and the police officer, clearly not interested, said it would be taken care of, just not now. It was afternoon and over six hours had passed since the bite, with only 18 left. I called our chief of police at his home.

Listening to my sad account of what had transpired, the chief agreed his officer failed to comply with the law and was amiss. The chief said he would contact me in an hour to update me on what was being done.

The chief must have had a nice chat with his police officer because less than an hour later the officer called me. He said the man I saw with the dog was not the owner but the brother of the man who owned the dog. The owner, his wife, and his kids were away for the weekend, but the brother was able to contact them (after being told to do so by the officer) and the inoculation certificate was located. The police officer was on his way to the veterinarian's office, which verified the vaccination against rabies. My wounds healed, but the owners had to go to court (I was the prosecution's witness) and fined for negligence of care (the brother was told to keep the dog locked in the back yard, which he failed to do). This was one encounter with the dangers of running.

The following year, a couple of days after Christmas, I was ending a run, less than a block from home. Suddenly I felt a hot stab in the back of my right thigh, causing me to stumble, but not fall. I had just been shot. I had heard a muffled crack from the back yard of the house I just passed. Pulling my handkerchief out of the pocket of my running shorts, I placed it over the now bloody wound and shuffled home. Anita cleaned and bandaged the hole and, as before, drove me to the ER, where the injury was disinfected, treated, and bandaged. Because it was a gunshot wound, the

Christmas in San Antonio in 1978. Front row, from left: Bob, Anita, Karen; back row, from left: Julie and Susan.

police were notified. During the police interview, I quickly identified where the shot came from.

I later learned I was shot with a .177 caliber air rifle (CO2 charged) by a young boy (maybe 12). He had received the air rifle for Christmas, but his parents forbade him to use the gun until they could take him out to the country to shoot it. Apparently, that didn't sit well with him, so when they had gone shopping, he retrieved his rifle. He then tacked a paper target on a wooden gate in the back yard (facing the street), placing it between the open slats, so the target had no backing to stop the pellet. My leg did that. His parents took the rifle away from him. I recovered from the second gunshot injury to that same leg.

Is My Sergeant a Serial Rapist?

One afternoon Rose came into my office and said that a gentleman, a San Antonio Police Department detective, wanted to see me. I said to show him in. Introducing himself, he said that he was part of an investigation regarding the sexual assaults of a few young, single women who had been attacked in their apartments. While there were no witnesses to the actual assaults, the same vehicle and person had been seen in the immediate vicinity of some of the victims' abodes. The person was described as circumstantial, dark hair. The vehicle was identified as a two-door, dark-colored muscle car with a racing stripe down its middle. A few days ago, a walking patrol officer saw such a car on the streets of San Antonio and wrote down the license plate number. A search of Texas license plate numbers assigned to a dark muscle car yielded a suspect. A medium built male in his twenties with dark hair was my sergeant, Roberto Perez.

The detective also informed me that the same vehicle was seen parked near the scene of one attack at the time of the assault. I exclaimed, emphatically, that Roberto was no rapist. Somehow there was a mistake. The investigator continued to explain that the case was going to be presented to a city grand jury by the district attorney's office in a few days. Sergeant Perez would not be informed of this, but I could be a witness on his behalf.

The grand jury process is mostly a confidential procedure to avoid embarrassing a person being considered for committing a crime if they are innocent. The grand jury is a group of empaneled citizens (usually serving for several weeks) whose job is to listen to evidence presented by the DA's office to determine if there is sufficient substantiation to conclude that the person did commit a crime. Typically, the only attorneys present during the hearings are those from the DA's office. The prosecutor presents the evidence alleging the crime and the perpetrator, and then witnesses give their versions of what happened. It is the job of the grand jury to determine if sufficient evidence exists to indict the person suspected of committing the crime. In the case of Roberto Perez, all the evidence against him was circumstantial, as no one and nothing could show he was the one who assaulted the women.

The detective said I could be a witness for Perez at the grand jury hearing. I asked for the dates, time, and locations of all the attacks, which were provided to me. After receiving this data, I met with Pete and explained what was going on. Our mission was to determine where Roberto was at the time the assaults took place. We found the following.

At the time of one rape, Roberto was a few hundred miles away, TDY (temporary duty), attending a counseling conference at another Army post. His headquarters company commander provided a copy of his orders and a quick phone call confirmed he was in attendance. During another attack, he was on leave in Pecos, Texas, where his home is. My wife Anita and I once landed at the Pecos Airport for fuel, and we borrowed a car to visit his parents. Another brief phone call established he had been physically in Pecos, 365 miles away. A copy of his leave orders was obtained from his company. Pete looked at the address where Roberto's car was identified and immediately recognized where it was. He knew that Roberto had a favorite restaurant he frequented, and the owner (and staff) knew Roberto. His car was identified in the restaurant parking lot. The owner was unable to positively state that Roberto was in the restaurant during the attack but did say he was there one evening during that week. He did establish that Roberto patronized the eatery regularly so his car often would be in the parking lot.

As a witness at the hearing, I explained who I was and my relationship to Sergeant Perez. I explicitly stated he was no rapist but an honest, law-abiding person. I then presented the evidence I possessed showing that on two dates of the attacks, it was impossible for him to have committed the crimes. I presented why his vehicle was identified near the scene of another assault in the restaurant parking lot. I submitted copies of Roberto's orders and information from the restaurant owner. I confirmed that everything I presented on the sergeant's behalf could be verified.

A few days later the detective called me to say that Roberto would not be indicted. Roberto left the Army about the time I retired. He enrolled in the University of Texas at Austin and enlisted in the Texas Army National Guard. For one summer he attended the National Guard OCS and, even before graduating from UT Austin, was commissioned a second lieutenant. Upon graduation, he became employed full-time as a National Guard officer. I was told that, a couple of decades later, he retired as a full colonel. I never told him that he had been a sexual assault suspect.

Research

THERE IS "PRACTICAL" RESEARCH AND "ACADEMIC" RESEARCH

All my research was practical or applied. I was constantly exploring, examining human behavior in particular situations. My quest for understanding what people did began with my studies on the prevalence of adjustment difficulties among Vietnam veterans. Next came investigations into how recruits who completed the process of becoming soldiers compared to those who could not do it. I studied the psychological effects that being a POW had on captured soldiers. I scrutinized the families of Vietnam vets, wanting to know how the war the husbands and fathers participated in affected the wives and children. By the mid- to late 1970s, my thirst for research expanded into the realm of world-class athletes and coping skills of pilots in the cockpit. All my inquiries were conducted by scientifically exploring how people reacted in specific circumstances, attempting to recognize what those who succeeded did versus what those who failed, did differently. My quest was to determine how and why humans performed as they did in defined conditions. In summary, all my research was applied and practical, providing answers so we as psychologists could share what we learned to improve the success rate of those involved. This was my rationale and guiding principle for conducting research.

The "practical" aspect of some of our research at CMHS was to understand "which" or "why" soldiers behaved the way they did. Our collected data could help identify soldiers who were most likely to experience problems during training. We could show commanders which soldiers could face difficulties and how to identify them before their problems got out of hand. We could then present commanders with ways to manage stressful issues and explain how CMHS could help the floundering soldiers. Our research could identify problem areas so we could generate remedies or suggest preventive strategies.

Unfortunately, this approach was the reason a colleague was terminated from his psychology PhD program at the University of Texas at

Bob, on the right, swearing in James Warren as a second lieutenant in the Army Reserve (U.S. Army photo, 1979).

Austin (UT Austin). I had a young man, a sergeant in the Army Reserve, working with me as part of his reserve obligation. He was a doctoral candidate at UT Austin who collaborated with me as a reservist, but also as part of his psychology practicum. He had been a sergeant and a mental health counselor who left the Army to go to graduate school. While in graduate school he was commissioned in the Army Reserve. His wife was a captain in the Army, a psychiatric nurse assigned to the in-patient psychiatric service in BAMC.

As a sergeant in the Army Reserve, he was assigned to the CMHS to fulfill his reserve duties. Along the way, because of his working toward his PhD, he was eligible to become commissioned as an officer. On 8 August 1978, I commissioned James Warren as a USAR second lieutenant.

Lieutenant Warren was a highly motivated and intelligent person who shared several research projects with me. He was energetic and extremely dedicated to working with me on applied research. Unfortunately, UT Austin Psychology Department professors were not a fan of applied research.

As a brand-new psychology graduate student, in the first semester of my master's curriculum, I applied to the doctoral psychology program at UT Austin. I was summarily rejected as having been in the Army so long I was incapable of thinking. I re-applied after I received my degree and began working as a psychologist; this time I was accepted. I enjoyed the perverse pleasure of turning down the opportunity of attending UT Austin, explaining its program was not good enough for what I wanted. Regardless of where PhD Psych graduates at Austin gain employment, the department maintained that it graduates academic researchers, not clinicians. And this is what got Warren kicked out of its program.

Warren had spent almost two years working with me doing both clinical work and research. He enjoyed the research as much as I did. Furthermore, he saw a practical use for what we looked at and devoted quite a bit of his practicum energy toward that end. All he had left at Austin was his doctoral dissertation. Having been intimately involved in research examining Army problem areas and seeking better means to solve these problems, he became committed to practical research. Regrettably, his professors did not share his enthusiasm for applied research and rejected every proposal he submitted.

Obtaining tenure is a goal for those who seek permanent positions as a professor. The old saying, "publish or perish," refers to the fact that most colleges and universities grant tenure (permanent employment) to those professors who complete research projects and get them published in professional academic journals. In my humble opinion, much research accomplished by university professors seeking tenure is not conducted with the purpose of obtaining practical information to solve real problems, but performed primarily to get published for gaining tenure. This is what my Lieutenant Warren believed and was not interested in doing.

He argued with his committee, strongly voicing his opinion against the theoretical research demanded by his teachers, firmly refusing to waste his time doing worthless research just to get his degree. He was dismissed from the program.

Warren told me what happened. I then had a long talk with him. I told him my feelings about academic research and my misgivings. I continued to explain that unless he did what his professors wanted, he would never graduate; he would not be able to work as Doctor Warren and he would always be working for someone else (who had the PhD). After he received his degree, he could do any research he desired. Without the degree, his research opportunities would be severely limited. He understood what I was saying and agreed to beg to be allowed back in the program. I said I would go to Austin to personally plead for his return.

One afternoon I flew to Austin and met with the psychology department chair. I explained why Warren acted the way he did; he would apologize. I requested that he be reinstated. The chair agreed, but only if Warren came to embrace the type of research his professors wanted. Warren met with them, capitulated to their demands, and was allowed back in the program. With his new research demands, he was unable to return to BAMC but did graduate.

Is Applied Research Worthwhile?

Poignantly, some twenty years later, I was a university journalism professor, teaching a class in media management. As part of my interests (I had obtained a master's degree in Business Administration and Management from Webster College ... now Webster University ... in December 1978), I conducted research examining the management of mass communications businesses (radio and TV studios, newspapers, and magazines). My project studied the regulatory and personnel difficulties managers faced in hiring and maintaining employees toward the end of the twentieth century, a classic example of practical research.

This paper[3] was presented in a regional journalism academic conference and then published as a chapter in a media management book. At the conclusion of the conference, all attendees were assembled for the announcement of the "best" research paper presented. Sitting behind me were two older professors discussing the paper I presented (they were unaware its author was sitting in front of them). Their feelings were that the paper had no place in this conference as it was not academic research, hardly worth being presented. A few minutes later this paper was announced as the "best" research presented at this conference.

How Effective Is the All-Volunteer Army?

In 1975, while at Fort Polk, I conducted several studies which examined differences between Army volunteers who completed Basic Combat Training and those who failed. By 1979, the all-volunteer Army was in its sixth year. A major concern was whether or not it worked. Current research revealed that more recruits in 1979 were discharged during BCT than in 1978. Another study showed that while thousands of young people were enlisting to build their dream, most became dissatisfied and disillusioned. This study concluded that the Army was attracting many applicants from lower economic groups with lessened mental abilities. They were unprepared to succeed in the military and unable to adapt to the rigorous demands of the armed forces. These new volunteers bring to the Army a legacy of negative social values reflecting poverty, economic exploitation, poor education, discrimination, social instability, and corruption. The researcher believed that the values and attitudes of many of those volunteers were incompatible with the requirements of sustaining an effective, disciplined, reactive Army.

Fort Sam was a major training facility for new soldiers being prepared to serve in a variety of entry-level medical fields. If a trainee was deemed unable to adapt to Army requirements, the soldier had to be evaluated by CMHS counselors prior to being discharged. Lieutenant Warren and I were interested in why most soldiers could finish their training, but others could not. Together we established a study[4] to determine why. Our research was conducted during the summer of 1979.

During this time 106 soldier trainees were seen by CMHC counselors. Sixteen were recommended for discharge due to their inability to adapt to the Army environment. Our study collected biographic, demographic, and clinical data on each soldier seen. We then compared our data with those who stayed and those who were discharged. We next compared this 1979 data with that of my 1975 studies at Fort Polk. We also had to recognize that there was a four-year time difference and the trainees themselves were different. At Polk all the soldiers seen were in BCT (initial Army training) while at Fort Sam our soldiers were in advanced training as they had already completed BCT. Additionally, those soldiers at Polk were destined for the combat arms while the Fort Sam soldiers were all in medical training, and this cohort included female soldiers.

Despite these noteworthy differences, many variables were stable across both groups. Our results proved to be both useful and instructive. Both studies revealed that individuals with poor pre-service adjustment patterns exhibited the same behaviors in the Army. But one difference seen between the two groups was that in 1979, the unsuccessful soldiers experienced increased family dysfunction and a higher incidence of personal psychiatric problems.

Our findings reinforced earlier conclusions that more individuals enlisting today were not capable of being successful soldiers due to pre-service conditions and behaviors.

Female Adjustment in the Modern Army

Virtually all the young soldiers I saw as a psychologist at Fort Polk were males. At Fort Sam, though, many were females, both young trainees and career women. My interest in why some soldiers succeeded while others failed now extended to women. Being around females was not unusual for me. I had two sisters and no brothers. In my immediate family, I was the only male (one wife and three daughters), so, for most of my life, females were a big part of it. By the late 1970s, the Army considered recruiting quality females as one way to maintain an effective fighting force.

My study[5] examined adjustment problems encountered by female soldiers (trainees and permanent party), then compared the research findings to male peers to determine if women soldiers differ in their method of coping.

Biographical and demographic data collected showed differences between male and female soldiers. Females were younger and better educated than the males. More females were single or divorced. Possibly the females were better educated because all females had to possess a high school diploma. The females had fewer psychiatric problems prior to enlisting. While the males experienced more psychiatric difficulties both prior to the Army and during training, the women soldiers were seen as having more adjustment complications in the Army. Women would seek help from our CMHS more often than men, while the latter were reluctant to recognize emotional conflicts. Also, while no single psychiatric diagnosis defined males unable to adapt to military service, the females most often experienced adjustment reactions. The percentage of women seeking CMHS support was much higher than that of the men, but so was their perception that the best solution to their problems was being discharged.

In summary, the methods of coping might be different, yet males and females unable to adjust to the military were not seen as that different.

Other Research

When I returned to active duty to become an Army clinical psychologist, the only information on what Army psychologists did, where they could be assigned, or what career opportunities were available came from talking to an Army psychologist who had been on active duty for a couple of years. One goal I had as the HSC psychology consultant was to create a career guide for Army psychologists. To this end, early in my career practicing psychology in the Army, I began to collect information on what Army psychologists do. By the end of 1981 a 27-page booklet[6] was created and published, providing virtually everything a psychologist would want to know to enjoy a career as a clinician or researcher in the Army.

This booklet, *A Career Guide for the Army Medical Department Psychologist*, was the combined efforts of several Army psychologists. While I was the editor-in-chief, three other Army Reserve psychologists were associate editors (Major Andrew S. Martin, PhD; Captain A. David Mangelsdorff, PhD; and Captain Thomas R. Dorworth, PhD) and several other Army psychologists contributed to the content. The final version was a project of the AMEDD Plans and Policy Task Force, chaired by Major Timothy B. Jeffrey, PhD.

This booklet provided information and guidance to Army Medical Department psychologists (of which there are three types: the clinical psychologist, the research psychologist and the clinician who has completed a clinical internship but not a dissertation). It provides a step-by-step guide to assignments, promotions, further training available, and rules and regulations applicable to a career in the Army. It provides an overview of various jobs available to psychologists, varying from combat units to Army hospitals to medical centers or various research facilities.

A special section on how to get ahead in the Army was contributed by the senior psychologist in the Army, Colonel Robert S. Nichols, PhD. He defined "getting ahead" as getting promoted, acquiring professional credentials such as getting licensed, acquiring a professional reputation (in and out of the Army), and getting increased responsibilities and better jobs. He covered methods for achieving this success, and included a list of what to do and what not to do.

This booklet is the first of its kind and one of the most valuable resources for both the brand-new psychologist entering the Army and senior folk like me. I was proud of this legacy I left as it was published right after I retired from the Army.

Mental Health Programs

Most of our work at CMHS consisted of seeing patients or clients. The mainstay of our existence and the bulk of what we did was sit down with a person who was experiencing some form of difficulty within his or her life. Sometimes this unwanted behavior was present in the patient's work environment, other times in their homes with their families and at other times in their personal lives, outside of work. Our job was to help the person in the chair in front of us to recognize what behaviors were causing problems, why, and how to change. Sometimes we helped the person to replace unwanted behaviors with more desirable actions, while at other times we could intercede and alter the environment in which the person must function. Sometimes our patient saw us voluntarily and other times was referred by their commander or supervisor. For whatever the reason, the help we provided was reactive: something was not right and then we were called on to fix it.

Under my predecessor, this was the only assistance CMHS provided. As a community psychologist, I was trained to recognize problem areas within the society we served and to become proactive by developing programs to eradicate the difficulties before they became so bad, the victims had to see us.

Therefore, with the help of my staff, we began to determine how we could develop programs to address problems in the community and stop them before they came to us. Essentially, we created two types of programs. One was a training platform for students who were interested in working in a community mental health setting or as clinicians. We trained graduate students in social work and psychology as well as military men and women in their second year of training to become a physician's assistant (PA). We also ran a mutual-based training program for reserve psychologists. Some met with us once a week and others would serve their annual two weeks of active duty with us. I say "mutual" because they would learn from us how to manage a community mental health clinic and they would provide for us advanced education in counseling and clinical therapy and psychological testing.

The second type of program was to assess a need in the community we served and then develop a syllabus or seminar or curriculum or course to train those members of the community with the problem so they could remedy the situation themselves without coming to us.

Some of our programs addressed stress management, adjustment of Army medical school enlisted students, and sexual assaults and rape counseling. We created and held a 10-week, 20-hour abnormal psychology course for mental health counselors (MOS 91G), seminars for preparing 91Gs for their annual proficiency tests, weight control clinics, clinics for commanders on handling behavioral issues within their commands, and a variety of specialized training sessions to provide assistance within our community so the people involved could ward off issues before our intervention was required. Some of our seminars were recorded by Health Services Command and then shown via an HSC TV network to other Army hospitals and medical centers.

Two programs our CMHS created were accepted at the Army level as worth sharing with the rest of the Army. They were or sexual assault program and the psychiatric training of the Army PA students.

The Army's Physician Assistant Clinical Program

In the mid–1960s, Duke University initiated a program to train people as physician assistants because of a shortage of doctors in the U.S. The physician's assistant (PA) was like a medical expert between an RN and a physician. The program took two years: one year of academic schooling and a year of practical experience, like the internship of a doctor. The PA could practice medicine alone, but under the supervision of a physician, treating minor injuries and practicing routine medicine.

The Army adopted the program in 1971 with the academic year taught at Sheppard Air Force Base in Wichita Falls, Texas. The second year of clinical OJT would be at selected Army medical centers. Upon completion they would become warrant officers. Some PA students would spend their clinical year at BAMC where they would rotate through various major medical departments. Their rotation in psychiatry was four to six weeks, during which they spent most of their time in both the psychiatric outpatient and in-patient services. They were assigned to my CMHS for a week.

Initially most PAs would spend their time at a troop medical clinic or the medical unit in a combat division. In their Department of Psychiatry rotation, though, they would be seeing mostly retired military or their dependents, not young soldiers. At our CMHS, young troops are what they treated. They were working with soldiers just like they would be in their first assignment, not retired people. The PAs requested most of their rotation through psychiatry be in CMHS, treating young soldiers. Their request was accepted, so now most of their psychiatry rotation was completed at CMHS. All the PA students we supervised were outstanding. Medical background experiences required to be accepted into the PA program were extensive. We even had some senior nurses training to become PAs. The program was a winning situation for us as a clinic and for the PA students. At the end of their rotations at CMHS we were sorry to see them leave.

Our Program on Sexual Assaults

As more women entered the Army, the incidence of sexual assaults also increased. As Sergeant Perez learned from his female friend who worked in the ER, dealing with rape victims was sort of a hit-or-miss situation depending on who was on duty when the victim arrived at the ER. There was truly little standard protocol in place, so different staff treated the victim in dissimilar ways. Our staff set out to create a standard procedure for treating sexual assault victims. The victims presented with different feelings and behaviors after being assaulted. Some were angry; some blamed themselves; others became withdrawn and depressed; a few presented an outward semblance of being calm and in control, while internally they harbored a wide range of hidden responses. To treat a victim responsibly, the healers needed to understand what the victim was going through, how they felt, how they viewed themselves and how they perceived others responding to them and what happened.

What we had to do was honestly viewed as a major undertaking that could take a long time to install throughout Fort Sam. But two things we could initiate immediately which would be a big step in the beginning. Everyone at CMHS was assigned a mission with the singular goal of establishing a single protocol for treating sexual assault victims in the most supportive way possible. Our first question was, where do we begin?

Who did we represent? The Army and the victim. We should begin at that point where a sexual assault victim is most likely to encounter the Army: either the Military Police or an Army medical facility. We now realized that each facility may serve a different function. The MPs might focus on establishing a crime was committed and collecting evidence, while the medical people may want to assess physical damage and treat that. What may be left out? The psychological state of the victim. A single trained support system should be in place to become the victim's advocate, to help her or him readily navigate the legal and medical system successfully without adding to the trauma and psychological and physical insult the victim has endured.

The legal and medical systems may have competing goals, but they must be made compatible. The victim must have a support system in place that will never desert the victim. We understood where we should focus our efforts. We needed to get the medical staff and the military law enforcement officials to each understand the other's missions so they could work together, not against each other. We needed to train each group on how to best help sexual assault victims. Initially our enlisted counselors set up an on-call system where one counselor (and a back-up) would be available at any hour to go to the ER or the MPs to immediately assume the role as the victim's advocate.

Collectively we created a guidebook for treating a sexual assault victim. This became our training manual for teaching medical staff and MPs what to do and how to obtain a victim advocate, a counselor who would not leave the victim alone.

We taught the medical staff and the MPs the several items that should be considered by all of those helping the victim. Does the ER have evidence collection kits? Is the victim examined for other injuries? What pregnancy options are available and what about sexually transmitted infections? Confidentiality must be foremost in the treatment plan and the victim must be assured it is never their fault. The feelings of the victim should be validated and respected. Follow-up appointments must be made, and a permanent counselor selected to aid the victim. As soon as possible, any legal recourse should be explained to the victim.

All of this was quickly established and implemented by our staff. But this was only the beginning. From the hospital and MPs, we wanted to go further. We developed a program to train commanders and supervisors on how to handle sexual assaults within their units or services. We trained volunteers to serve as victim advocates, relieving our small staff of always being on call. Finally, we developed a total sexual assault treatment program for all of Fort Sam. What we created became a prototype for Health Services Command which was made available to every Army medical treatment facility throughout the United States and the Panama Canal Zone.

These were the services provided at CMHS. My staff did the work; my job was to enlighten, encourage, and allow them to grow and develop, and allow our CMHS to provide the best services possible. I was convinced that we did exactly that, and I was immensely proud of all their accomplishments. We had together come a far distance from the staff I initially inherited. This was easily one of the best jobs I ever had.

But as 1980 rolled along, other career concerns began to take precedence over what my future would look like. I had previously received a letter from Army Personnel informing me of the regulations requiring mandatory retirement after 20 years of active duty for reserve officers. By September 1981, I would have accumulated 20 years of active military service.

18

Non-Military Endeavors (Moonlighting)
Why?

During my assignment to Fort Polk (see Chapter 7) I began engaging in non-military, off-duty work by teaching psychology courses for an on-post university program. Assigned to Fort Sam Houston, I hoped to continue working in the civilian sector, off-duty. Why?

There were two obvious reasons: extra money, and undertaking professional tasks beyond what I could do in the Army. As at Polk, there was no disagreement from local psychologists for me to work in private practice. Initially, at Fort Sam, I began teaching graduate courses, then moved into management consulting. Additionally, upon moving to San Antonio, I still had two more years on a three-year special education contract with the Beauregard Parish School district in DeRidder, Louisiana.

During my six years at Fort Sam, I was engaged in four totally different areas of off-duty vocational endeavors, which were professionally satisfying, lucrative, and a lot of fun for me. These areas consisted of teaching, the special ed project, management consultation, and investment in a small apartment complex.

Teaching

I engaged in two different ways of teaching, one as an off-duty paid professor and the other as an Army psychologist assigned as an adjunct professor to schools associated with Army medical institutions (no extra pay).

When I began my job as the Health Services Command psychology consultant, a colleague, the social work consultant, asked if I wanted to earn some extra money teaching graduate courses. Fort Sam had several colleges and universities from around the nation with local education degree programs being offered through the Post Education Center. While each program was managed locally by paid, full-time employees, the faculty were all part-time adjunct teachers. All were academically qualified to teach their subject. The social work consultant taught for Webster College (now a university), with the home campus in a suburb of St. Louis, Missouri. It needed a PhD psychologist to teach some counseling courses, so I applied and was hired. I taught there for almost three years, quitting only when I enrolled in its master's degree program in business in January 1978.

When I left HSC and became the chief of Psychology Services at Brooke Army Medical Center (and later chief of CMHS), the medical center was, in addition to a major Army medical center, a teaching hospital. And the teaching was not just for physicians. It had interns and practicum students in hospital administration, psychology, social work, and the second (practical) year in the education program for Army Physician Assistants. Because of this collaboration with several local institutions, many senior Army medical professionals also held academic teaching appointments at these schools. These were not paid appointments but on-duty assignments as Army medical officers.

These relationships with the department heads in various degree programs led to my being hired as a paid adjunct off-duty professor. At the same time I became the mentor of different interns working on graduate degrees in counseling, psychology, and social work. I was not paid to serve as their intern or practicum supervisor (although I graded them), as this was part of my regular duties as an Army psychologist. In turn, we received free work from the students and in every case their work was superb, so we got the best of the deal. Additionally, some did research with me and became authors of published or presented research papers.

I began teaching for Webster College graduate programs at both Fort Sam and at Laughlin Air Force Base at Del Rio, Texas, 160 miles west of San Antonio. Webster would charter a Piper Cherokee six, a single-engine six-seat plane, for flying three to four professors to Laughlin Friday afternoon to teach an evening class and a second class on Saturday morning. The chartered plane would then fly the professors back to San Antonio. All of us were either Army or Air Force officers, but I was the only teacher-pilot, so they wanted me in the right seat, next to the pilot. Our charter pilot was also a certified flight instructor, so he let me fly. He would take off and then let me fly, and as we approached Del Rio, he would assume command. Because he was a CFI, he signed my logbook to attest that these were training flights. I have several dozen hours flying a Cherokee six with not a single landing or take-off.

After supervising several interns or practicum students, I was asked to teach graduate courses at St. Mary's University, Trinity University, Our Lady of the Lake University, and the University of the Incarnate Word. All these schools had graduate students working at either the BAMC Psychology Service or the Community Mental Health Service. All paid me to teach evenings or weekends.

Because Brooke Army Medical Center was also a teaching hospital, many senior medical staff also received teaching appointments at other San Antonio medical or health institutions which also taught medical professionals. I was a Clinical Assistant Professor of Psychiatry at the University of Texas, San Antonio Health Science Center in the medical school where I taught classes in community mental health and supervised PhD students doing their APA internships. The Bexar County Hospital District appointed me as an affiliate member in the Department of Psychiatry. St. Mary's University of San Antonio appointed me as Lecturer in Human Services in its Department of Human Services. All were actual teaching or supervising positions, without pay, because of their teaching arrangements with Brooke Medical Center. These appointments involved mostly supervising students doing internships or practicums at Brooke and occasionally presenting specialty seminars at the schools listed above. The work was fascinating and the students bright and eager to learn. This was a very enjoyable benefit to being a psychologist at an Army teaching hospital.

Management Consulting

This endeavor is described as helping organizations improve performance or efficiency, or increase productivity. Sometimes management consultation is employed simply to make the workplace environment a better place to function. The consultants come from a variety of backgrounds, such as engineering, finance, production, management, administration, economics, marketing and advertising, public relations, and of course the behavioral sciences. In fact, over the past century, behavioral scientists have contributed much to the theory and practice of managing people.

In the early 1900s, Frank and Lillian Gilbreth were able to show managers how to increase production efficiency by regulations and consistency. Frank and a daughter authored *Cheaper by the Dozen* about the Gilbreths and their family of 12 children (later adapted for film). In the 1920s, social worker Mary Parker Follett began the study of organization behavior. At this same time, Harvard sociologist Elton Mayo began creating motivational theories (the Hawthorne effect theory). In 1943 psychologist

Abraham Maslow posited his theory of the Hierarchy of Needs, in that until basic human needs are met (food, shelter, etc.), higher aspirations will not be sought.

In 1959, psychologist Frederick Herzberg presented his theory of motivation and hygiene, about motivation and job satisfaction. A year later psychologist Douglas McGregor described his philosophy of two ways to manage (good or bad) as the X Y Theory. Clearly behavioral scientists have been actively involved in industrial and organizational psychology since World War I, when job selection methods were devised to determine the best way to train and assign men during the influx of enlistments at the beginning of the war.

My involvement with management consultation began with my use of the Army's organizational effectiveness programs. I began working with military organizations during my time at William Beaumont, which continued at Fort Polk. As the Health Services Command Psychology Consultant, this practice stopped, but I began to teach Army behavioral scientists how to conduct a command consultation. When I returned to practicing psychology at Fort Sam, I picked up command consultation again.

Fort Sam, though, was mostly populated with individuals connected to Brooke Medical Center and/or the Army's Academy of Health Sciences. Yes, there were support troops (law enforcement, maintenance, administration, logistics, etc.) but almost everyone else was somehow involved in Army medicine; there were no combat units. This meant that my market for consultation was extremely limited. But I was able to turn to the civilian population for what I wanted to do.

Private Practice

The local civilian psychologist I worked with on the evaluation of the Olympic athletes invited me to join him with some consultations with civilian business organizations. He was working with them on efforts to increase efficiency or production and improve management skills. I was able to secure Army permission to work with my friend during off-duty time.

I thoroughly enjoyed this work. Our clients were educated, affluent, astute, and enthusiastic men and women to work with. They appreciated our areas of expertise, passionately accepted our analyses, and adopted our suggestions wholeheartedly. For me, this was an area of psychology that was exciting, energetic, personally rewarding, and professionally challenging. As I was within four years of possibly retiring, this was a potential opportunity after the Army.

Pace Picante Sauce

My wife, Anita, worked for Margaret Pace, an affluent and prominent San Antonio socialite, whose family was associated with the San Antonio Pearl Brewing Company. Anita was Margaret's administrative assistant, helping administer and manage all Margaret's schedules of activities and her investment portfolios.

Of medium height, slender, with short dark hair, Margaret Pace was attractive, intelligent, and in her mid-fifties. A fine arts graduate of the H. Sophie Newcomb Memorial College of Tulane, she married Tulane graduate David Pace in the early 1940s. A World War II Army Air Corps pilot, he became a food entrepreneur in San Antonio after the war. When he was growing up in Louisiana, his family produced syrup from sugar cane. He began making syrups, jellies, and other condiments. Together Margaret and Dave created Pace Foods in 1947. Of all his food products, one, a salsa (a condiment or dip for Mexican dishes), Pace Picante Sauce, sold more than his other condiments. A $150,000 loan from Margaret's mother in 1951 allowed the Paces to build a new production facility.

The source of the actual picante salsa formula is controversial; David's family claim it is an old family recipe, while others state it is a variation of a local salsa David admired. Margaret said that it came from a recipe from a hotel her family owned in Mexico. Over the years the salsa became a best seller, with sales increasing each year. Margaret, being an artist, designed the label and the company logo. David tried to trademark the name "Pace Picante Sauce" but could not because of the familiar words "picante" (Spanish for spicy) and "sauce." David then created the unique hourglass-shaped bottle for his sauce.

David and Margaret had two children: a son, Paul (a hand surgeon living in east Texas), and a daughter, Linda. Linda married Kit Goldsbury, who joined Pace Foods in 1969. In 1976, Margaret and David divorced, partially because of some of David's behaviors. Each retained half the company.

Even though Pace Picante Sauce was thriving in a hot market (the most sales were in the Middle East), the company was not managed very well; sales were up, but income was not. This distressed Margaret, as she envisioned the growing company as an inheritance for her two children, yet financially it was not doing as well as it should. As half-owner, she tried to make changes in the operations of the company but was thwarted at every move.

In San Antonio, David was on a first-name basis with the movers and shakers of the city. The leaders in San Antonio legal and banking circles were all friends. The Pace Foods board members were all cronies who admired David and saw Margaret as an ignorant pest. Her requests were ignored and her desires for company information disregarded; essentially, she was shut out from every aspect of the company. As half-owner, she was able to secure financial data and the financial mismanagement was clearly visible. Fearing there would be no company for her children, she shared her concern with Anita. This is when I entered Margaret's life, in early 1977. Together, Anita and I became consultants to Margaret, assisting her to gain more influence in the future of Pace Foods.

Initially we served as a sounding board for her concerns. Our original task was to help her understand what was happening and provide suggestions on how to deal with the board that discounted her company ownership. Her treatment by her ex-husband and the board angered her and our attempts to have any effect on the company management were constantly snubbed. Something else had to be done.

We explained to Margaret that she had three options: she could stay on her current course, and continue being ignored. She could just quit and let the company flounder, financially, as it was doing. Or she could buy David out and assume total control of the company.

She realized that continuing as she had been doing was a waste of time. Giving up was not something she would accept. She then explained why she could not buy David out. Every legal firm in San Antonio was his friend, so none would represent her in a buy-out. She would need a loan and David was a buddy of the heads of all the banks in the city, so none would lend her the money. She agreed that buying out David would be the best solution for her, but she reiterated that he would never sell, and she didn't have the money, even if he agreed to sell. We assured her it probably could be done.

Anita and I had access to several years of financial and sales data which clearly demonstrated the financial records of the company were in disarray. The balance sheets of a company represent the financial picture at the end of the day. Balance sheets consist of two sides of a company: one is assets (everything a company owns); the other is liabilities and shareholders' equity (debts and shareholders' financial ownership). In Pace Foods' balance sheets, numerous discrepancies were noted. For the most part, these errors were not attempts at fraud but rather were results of careless record keeping. As an example, Anita and I found a local bank account on the 31 December balance sheets showing deposits of over $300,000. These monies were not listed on the 1 January balance sheets. Essentially in one day, the company had lost track of more than $300,000. While this money existed in a bank account belonging to Pace, the documentation was lost, so the company possessed more than $300,000 which it no longer recorded.

A careful examination of all the company's financial and market records showed several instances of financial record-keeping blunders. Actually, the company had quite a bit of cash lying around, especially in retained earnings. David Pace had interests beyond Pace Foods, such as his chair company (he designed a chair for which he held a patent). From a sales point of view, the company was doing great. Production was high, revenues were increasing but, unfortunately, the record-keeping was dismal, bordering on nonfeasance.

Anita and I sought advice from community bankers and attorneys we knew. Since Margaret was unable to use local legal and financial services, we inquired where we could locate qualified professional help. The answer was Houston, Texas. We contacted a legal firm which had expertise in business acquisitions, and an investment bank which made loans to purchase businesses.

Anita and I prepared detailed documents for Margaret, the bankers, and the attorneys. The strategy was to provide the attorneys with enough information to convince David to sell his share to Margaret (or be charged with nonfeasance) and to present enough financial and sales data for the bank to place a valuation on Pace Foods.

On Saturday, 15 October, Anita and I flew in a rented Cessna 150 to Houston Hobby Airport. We met with the law firm representing Margaret and the investment bank. Because of the confidential aspect of her acquisition, we met on a weekend. With everything turned over to the two professional institutions, our involvement with Margaret's acquisition of the company was completed. The company was valued at $4 million, so in late 1977, Margaret paid David $2 million for his half (and most of that loan was recovered from Pace Foods' retained earnings, after the sale).

Upon acquiring total ownership, Margaret selected Kit as president. Margaret remarried in 1981 and sold Pace Foods to her daughter and son-in-law for $14 million. Kit expanded and revamped the company so that by 1991 Pace Picante Sauce was the number one selling condiment, with sales around $173 million. In 1989 Kit and Linda divorced, with Kit buying Linda's share for $95 million. In 1994 Kit sold Pace Foods to Campbell Soup Company for $1.12 billion.

Anita was asked by Margaret (after she was sole owner) to go to the Pace Foods headquarters and work with the office people to get the financial and other records corrected, and to show the secretaries how to properly keep the books. With Margaret's life on track, her need for Anita decreased. Spending almost a year working with Margaret and successfully engineering the sale of a national, multi-million-dollar business led Anita and I to consider starting a part-time management consulting business.

There was one major problem, though: we had limited knowledge of the business world or its language. As more time was spent studying Pace Foods' finances, we realized our expertise in business restricted our abilities as management consultants.

Graduate School.... Once Again

To remedy this glaring personal deficit, we investigated obtaining graduate degrees in business. In January 1978 I enrolled in a Master of Arts degree in Business Administration and Management in Webster College at Fort Sam. Now the program is the Master of Business Administration (MBA). It was an accelerated degree program, specifically designed for military people who moved around quite a bit. Classes were at night or on weekends, with intense homework (I spent about 20 hours a week on just my finance class). I graduated in December 1978 with a 4.0 grade point average. Now I could speak business with a fair degree of authenticity.

At this same time Anita enrolled in graduate school at Trinity University in San Antonio. She earned her Master of Business Administration degree in August 1980 with a 4.0 grade point average.

In 1979 I requested authorization from the Army for me to join Anita to engage in off-duty management consulting, specializing in company evaluations, program design and staff development. That year Anita and I formed Worthington and Worthington Management Consultants, a part-time endeavor for both of us. Over the years we served a variety of businesses and organizations such as a state banking institution, a large aviation business (sales, charters, aircraft servicing, flight training), and government entities.

133 Claremont

Probably the single most critical area of my master's degree was the finance coursework. It was extremely hard; I spent about 20 hours each week on homework. But what I learned has become an important part of my life—how to make money using money. Essentially my finance professor taught me how to make money by leveraging. Leveraging involves using a small amount of your money along with borrowed money to acquire an investment.

Upon graduation, I wanted to use my new knowledge by investing in a business. I examined my background, interests, and skills which I possessed. I enjoyed building; in the past decade I had rehabbed or enlarged five houses, earning a profit when they sold, but investing in another house did not seem like a money-making proposition. Possessing several homes would make more money but be very costly to acquire. Owning one apartment house would place several renters all together, under one roof and in one building. I began to gather information on becoming an owner.

San Antonio, a city of almost one million residents, was the tenth largest city in the U.S. Its apartment association was also the tenth largest in America. Apartment buildings in the city were plentiful and several were for sale each week. For my first look at one for sale, I hired an engineer to take me with him and show me how to structurally evaluate the building to determine its stability. I then began a quest which took about six months.

In July 1979 I had found an apartment building ten minutes from my home, situated between Broadway and Fort Sam on 133 Claremont. Two to three decades previous, the area was nice, with proud homeowners and large houses. Over time many homes were converted into small apartments and the neighborhood became a haven for drug addicts and dealers. I went to the city zoning department to determine what lay in the future for the area and I was pleasantly surprised. A program was in place to eradicate the drug usage and to rehab the neighborhood. Increased law enforcement emphasis on drug usage had begun. A large residential city park was to be redone and code enforcement was going after land and building owners to clean up their properties or face severe fines. I bought the building.

Susan, Karen, Julie, and Bob on the River Walk in San Antonio, 1980.

Situated on two and a half lots, the two-story building was structurally sound, housing four single-bedroom apartments and two studio units. The place needed a face-lift, in and out, but the price was right. My plan was to combine the two first-floor studios with the adjacent apartments, creating two, two-bedroom apartments.

The owner had to sell and was in such a hurry that he was selling at a bargain price. On 25 July, for $10,384 cash, Anita and I became owners and managers of a small apartment building. The total sales price was $37,688 because we assumed two loans of $27,688. Borrowing money from Julie's and Karen's college funds (each had a signed contract and we paid them a favorable interest rate), I had the money for remodeling the building.

True to its plan, the city did rehab the neighborhood. Property owners who had neglected their upkeep were convinced by the city it was cheaper to clean up than to pay the fines. Several apartments changed hands and rehabbing became a familiar scene on Claremont. One small apartment building next door was purchased right after mine and the new owner poured a mint into redoing the building. It became the nicest on the street and tenants were located immediately. This area had truly turned around.

The entire building was remodeled. Rather than refinishing the small studio bathrooms, I just shut off their water and boarded them up. All floors had been painted and eventually covered with cheap carpet. Sanding revealed fine oak floors, which we varnished. Twelve-foot ceilings and tall, wide windows with natural wood floors offered an inviting place to live. The rental income—minus the debt service, reserve, and maintenance costs—still provided several hundred dollars of monthly profit.

I became a director in the San Antonio Apartment Association and in 1980 was selected as the small-apartment owner of the year. I also wrote a column on small apartment ownership and management for the SAAA monthly magazine (which, after my retirement from the Army, blossomed into a syndicated column for several apartment association magazines around the country). Through SAAA I met the president of a loan company and he inquired about my building. He asked about the current (assumed) loans, and suggested I consider refinancing. Explaining the process, he said I could refinance for more than I had in the property, pay off the two loans, and walk away with at least $20,000 in cash.

The building was refinanced in September 1980 for $48,000. The loans were paid off, and, after lending and closing costs were covered, Anita and I pocketed $21,833.

After I retired from the Army, long-distance ownership became tiring, and the previous profit was lessened by hiring a local property manager. As it was no longer the money machine it used to be, we decided to sell. The apartment industry in San Antonio was at a long-time high. Demand far exceeded supply. A recently retired high school shop teacher and his wife bought our building in December 1981. They paid $76,000 for it; after paying the refinanced mortgage, we received $28,000. During the two and a half years of ownership, we also received several hundred

Photograph showing Bob as a director of the San Antonio Apartment Association, on far right (San Antonio Apartment Association, 1981).

Anita as the manager of the Fox Photo National Warehouse in San Antonio, 1980.

dollars each month as profit. During our ownership, appreciation turned our original $10,348 investment into $50,000 via refinancing and selling. It was such a worthwhile investment for us that after I retired from the Army, Anita and I began investing in small real estate development projects.

Anita's New Job

After Margaret Pace assumed ownership of Pace Foods, concern over the company lessened. Anita's work managing her investments and volunteer work turned more into bookkeeping than problem solving. Now Anita's responsibilities required less time.

In 1980 Anita joined Fox Stanley Photo, Inc. as a full-time employee. Fox Photo was a national chain of photo stores and several commercial photo finishing plants across the country (prints made by Fox were noted by their round-bordered corners). She was hired as manager of the national Fox warehouse, responsible for stocking all the Fox retail camera stores. She was a pioneer, being the first female senior manager hired by Fox. She quit Fox upon my retirement in the fall of 1981 because we moved out of the city.

But the two of us continued with Worthington and Worthington as a part-time endeavor, using both our new-found business degrees and my psychology and management backgrounds to attract new clients and keep us busy.

As we approached 1981, mandatory retirement loomed. Anita had an excellent job, and our consulting business was expanding. Could I remain on active duty? Would I be forced to retire? What would I do? The business world was beginning to appeal to me more and more.

19

Retirement

When It Began

In late 1979 I received an official letter dated 14 November. It stated that based on the provisions of AR 635–100 (Army Regulations) my mandatory retirement date had been established as 1 October 1981. As a reserve officer on active duty, I could not serve beyond 20 years on active duty.

There were exceptions to this regulation as needed; professional officers such as attorneys, doctors, chaplains, nurses, and others (to include psychologists) could receive a waiver to remain on active duty beyond 20 years. For this waiver to be approved, the officer must have expertise and skills in short supply in the Army.

Upon learning of my mandatory retirement, the BAMC commanding general offered to approve a waiver for me to remain on active duty beyond October 1981. Because the retirement date was almost two years away, Anita and I felt no rush to decide my future. But 13 months later, a major event occurred which could impact seriously on any retirement decisions we made: DOPMA.

DOPMA

The Defense Officers Personnel Management Act of 1980 was Public Law 96–513, an amendment to Title 10, U.S. Code. Created by Congress and signed into federal law by President Carter on 12 December 1980, it was to become effective on 15 September 1981, a few days prior to my mandatory retirement.

During World War II the Army could promote officers at the command level. Promotions came fast and at the end, the Army was saturated with senior officers. Something had to be done to better control the acquisition, retention, termination, and retirement of military officers. In the next 30 years two different major Congressional acts were created to unify the management of the careers of military officers. But by the mid–1970s, officer career management was still in a turmoil.

The active Army (the Army of the United States) comprised officers from differing military organizations such as Regular Army, reservists, and National Guard officers, each with its own promotion systems. Added to this hodge-podge of officer career administration was the end of the Vietnam War, the end of the draft, and the new all-volunteer Army. Additionally, the size of the Army in the mid–1970s was so bloated for peacetime that many officers had to be terminated (mostly officers who flew helicopters in Vietnam).

Causing more confusion regarding the military careers of the officers was a distinct difference in career management philosophies between the Army and the Naval services. For example, in early 1959 I was a U.S. Marine corporal, and my company commander was a Marine captain. Six and a half years later (mid–1965) I ran into my former commander, and I was now an Army captain, and he was a Marine major. A few years later I was now a major and he was still a major.

DOPMA was created to stabilize officer personnel management across the U.S. military, set ceilings for the number of field grade officers, and codify rules on separation and retirement. It established how and when lieutenant colonels or commanders (U.S. Navy) could be promoted to full colonel or captain (Navy) and set the number that could be promoted to 50 percent of those eligible (having 21 years of commissioned service). So how did this impact me?

Under DOPMA, all officers on active duty more than 10 years would be treated as Regular Army, so no more reservists or National Guard. There would be a single promotion policy for all officers. This meant my reserve commission would be converted to Regular Army. Retired Regular Army officers had severe limitations on pay if they became employed in a federal job. This did not apply to reservists. I would become eligible for promotion to full colonel after 23 August 1982. Because of my date of rank as a lieutenant colonel I would be at the end of the annual promotion list (if I was selected).

So, I could be promoted in late 1983 and retire as a full colonel. Well, no. There was also a new Army regulation: for an officer to retire as a colonel, he/she had to serve in that grade for three years. So, if I elected to remain on active duty and retire as a colonel, I could not retire until late 1986, five years after my 20 years of active duty. Instead of retiring at age 44, I would have to stay in until I was 49.

The first question was: am I promotable? The answer was yes. My competition would only be officers of my branch, the Medical Service Corps. This included professionals in the behavioral sciences, pharmacists, optometrists, podiatrists, health facility administrators, medical evacuation pilots, laboratory scientists and medical scientists.

I believed I was highly qualified. Most of my fellow MSC officers had spent a career in their professional fields, and very little time in other parts of the Army. All my officer efficiency reports as a psychologist were perfect. I had served as a hospital psychologist, service chief and at the top as a major Army command psychology consultant. In addition, I had three graduate degrees, had commanded an Infantry company, endured three combat tours, had numerous combat decorations including seven for valor, and was a graduate of the Army Command and General Staff College. I was convinced being promoted was not an issue for me. Staying in another five years, however, was.

Anita and I had many lengthy discussions about this. Should I stay in or get out? What would be the reason to stay an extra five years? What would I do if I retired in 1981? These were the questions to be answered as 1980 rolled into 1981. What could I do after the Army? What did we want to do as a family? Where would we live?

Another prime concern: college for our daughters. In January 1981 our oldest, Suzi (now Susan), was a twenty-year-old junior at Tulane University. She had a full Air Force scholarship as a potential USAF scientist. Her major was computer science. Our cost for her education was minimal. Our middle daughter, Julie, would enter college in the fall of 1981 and our third daughter, Karen, would start college in 1986. What should we do?

Susan's high school graduation, 1978. Bob, Julie, Susan, Karen, and Anita.

Time to Retire?

By October 1981, I would have been in the military (Marines and Army, active duty and reserve) for over 24½ years. In five more years, what could I ever achieve? The top job for an Army psychologist was as the psychology consultant for the Army Surgeon General, assigned to the Pentagon. My old mentor, Dick Hartzell, when he held that position, lived in Annapolis, Maryland, and drove over four hours each day, traveling back and forth to work. Twice I had been offered that assignment and twice had been able to refuse it. I never wanted to have to drive more than 15 to 20 minutes to work so I had no interest in working at the Pentagon.

Anita and I knew I could make more money as a civilian than as a colonel so five more years was not financially worth it. Wearing eagles instead of silver oak leaves was attractive, but the additional time seemed a steep price to pay. So now, in early 1981, the question was no longer whether to stay in the Army, but what to do as a civilian?

Managing the mental health clinic was invigorating and was an excellent job. I enjoyed command consultation and training our grad students and PAs. The several mental health programs we operated were interesting and exciting. Seeing patients, though, was becoming less appealing. It seemed like more and more patients with behavioral problems came to us to fix them. Their expectations seemed similar to that of a person with a broken arm who sees an orthopedic surgeon; the surgeon places a cast on the damaged wing and says, "Come back in six weeks. Your arm will be healed by then and we will remove the cast." The patient does nothing but wait for the six weeks to pass and then the arm is restored.

Many patients came to us for help but expected us to do the work, without any involvement in the process. I was beginning to tire of this. On the other hand, I did enjoy the off-duty management consulting I was doing. Anita and I would be tasked with evaluating a business organization that wanted to improve its functioning. We would go in and evaluate the organization (leadership roles, internal communications, management style, and standards of performance). We would detect areas of weakness as well as strengths. We would report our findings to top management along with our recommendations for capitalizing on the strengths and minimizing areas of limitations. We would prepare a training schedule, write its training textbook, and institute an instruction program.

We considered turning our part-time consulting business into a full-time effort for the two of us, but decided against it. With two daughters in college simultaneously, we wanted a more reliable source of income. Turning the consulting business into a full-time enterprise was enticing but we needed a steady, guaranteed source of revenue to supplement my Army retirement income.

I was beginning to enjoy the business world more than clinical psychology. I thoroughly relished teaching (and was good at it). Why not be a management professor in a business school? I had a graduate business degree and had owned and managed two businesses. I was eligible to teach in a college setting, as I had a PhD and an amazing résumé of academic papers presented and published. Besides, most modern management theorists were psychologists, right? By the end of January Anita and I decided I would seek employment as a business professor.

The premier means of posting teaching positions available in colleges and universities was in *The Chronicle of Higher Education*, a monthly periodical devoted to academic news, information, and jobs. I began subscribing to that publication. Academic business journals also provided ads announcing existing teaching positions. Anita and I agreed that we loved the Southwest and had no desire to move elsewhere, so my job search was limited to four states: California, Arizona, New Mexico, and Texas.

Site visits at three schools were quickly arranged: The Naval Postgraduate School in Monterey, California; Embry-Riddle University in Prescott, Arizona; and Eastern New Mexico State University in Portales, New Mexico. My first visit was to Monterey.

The Naval Postgraduate School

The Naval Postgraduate School began in 1912 as a postgraduate program associated with the U.S. Naval Academy. In 1951 it moved to Monterey's old Hotel Del Monte, a luxury resort hotel built in 1880. The Navy had leased it for training during World War II and then bought it. As a fully accredited institution, the school offered graduate degrees in management and engineering. I was familiar with the school and Monterey as my family and I lived in Monterey while I attended the Defense Language School at the Presidio of Monterey in 1965. But as I was to learn, that was 16 years ago, and changes had occurred.

I should have realized things were different in 1981 when I crossed the Colorado River into California. At 6000 feet above the desert near Needles, California, in my plane, I noticed the ground was brownish and a little blurry. Not paying attention, I focused on landing at Monterey, but as I approached the Pacific Ocean at Monterey, I realized the blurry ground was due to smog. After landing, I took my rental car to the hotel where I had reservations. Driving downtown, I passed Dennis the Menace Park, a favorite playground for Suzi and Julie. It was a pleasant area of safety for kids. This time, though, the stream of heavy traffic seemed to turn the park into a smoggy danger zone, surrounded by speeding cars.

The next day I had my interview. The position was for a professor of management, and as I learned, the school preferred teachers who possessed a military background since its students were primarily Naval officers. I met with three professors, who already had my résumé and were familiar with my background. We discussed what my responsibilities would be, and how they fit perfectly with what I wanted to do. I was impressed with the school, the curriculum, and the professors I met. I had loved Monterey when I lived there and believed it would be a good move and an excellent job.

After the interview, I was able to spend some time with one of the professors who was a recent business professor from a college in the Midwest. He enjoyed teaching here but explained that despite almost doubling his salary, he could not afford a house for his family within an hour's commute from the school.

Monterey in 1965 was a town of 24,500 residents. First discovered by Spanish explorers in 1602, it became the port of entry for California in the 1700s, due to its location on Monterey Bay. In 1965, when I lived there, the national Defense Language Institute and the Naval Postgraduate School were two of the town's largest employers, as they were in 1981. Monterey was the nicest place I had ever lived during my military career (San Antonio was a close second). Fort Ord, just north of Monterey, home of the 7th Infantry Division, was the largest Army post and the most desired due to its beautiful location on the Pacific Ocean.

In the early 1900s it was a major fishing location which dried up in 1950s because of overfishing. From the 1930s to the 1950s, it was home to many internationally known writers such as Henry Miller and John Steinbeck. When the fishing industry collapsed, the large canneries along the Bay were abandoned, as well as the Fisherman's Wharf. By the early 1960s, though, Cannery Row and the wharf became valuable real estate projects. They were beginning to be turned into restaurants and shops, which are exceptional tourist attractions. Getting around town was easy and uncomplicated. With nearby Carmel and the famous 17-mile drive, the Monterey area was an ideal place to live: historic and interesting, with many things to do and places to visit. And the climate was perfect for me: mild (mostly the 50s to 60s, year-round) and moist.

In 1981 Monterey was not the same. Traffic was horrendous, with ample smog. Navigating around town had become complicated. The place had grown by over 3000 people and was no longer the ideal place to live (at least for me). After the interview I drove all over Monterey and returned to the hotel. Calling Anita, I described what I saw. I explained that I was told I was the top candidate for the job, but Monterey was not what we wanted. She agreed, so the next morning I called my contact at the school and explained that while the teaching position was exactly what I wanted, Monterey was not where my family and I wanted to live. Boarding my plane, I flew back to San Antonio, disappointed that the teaching position at the Naval Postgrad School did not work out.

Embry-Riddle Aeronautical University

My next interview was with the dean of Academics at Embry-Riddle Aeronautical University, located in Prescott, Arizona. Beginning as an aviation flight school in Cincinnati in 1926, it closed in 1930, only to reopen in Miami, Florida, in 1939. It moved to Daytona in 1965 and became a university in 1968. In 1978, Embry-Riddle established a second campus (taking over a vacant college) in Prescott, a small city in the high desert of central Arizona.

Prescott College had a small campus, built in 1966, but because of fiscal mismanagement it closed in 1974. Embry-Riddle established a second location by acquiring this relatively new college campus. One reason for the acquisition here was that this area had over 300 days of sunshine for flight training. The school offered undergraduate and graduate degrees in aviation management and aerial transportation as well as flight training for students to become certified as commercial pilots.

I had applied for a management professor vacancy, citing my background as a manager, my experience in aviation, and my PhD as well as a graduate degree in business. I was invited to visit the campus. The position interested me for three reasons. First, it was a teaching area I was qualified to occupy. Second was the location. My family lived in Flagstaff for two years, and since Prescott was only 95 miles away, we had spent considerable time in Prescott and the surrounding area, camping, fishing, and exploring old mining ghost towns.

Love Field, at an elevation of 5045 feet, was a multi-instrument, three-runway airport. Embry-Riddle had training planes based there, as well as hangars and maintenance personnel. I was sure I could work out a place to hangar my plane and find mechanics to maintain it. This was my third reason for wanting to teach at Embry-Riddle.

After I landed at Love Field, a car with a driver met me to take me to the campus, about three miles away. I was escorted first to a very nice VIP suite in a building on campus to place my baggage and then taken to the dean's office. Upon entering, I was very surprised.

Facing me was what looked like a teen-aged girl. She was the dean of

Academics and a recent mathematics PhD graduate in her mid-twenties. I learned that she was unable to obtain any mathematics teaching position but was hired this past fall as the dean of Academics for this Prescott campus. This should have been my first clue about Embry-Riddle.

She welcomed me to the school, and we discussed the university, its mission, its faculty, and its students. During our conversation I found that Embry-Riddle had no planes, no hangars, nor any mechanics. Everything was leased, so all the students and instructors had to do was enter the planes, fly them, and then park them. Embry-Riddle owned nothing related to flight training. That terminated my third reason for working there.

Much of our time together was spent with me covering my education, my experience in management, and my teaching credentials. She said someone would take me on a tour of the campus and I would be her guest for dinner at a local restaurant. The next day I would be interviewed by four management professors and be taken around the classrooms. I spent the rest of the afternoon walking around the campus with my guide, noting how new everything looked. After all, this place was only 15 years old.

The next day, I met with four professors. Two were retired FAA employees and two were retired Department of Transportation executives. All had grown up in the Prescott area and wanted to retire there. They all said that if they were not drawing a federal retirement check, they could not afford to live in Prescott. When I asked why, they said that Embry-Riddle didn't pay much.

The curriculum, the classrooms, and the experiences of the four professors impressed me. I commented on the school not owning any airplanes, but was told that as an employee, I could fly two hours a month at a greatly reduced rate. I explained that since I owned a plane, paying to rent a plane didn't make sense to me. I enjoyed my interaction with these men, realizing they all loved what they were doing and how much they liked teaching here. The environment was modern and conducive to learning; the students were mostly motivated, excellent scholars; and life in Prescott, if one enjoyed outdoor activities, was gratifying.

After lunch with them, I returned to the dean's office. We talked for a while; she was seeking my impression of the campus and how I saw the professors. I replied I admired its management academic program and its faculty, and living in Prescott really appealed to me. She asked a couple more questions about me and then handed me a contract.

I was dumbfounded. As a lieutenant colonel I was making about $38,000 a year. This nine-month contract for an assistant professor (a full year for a university professor, although some professors could teach during the summer, earning extra income) was only for $15,000. I asked if the salary offer was negotiable and was told no. That offer was firm.

I now understood exactly what the four professors meant when they said that, without their government retirement checks, they could not afford to teach at Embry-Riddle. Typically, a dean of Academics is an older person with a background in teaching and education administration. I then realized, based on my limited knowledge of how Embry-Riddle paid its employees, that its pay for the dean of Academics would never attract a senior faculty member, so it had to hire a new PhD with no teaching or college administration experience. Thanking the dean, I explained that I would have to discuss the offer with my wife. She accepted that, stating the contract would be valid for a week.

A ride took me back to the airport and I winged my way back home. Anita and I considered the contract for a few hours. My retiree income would be just under $20,000 a year. To equal my pay as a lieutenant colonel I would have to make, at the minimum, $18,000 annually. Fifteen thousand just wouldn't cut it. I called the dean the next day, thanked her for the courtesy of inviting me to campus but explained that the salary offered was not enough for me and my family. No counteroffer was presented, so we said goodbye. Looking at higher-education pay scales for professors as documented by *The Chronicle of Higher Education*, I found the salary offered by Embry-Riddle for an assistant professor position was in the bottom five percent of university salaries.

Eastern New Mexico State University

By mid–March I was becoming concerned. Both job interviews had been very unsuccessful. I only had one left. A management teaching position had been advertised by the School of Business at Eastern New Mexico State University. The dean said he would be attending an academic business management conference at a hotel in New Orleans and I could be interviewed at the conference.

When we met, I was informed that due to budget issues the position was no longer available. But, he said, he knew another dean who did have a need for a management professor. He explained that the dean, Jerry Miller, was at the conference, and he could introduce me to the dean of the Business School at West Texas State University (WTSU) in Canyon, Texas.

In the area where publishers displayed textbooks, I was introduced to Miller as he was handed my résumé. Of average height and build, with longish, sandy-colored hair, bespectacled with an open smile, he was about my age (almost two years younger). Friendly, quick-witted, he was a man in motion. Explaining he had to go to a publisher's open house, right now, he thanked the other dean and invited me to join him, and we could talk at the party. He led me through a door to a set of steps. Through another door, we entered a corridor leading to the hotel guest rooms. As we turned into the hallway, I saw a beautiful blonde co-ed standing there, and Jerry hugged and kissed her. I was mortified; here was a dean, cuddling a young woman, maybe one of his students. I was introduced to Jeane, his wife. While she looked like a young grad student, she wasn't; they had three pre-teen sons. We entered the publisher's suite.

The room was full of business professors. Jeane knew most of them and began to mingle while Jerry and I grabbed drinks and sat on a couch in a corner. Rapid-fire questions followed. Jerry described the position available: a management assistant professor position starting in the fall. He expounded on what he wanted, saying he had had good luck hiring retired military officers in the past, so he wanted more information on my teaching background.

Citing my teaching experience, I described classes taught at St. Mary's and Our Lady of the Lake, and supervising grad students at Trinity, all in San Antonio. I asked if he wanted me to contact the deans I worked for to call him; he replied no, he would do that. Rising, he appeared eager to leave; glancing around for Jeane, he said he had another appointment, but he would get in touch with my deans and get back to me in a week or so. They left as quickly as they had arrived.

One week went by with no call from Dr Miller. Another week and still no call. Finally, I called Dean Miller and asked if he had talked to the deans. He replied yes, but they said they never heard of me, so he was leery of me. I asked who he talked to, and he said the dean of each business school. I responded that I never taught for the business schools; I taught in the behavioral science departments. He said, "oh." Quiet reigned. I said I would ask each dean I worked for to call him, and he said okay. He did not seem nearly as anxious about me as he did in New Orleans. I felt that he was no longer interested in me. He said goodbye and hung up.

That evening I explained to Anita what happened, thinking my opportunity to get interviewed just went away. The next day I contacted each dean I worked for, explaining what had happened, and asked each one if they would contact Miller on my behalf. Each said they would.

A few days later I received a call from Jerry Miller stating that three deans contacted him and gave me glowing appraisals for both my teaching skills and my ability to manage the graduate students. He said he was impressed by the reports of the deans and their beliefs I would be an outstanding business professor. He invited me to come to WTSU for a formal interview in April. I was astounded and almost shouted with joy, but retained my composure.

West Texas State University

In early April I flew to Canyon, landing in the late afternoon, on a short dirt strip just north of the town since the closest airport was in Amarillo, about 20 miles away. Jerry met me there and said we would have dinner with two other professors, and then we would talk. The next morning I could tour the campus and the business school.

Jerry and I met two other professors at the Railroad Crossing restaurant near the WTSU campus. The modest city of Canyon (population 11,000) began as a small community in the late 1800s. Located in the West Texas Panhandle, it is 19 miles south of Amarillo and 12 miles west of Palo Duro Canyon, America's second largest canyon (being 120 miles long). While catering to workers who commute to Amarillo and local ranches, Canyon was also the home of West Texas State University.

WTSU, with around 8000 students, offered undergraduate and graduate degrees in many fields. Founded in 1910, it became a state university in 1963. The School of Business had departments in management, marketing, finance, accounting, and economics, granting both bachelor and graduate degrees in business. The faculty comprised tenured, non-tenured and adjunct (part-time) professors. One of WTSU's more famous members was artist Georgia O'Keeffe, known as the mother of American modernism art, who headed the Art Department from 1916 to 1918.

The other two professors were both retired military lieutenant colonels. One was a former Air Force pilot who taught statistics; the other was a former Army logistics officer, now a management professor. Ironically the Army professor had been a good friend of John Paul Vann, the controversial retired Army Infantry lieutenant colonel, a former Vietnam combat advisor who became a State Department Advisor in Vietnam with the equivalent rank of major general. Vann died in 1972 in a helicopter crash in Vietnam. I worked for Vann during my second tour in Vietnam as a combat advisor.

The two were graduate students together at Syracuse University in New York in 1959 when Vann was accused of raping a 15-year-old girl. During the military investigation, Vann was able to cheat a lie detector test, so the charges were dropped. Vann received an MBA while his friend (the WTSU professor) received a PhD.

During dinner I asked all kinds of questions surrounding the transition from Army to business professor. Both him; retirement to WTSU. Jerry mostly listened. Both retired colonels indicated their choice to teach was a wise one and that WTSU was the best place to work. I came away from the meal with a much better understanding of the move from the military to academia, and an appreciation of how nice it would be to teach at WTSU.

Prior to my departure the next day, Jerry explained how much he enjoyed having retired military officers working for him. He said he found them intelligent, educated, sophisticated, experienced and with personal values consistent with the values of WTSU. He also stated they were excellent teachers. We also discussed what courses I felt qualified to teach and which ones I wanted to teach. I mentioned management, business strategies, and small business operations, at both undergrad and grad levels. He thanked me for coming, said he was impressed with me and would contact me soon. A few days later I received a nine-month contract (signed by the president) in the mail for a tenure-track assistant professor of management for $19,000. The attached letter also indicated that summer teaching opportunities would be available for additional income.

If we moved to Canyon, what would Anita do? She had an investment in her graduate education and was very successful managing a national warehouse. If I took the job at WTSU, she would have to quit her job at Fox Photo; then what?

We decided to move Worthington and Worthington to Canyon, where it would become a full-time business. Anita would become president and I would work for her. Anita and I agreed the move to WTSU would be ideal for everyone, so I signed the contract.

What Now?

In less than four months we had a lot to do. My official retirement date was 1 October, and we were now in May. Our daughter Susan would enter her senior year in Tulane in August. Julie originally was headed to Northern Arizona University but now considered WTSU. She was offered a scholarship, and as I would be a faculty member, she would also receive a significant tuition discount. Karen would be entering eighth grade in the fall.

We had a house to sell in San Antonio. But the real estate market was excellent for sellers. Six years prior, we bought one of the smallest but nicest homes in an excellent neighborhood. But we now had for sale one of the nicest, largest homes in an excellent neighborhood, which should be easy to sell. We also had to purchase a home in Canyon and then pack everything up and move.

Julie's high school graduation, 1981. From left: Susan, Julie, and Karen.

My replacement would be a lieutenant colonel psychologist, currently the chief of the Psychology Service at Tripler Army Medical Center in Hawaii. Additionally, assuming the position of the Health Services Command Psychology Consultant, he would arrive in mid–August.

My last day at work would be Friday, 14 August, with the next few days clear for out-processing Fort Sam. Thursday, 20 August would be the first day of terminal leave (vacation time before retiring). On that day the family would depart San Antonio to start another episode of our lives. Julie decided to attend WTSU (where she met her husband-to-be, Steve).

Several weekends during the summer, Anita and I would depart on a Friday afternoon, fly in our plane to Amarillo and spend the weekend in Canyon looking at houses. By the third visit, we made a purchase offer on a house close to the university, which was accepted.

Our house in San Antonio sold quickly. A wealthy cattleman, who owned a large ranch about 100 miles southwest, needed a place for his family to stay while visiting or shopping in the city. We bought the house for $51,500, and spent $8400 adding a two-room single bathroom wing to the house. We sold the house for $130,000, a 117 percent profit. Anita and I flew back to San Antonio on 11 September to close on the house we sold there, returning to Canyon the next day.

Leaving the Army was not difficult (twice before I had left active duty, once as a Marine in 1959, and again as an Army major in 1969) because entering a new career was stimulating and exciting. There was no retirement ceremony as I left the CMHS before retiring (but the staff did throw a very nice retirement party for me). In the mail I received a package containing orders for the Army Legion of Merit medal, the second highest award for meritorious service. What impressed me most were the comments regarding my performance on my last officer's efficiency report. The statement began:

> "Lieutenant Colonel Worthington's credentials, talents, and abilities are so numerous, protean, varied and ostentatious as to truly defy description. Were he a football player, his number would be retired along with him, out of respect for his accomplishments...."

Twenty years of active duty, almost five years of active reserve, three combat tours, and 27 medals later, it was time to say goodbye. Very little of this time was horrible (my year as a company commander comes to mind); most was gratifying, such as my time as a combat advisor and the decade as an Army psychologist. My uniform was relegated to the back of my closet, where it resides today. I did don it once more to commission my daughter Susan as a second lieutenant in the Air Force, nine months later. Plaques and honors bestowed were packed carefully in boxes, now lying on the shelf of a storage unit. My military ID card went from Active Duty to Retired as I moved into another phase of my interesting existence.

As I have done more than once before in my life, I terminated one aspect to enter another. I was no longer a soldier, no longer a clinical psychologist, but now a university business professor. Yet, I remain indefinitely a lieutenant colonel, an achievement I will treasure forever. Anita and I had endured rough times as well as smooth sailing. As we departed one life to move into another, we looked forward to new, different, exciting, rewarding, and fulfilling times ahead. Which is exactly what happened.

Epilogue

My Army retirement and move to Canyon, Texas, to become a business professor was just another new adventure in our lives. Anita worked full-time as the president of Worthington and Worthington Management Consultants. Two daughters were in college and the youngest was still at home and attending school. Our new life was going well.

I traveled quite a bit as an Army psychologist, and as the Health Services Command consultant, to conferences, conventions, and professional meetings. All these trips were on official Army business; therefore, my expenses were reimbursed by the Army. Now, as a civilian, my flying costs came out of my pocket; I needed a business reason to fly, so I became a part-time editor (working at home) for a weekly national aviation newspaper, which meant my costs for owning and operating a private airplane were a legitimate business expense because flying was necessary to write articles and attend aviation conferences. I also continued full-time teaching at WTSU.

As more requests came to me for magazine articles, I reduced my teaching load to half-time. My magazine articles expanded from aviation to business, travel, firearms, motorcycles (I was a motorcycle rider) and 4-wheel drive vehicles (I had owned several Jeeps). Worthington and Worthington also grew as more corporate and government contracts were signed. Anita and I co-authored several business books and travel articles.

There were enough writing assignments for full-time work; potentially, another career change. The winters in Canyon were brutal (for people who enjoyed the sunny and mild Southwest) and Anita and I became empty nesters. Our middle daughter graduated from WTSU in 1985 and our youngest left for college in 1986. It was a suitable time to consider another adjustment to our lives. Anita and I decided to close our consulting business; I would leave WTSU, and we would move to a warmer climate.

In 1987, we made the move from Canyon to Las Cruces, New Mexico, where I wrote full-time and taught part-time after being invited to join

New Mexico State University as a visiting business professor for a year. I was only required to teach classes (not serve in other faculty capacities), so I had plenty of time to continue writing articles for a variety of magazines. After my visiting professorship ended, though, I realized how much I missed being in the classroom.

In 1989 I joined the faculty of Journalism and Mass Communications at NMSU. It was another teaching subject change for me, but as I had years of professional writing experience and a business background, I was asked to run the advertising degree program and teach several writing courses. In 1997, at age sixty, I retired as a journalism professor.

My writing career has endured through several "retirements," and today, with more than 2,600 publications, I continue writing. Over the last several years I have written a regular column, *The Left Seat* (the seat in the plane where the pilot sits), in aviation magazines; authored a few non-fiction books; and produced a movie. The first of my trilogy of military career books—***Under Fire with ARVN Infantry*** (2018), about my job as a combat advisor in Vietnam—earned a gold medal award for Excellence in Literature from the Military Writers Society of America. The second book, ***Fighting Viet Cong in the Rung Sat***, describing my second tour in Vietnam as a combat advisor, was published in 2021. This third book, which follows my career as an Army psychologist, is the last in the trilogy. I also produced a 2019 documentary film: ***Combat Advisor in Vietnam***, with all footage filmed by me in Vietnam. My next book will be about my 40 years in the left seat.

My military legacy continues. My daughter Susan served as a captain in the U.S. Air Force. My granddaughter Megan graduated from West Point; she is an Army captain, currently a company commander, and is on her third tour in the Middle East. My grandson, Matt, an Air Force Academy graduate, is a first lieutenant at Wright-Patterson Air Force Base.

My wife, Anita, passed in 2021 and I reside in Las Cruces, New Mexico.

Visit my web site at ***www.BobWorthingtonWriter.com.***

Military History

Elliott Robert "Bob" Worthington retired from the U.S. Army in October 1981, four and a half months shy of 25 years of service as an enlisted man, NCO, and officer. His military career began when he dropped out of college to enlist in the U.S. Marines in February 1957.

After Parris Island boot camp and Infantry training, he was assigned to the 10th Marines, an artillery regiment in the Second Division at Camp Lejeune, North Carolina. He was assigned to a 4.2 inch mortar battery and went on a six-month Mediterranean cruise as part of the USMC reinforced marine Infantry battalion, trained for combat assaults as needed anywhere in any countries facing the Mediterranean Sea.

On 15 July 1958, his unit completed a combat amphibious assault on the city dump of Beirut, Lebanon as part of the U.S. Operation Bluebat, to stop the war being fought in Lebanon by outside countries. The Marines remained several months, and in the fall, Bob returned to the States. While in the Marines, he met Anita Elliott, a Washington, D.C., college student; they dated.

As a corporal, he left active duty in February 1959 to return to Dartmouth College. He and Anita married in September 1959 as he entered his junior year. During his senior year at Dartmouth, he was employed as a regular, full-time police officer with the Hanover, New Hampshire Police Department.

He was an Army ROTC cadet (as well as a PFC in the Army Reserve). Majoring in art, he graduated in June 1961, as a ROTC Distinguished Military Graduate.

Due to a mistake in his ROTC records, he was not commissioned in the Infantry, but in the Chemical Corps. After completing the Chemical Corps Basic Officer Course, he remained at Fort McClellan, Alabama, where he became a platoon leader in a Smoke Generator Company.

He requested a branch transfer to the Infantry, transferring to the Second Infantry Division at Fort Benning, Georgia, as a rifle company platoon leader in early 1963. That summer he attended Parachute School. On his third jump he broke his hip, was hospitalized for two months, and then received a one-year medical profile prohibiting his return to the rifle company. He became the battalion assistant personnel officer. An additional duty was as the battalion coach and captain of its pistol and rifle team. During the Fort Benning Post matches, one of Bob's pistol shooters was unable to shoot, so Bob took his place, winning the Post pistol championship. This led to his becoming the XO of the Division Marksmanship Detachment, and as a professional pistol shooter, he earned the highest competitive designation of Master. He held this position until his one-year profile expired and was assigned as the assistant operations officer in an infantry battalion. During the summers, the battalion was trained by a Special Forces team in unconventional warfare tactics; it also trained in helicopter tactics. Bob was promoted to captain in mid–1965 and then received orders to Vietnam as a combat advisor.

Bob attended the Military Assistant Training Advisor Course at the J.F. Kennedy Special Warfare Center at Fort Bragg, North Carolina, and then the Vietnamese language school at the Defense Language Institute at the Presidio of Monterey in California.

He served in Vietnam as a combat advisor in 1966–1967. After Vietnam, he was assigned to the Armor Officer's Career Course at Fort Knox, Kentucky, then attended the Army classified Nuclear Weapons Employment Officer Course. Assigned to Fort Benning, he commanded a Basic Combat Training company. It became the worse job he ever held, because of the overbearing battalion and regimental commanders he had. The assignment was so bad he decided to get out and attend graduate school, which required money. He knew if he returned to Vietnam as a combat advisor, he could save a lot of money.

He was promoted to major, which ended his command tour, and returned to Vietnam as a combat advisor from August 1968 to August 1969. At the end of his tour, he was released from active duty and began graduate school at Northern Arizona University.

He received his master's degree in Guidance and Counseling in August 1970 and joined the university as a staff counselor. After a year he entered the University of Utah Counseling Psychology PhD program. At the same time, the Army was anticipating difficulty with senior officers and NCOs when it transitioned from a conscript force to an all-volunteer force. The solution was to locate former combat arms officers and return them to active duty to receive doctoral degrees in the behavioral sciences, to help the Army move into an all-volunteer force.

He graduated with a PhD in Counseling Psychology and a minor in Clinical Psychology in August 1973 and received a one-year post-doctoral fellowship in community psychology at William Beaumont Army Medical

Center, in El Paso, Texas. While in the Army Reserve and on active duty, Bob attended the Reserve Command and General Staff college, graduating in the fall of 1974.

Assigned as the clinical psychologist at the Army hospital at Fort Polk, Louisiana, he stayed a year, then was selected to become the first Psychology Consultant for the Army Health Services Command, a flag command at Fort Sam Houston in San Antonio, Texas, overseeing all health care, health facilities and personnel in CONUS, Hawaii, Alaska, and the Panama Canal Zone.

A year later Bob was also assigned as chief of the Psychology Service at Brooke Army Medical Center, also at Fort Sam Houston (yet still the HSC consultant). During this time Bob became a member of the DOD Operation Homecoming, a five-year project following up on the adjustment of all military Vietnam repatriated POWs and a member of the Center for POW Studies (Bob headed the program to do the psychological evaluation of all Army Vietnam POWs). He served as a sport psychologist with the Olympic Modern Pentathlon Team and became a pioneer researcher on the psychological adjustment of Vietnam veterans.

Because of his considerable traveling to work with Army medical facilities and personnel in the States, Bob became an instrument-rated pilot and the Army paid him to fly his own plane. This led to him becoming an aviation psychologist, working with Army aviation. Because a lot of his work required management consulting within and outside the Army, Bob earned a master's degree in Business Administration from Webster University in 1978.

He ended his Army career as the chief of the Fort Sam Houston Community Mental Health Service (while continuing to serve as the HSC Psychology Consultant). Bob retired from the army as a lieutenant colonel in October 1981.

His military decorations include the Combat Infantryman Badge, the Legion of Merit, seven decorations for valor, the Purple Heart, an Air Medal, three Army Commendation Medals, and the USMC Combat Action Ribbon.

Bob became a university business professor, a full-time writer and then a university writing professor, retiring from the university in 1997. As a writer, Bob has over 2,600 publications, including several authored or co-authored books, and journal and magazine articles. This book is the last book of a trilogy depicting Bob's military adventures.

Chapter Notes

Chapter 1

1. See my books *Under Fire with ARVN Infantry* (2018) and *Fighting Viet Cong in the Rung Sat* (2021), from McFarland.

Chapter 4

1. Worthington, Elliott R., Major, "The Vietnam Veteran Anomie and Adjustment," *Military Medicine*, 141, 3, 1976, 169–170, and Worthington, "Post-Service Adjustment and Vietnam Era Veterans," *Military Medicine*, 142, 11, 1977, 865–866.

2. Worthington, E. Robert, "Demographic and Pre-Service Variables as Predictors of Post-Military Service Adjustment" in *Stress Disorders Among Vietnam Veterans*, Charles R. Figley, editor, Bruner/Mazel, 1978, 173–187.

3. Worthington, Elliott Robert, *The Vietnam Era Veteran, Adjustment, and Anomie*, University Microfilms, 1973.

Chapter 6

1. See Worthington, Elliott R., PhD, *Methods for assessing human aspects of an organization*, Organizational Effectiveness Forum, Human Resources Division, United States Army Forces Command, 2-76, 1976, pages 19–23; and Worthington, E. R., PhD, *What Constitutes Change?* Organizational Effectiveness Forum, Human Resources Division, United States Army Forces Command, 3-76, 1976, pages 41–44.

Chapter 8

1. Worthington, Elliott Robert, "Post Separation Adjustment and the Women's Liberation" in *Changing Families in a Changing Military System*, Edited by Hunter, Edna J., Families Study Branch, Naval Health Research Center, 1977, pp 61–73.

2. Worthington, E. R. (Bob) and Heffner, Gary J., *A Comparison of the Emotional and Psychological Adjustment of the Returning Veterans of Vietnam and Iraq*, paper presented at the sixth Triennial Vietnam Symposium at Texas Tech University—The Vietnam Center, Lubbock, TX, 12–15 March 2008 and Heffner, Gary J. and Worthington, E. R. (Bob), *Vietnam vs. Iraq: A Comparison of the Soldier's Experience. Preparation for Each War, the Fighting in Each war, and the Return Home for the Soldiers of Each War*, paper presented at the Sixth Triennial Vietnam Symposium at Texas Tech University-The Vietnam Center, Lubbock, TX 12–15 March 2008.

3. Worthington, Elliott Robert, *Adjustment Behaviors, Prior To, During and After Army Service*, paper presented at the 84th Annual American Psychological Association Convention, Washington, D.C., September 1976, and Worthington, E. R., *The American Soldier: Those Who Make It and Those Who Do Not*, paper presented at the Inter-University Seminar of Armed Forces and Society, Arizona State University, Tempe, Arizona, February 1976.

Chapter 11

1. See Worthington, E.R., *Psychological Adjustment of Army Repatriated*

Vietnam POWs, Proceedings, Fifth Joint Meeting Concerning POW/MIA Matters, USAF School Aerospace of Medicine, Brooks AFB, Tx, 19–20 September 1978; Worthington, E.R., *Psychological Adjustment of Army Repatriated Vietnam POWs* (an updated and final version of the 1978 paper), paper presented at the 87th Annual Convention of the American Psychological Association, New York City, NY, 1–5 September 1979, Worthington, Bob, "Returning to a World That No Longer Existed," *Vietnam Magazine*, vol. 32, No.6, 2020, pp 34–41.

Chapter 13

1. Worthington, E.R., *Sports Psychology Consultation*, paper presented at the 24th Annual Convention of the Southwestern Psychological Association, New Orleans, LA, 20–22 April 1978.
2. Worthington, E.R., and McCaffrey, Michael, *Sports Psychology: The Clinician and The Modern Pentathlon,* paper presented at the 86th Annual Convention of the American Psychological Association, Toronto, Canada, 27–31 August 1978.
3. Worthington, E.R., *Psychology Training for Olympic Athletes*, paper presented at the 88th Annual American Psychological Association Convention, Montreal, Canada, 1–5 September 1980.

Chapter 16

1. What I did to turn around this clinic was written and published as a graduate level business school case study, except the setting was described as a civilian mental health center. See Worthington, E.R., *Community Mental Health Center,* in *Strategic Management, Planning and Implementation, Concepts and Cases,* 2nd Edition, Byars, Lloyd L., Harper & Row, 1987, pp 814–825.

Chapter 17

1. Figley, Charles R. (editor), *Stress Disorders Among Vietnam Veterans*, Brunner/Mazel, 1978.
2. Kulka, Richard A., et al., *Trauma and the Vietnam War Generation*, Brunner Mazel, 1990.
3. Worthington, Bob, *Personnel Management Concerns for Media Managers*, in Readings in Media Management, Media Management and Economics Division of the Association for Education in Journalism and Mass Communications, 1992.
4. Worthington, E.R., and Warren, James, *The Volunteer Army and Initial Adjustment Problems*, paper presented at the Seventh Psychology in the DOD Symposium at the USAF Academy, 16–18 April 1980.
5. Worthington, E.R., *Female Adjustment in the Modern Army*, paper presented at the Seventh Psychology in the DOD Symposium at the USAF Academy, 16–18 April 1980.
6. Worthington, E.R. (editor-in-chief), *AMEDD PSYCHOLOGIST CAREER GUIDE*, William Beaumont Army Medical Center, 1981.

Index